Narrative's Journey

Writing About Women
Feminist Literary Studies

Vol. 16

PETER LANG
New York • Washington, D.C./Baltimore • San Francisco
Bern • Frankfurt am Main • Berlin • Vienna • Paris

Susan Gevirtz

Narrative's Journey

The Fiction and Film Writing of Dorothy Richardson

PETER LANG
New York • Washington, D.C./Baltimore • San Francisco
Bern • Frankfurt am Main • Berlin • Vienna • Paris

Library of Congress Cataloging-in-Publication Data

Gevirtz, Susan.
Narrative's journey: the fiction and film writing of Dorothy Richardson/
Susan Gevirtz.
p. cm. — (Writing about women; vol. 16)
Includes bibliographical references.
1. Richardson, Dorothy Miller, 1873–1957—Criticism and interpretation.
2. Richardson, Dorothy Miller, 1873–1957—Motion picture plays.
3. Feminism and motion pictures—England—History—20th century.
4. Feminism and literature—England—History—20th century. 5. Women and literature—England—History—20th century. 6. Sex role in motion pictures.
7. Sex role in literature. 8. Narration (Rhetoric). I. Title. II. Series.
PR6035.I34Z69 823'.912—dc20 94-24565
ISBN 0-8204-2510-9
ISSN 1053-7937

Die Deutsche Bibliothek-CIP-Einheitsaufnahme

Gevirtz, Susan.
Narrative's journey: the fiction and film writing of Dorothy Richardson/
Susan Gevirtz. - New York; Washington, D.C./Baltimore; San Francisco; Bern;
Frankfurt am Main; Berlin; Vienna; Paris : Lang.
(Writing about women; Vol. 16)
ISBN 0-8204-2510-9
NE: GT

To My Parents

Works About Dorothy Richardson by Susan Gevirtz:

"Wanderyahre—A Reading of Dorothy Richardson," *Praxis*, Spring/Summer, vol 1, no. 1 (New Brunswick, New Jersey: Rutgers University, 1987).

"Dorothy Richardson Taken Place," *Raddle Moon* 11, vol 6, no 1 (Vancouver, Canada: Vancouver New Writing Society, 1992).

"Recreative Delights and Spiritual Exercise: Pantheism as Aesthetic Practice in Dorothy Richardson's *Pilgrimage*," *West Coast Line*, no 9 (26/3) Winter 1992-3, (Burnaby B.C., Canada: Simon Fraser University).

The preface to *Narrative's Journey* was first published in *Mirage #4/Period(ical) #34*, (San Francisco, California, September, 1994).

"Figment of Appointment," forthcoming *Chain* / 3 (Buffalo, New York: State University of New York, 1995).

Also by Susan Gevirtz:

Milkhouse and Korean (Elmwood, Connecticut: ABACUS, Potes & Poets Press, 1991).

Domino: Point of Entry (Buffalo, New York: Leave Books, 1992).

Linen minus (Bolinas, California: Avenue B, 1992).

Taken Place (London/Cambridge, England: Reality Street Editions, 1993).

PROSTHESIS::CAESAREA (Elmwood, Connecticut: Potes & Poets Press, 1994).

Acknowledgements

It is a pleasure to name the many who have assisted me in the writing and publication of this book. I am grateful to the Hutchins School of Sonoma State University for granting me leave to work on the book and for providing a vital pedagogic community in which to practice and learn about what I love.

I thank Helene Moglen for her extensive, tolerant and illuminating engagement with the many stages of this work. Enormous gratitude goes to Stephen Heath for his continuous support and belief in this project. For their support at formative stages, I also thank the members of my thesis committee—James Clifford, Donna Haraway and Hayden White. Many thanks also go to Noel King who shared his fluency in Dorothy Richardson's London, particularly its Anglicanism.

I give special thanks to my friends who are also writers and have brought that perspective to their readings. First, thanks beyond thanks goes to Margy Sloan whose astute editorial suggestions and depth of engagement with the manuscript have been beyond measure, matched only by her unwavering and absolutely necessary belief in the project. I am also especially grateful to Kathleen Fraser, whose constant support, editorial labors and discernment made it possible to continue. Megan Boler's, Carolyn Burke's and Norma Cole's superb readings of the manuscript have also provided the sustenance to proceed and insights on how to do so.

In the spirit of shared readings and concerns I am also enormously lucky to have Esther Labovitz as my editor. She has approached this manuscript with an editorial acuity and deep respect for Dorothy Richardson's work, as well as for my own, which has made it possible for the book to take its final shape.

Through their big capacity for serious play, my students have infused many of the ideas in this book with an animate, palpable vitality—for that I am endlessly grateful. I especially thank Laurie Posner, whose contributions on every level have been profound.

I would also like to thank my sister and brother, parents and grandparents who, in ways they may and may not recognize, have provided the support to write—recently, and long before this book was even a thought. I also thank my friends who are more than family: Kim Collet, Margo Goodman, Deborah Gunther, Kristine Larsen, Ardath Lee and Lynda Marin—without whose support this book would not have been possible. Laurinda Gilmore has been the catalyst for focussing much of what has ended up on these pages; for that my gratitude exceeds words.

David Delp came into this project near its close. As my conspirator in everything from toothbrushing to manuscript reading, he has provided support and accompaniment beyond what I had imagined possible, and a vision of another life after this book infused with an optimism and tranquility I could not have pictured when I began this project.

— San Francisco, 1995

Table of Contents

PREFACE: Methods and Intent

> And in this book, rather as in a novel, summaries or generalized perspectives will alternate with scenes or analyses of detail filled with quotations, and with pauses in which the author comments on what has just occurred, and of course with frequent ellipses or omissions. But is this not the point of departure of all history?
>
> —*Tzvetan Todorov*[1]

> And what if, from a writer's perspective, purgatory were but an image of the crucial passage from a moment lived in the book to another moment, still to be lived in writing?
>
> —*Edmond Jabes*[2]

In *Pilgrimage* we do and do not meet a main character named Miriam Henderson—she is there when we meet ourselves in the act of reading and so she is never actually there without us. To name a book *Pilgrimage* is similar to calling it Motion Towards the Sacred—and since in the case of *Pilgrimage* the sacred happens to be language and writing, to name this book *Pilgrimage* was like titling it Reading.

A community of reading writers exists on the page, there ignited. This is a visceral and secularly religious event. It is, I believe, an event not to be sought or avoided. If one assumes that all writing is committed in relation to other writing, then the interpretation of any work has always already taken place. The interpretation is an intervention, a response, of its time, in its time—a reading that is always a set of circumstances located somewhere. The world is an already-interpreted place always ready for interpretation.[3]

I have opened *Pilgrimage*, again and again, as if its title were Reading. So I have expected that it would be a perpetual invitation to investigate and encounter the motion and nature of reading, or, as Miriam Henderson puts it, "the part about the journey." In this case, the title *Pilgrimage* also gestures toward a book whose subject is a reading arriving again and again at the shrine of itself. That is, a reading that has many origins and constantly evokes rereading. In this book then, I take the subject of *Pilgrimage* to be my reading of it, the history of that one's reading, but also the reading histories of the many others that precede, collide, coincide with, and have informed mine. Whether I or any other, the reader of *Pilgrimage* is always its subject. All of these readings and readers also meet the many passages in *Pilgrimage* in which we witness Miriam in the act of reading and responding to books. I read Miriam herself as the character of reading as much as the character of an actual woman. In the midst of this honeycomb of readings my question repeatedly proposes itself: How and why does *Pilgrimage* produce more reading and writing?

In pursuing this question I have been interested in an approach that does not embrace the contextless communion of the old new criticism or the conventions of argument. While theoretical apparatus has been extremely useful throughout these investigations, I have not attempted to speak from any one theoretical position or to provide a consecutive argument. My purpose rather has been to animate concurrent readings, to open fissures, and propose directions for thought. My investigation proceeds as much by analogy and association as by linear logic. To overlay a single theoretical framework or critical mode on the reading of *Pilgrimage* and the "Continuous Performance" writings would be to ignore and obscure the theories of reading and poetics that are developed and proposed in the work itself. Instead, it is Richardson's articulation of her theories of reading, writing, and viewing, as well as that which is present and unarticulated, which I wish, by this approach, to feature.

The focus of this book is not primarily, or only, on *Pilgrimage* or on the late 1920s "Continuous Performance" columns about the early silent cinema, but on the conversation between them. My intention is to investigate and analyze some of the textual relationships that arise in setting this constellation of Richardson's writings in the vicinity of one another. In an attempt to demystify and reveal, I have been most interested in the counterpoint that occurs between the two kinds of writing, the ways in which this ambidextrous writing project of Richardson's allowed or required that secrets be kept, lies be made. I have been interested, as well, in the function of and reasons for Richardson's invention of this particular kind of silent cinema in her "Continuous Performance" columns. In juxtaposing and comparing passages and techniques from both, I hope to illustrate the ways in which the writings on cinema articulate a poetics that is practiced as a "filmic" prose writing in the novels.

An investigation of Richardson's aesthetic practice and theories may shed some light on current relations to language, writing and reading, particularly in connection with issues of form and gender. Richardson's concerns and aesthetic innovations are manifest in what she called the "feminine" silent film, and in the technique she referred to as "feminine" prose. Both names suggest the analyses of the relations between gender, writing and viewing, with which her work is redolent. These concerns dovetail with a more contemporary feminist view that the form of any writing or representation registers its particular relation to the complex social hierarchy in which it is produced. Sharing this view, I have attended not only to what Richardson has said about the "feminine," but equally to the way in which the forms and structures of her work present a politics, a cultural relation. Throughout the writing of this book the how has been of as much interest as the what.

In telling the story of my reading of Richardson's work, I have focussed attention on that which is doubled, tripled, always becoming, disappearing, and asking for more. This has been my chosen field of conflict and the mode I have heard "...suggested or imposed by the subject itself."[4]

NOTES:

1. Tzvetan Todorov, *The Conquest of America*, Richard Howard, translator (New York, London: Harper Torchbooks, 1985), 4.

2. Edmond Jabes, *Dante's Hell* translated by Rosmarie Waldrop, excerpted in *AVEC*, vol. 7, no. 1, 1994. *L'enfer de Dante* (Paris: Fata Morgana Press, 1991).

3. Among others, Norma Cole and Susan Howe have focussed on the way in which reading becomes a kind of writing and vice versa. Especially resonant works: Norma Cole, "In the Time of Prosody: Introductory Remarks, the Browning Society," February, 1994; "OUR OTHERS," delivered at the Walker Art Center, December, 1993; Susan Howe, *My Emily Dickinson*, (Berkeley, California: North Atlantic Books, 1985).

4. Todorov: 4.

Monkeying With the Plot: In Lieu of a Biographical Note[1]

> Surely what fiction at its best, can do, is to arrange data, truths in their real relationship by a process of selection. Like an artist making a picture, something akin happens to us all as we get on in life. We see data of experience no longer chronologically, but rearranged in their true sequence. The past comes at last to life, transformed, rearranged, immortal.
>
> —*Dorothy Richardson*[2]

Dorothy Richardson viewed writing as a map of authorial consciousness. In *Pilgrimage* she does more than write an autobiography; she also makes a statement about writing itself by tracing a consciousness in action. For Richardson, all writing is autobiographical and her choice of an autobiographical form for her epic was made, in part, to highlight this idea. The many parallels between the consciousness and life of Miriam Henderson, the main character of *Pilgrimage*, and that of her creator literally manifest Richardson's idea that writing is a map of an author's psyche.

However, this does not mean that an easy equivalence can be drawn between Miriam Henderson and Dorothy Richardson. The Dorothy Richardson -equals-Miriam Henderson equation is present in *Pilgrimage* as one possible view and as bait. It is a parallel that Richardson both suggests and complicates in making Miriam occupy the character of a seemingly actual person, as well as that of an imagined writer writing and a reader in the act of reading. Just as *Pilgrimage* both is and is not autobiographical, Miriam Henderson is a locus of identification as well as disguise. A character who is a map of authorial consciousness is also a map of narrative strategy in action.[3] Indeed, among other things, Miriam can be seen as a locus for the spinning out and demonstration of theories of narrative.[4]

As I will elaborate in forthcoming chapters, it is possible to view Richardson as both setting up and dismantling any such simple parallel between Miriam and herself, her life and the life of *Pilgrimage.* The theories about time and narrative that Richardson asserts overlap closely with her theories about the subject and the relation between an author and a reader. For Richardson time existed more as a vertical simultaneous event than as a linear horizontal progressive unfolding. Consistent with these views, she conceived of a subject as having an unchanging "luminous center" but also to be multiple and always-changing in a protean fashion. All of these views have their counterparts in Richardson's aesthetic practice.

Thus, although *Pilgrimage* is certainly autobiographical, Richardson wishes in her technique—and in her ideas about reading and writing, readers and authors—to simultaneously set up and frustrate the expectations that accompany the genre of autobiography, one of which is the assumption that autobiographical writing is writing about the author.[5] Richardson strongly implies in the foreword to *Pilgrimage* that writing, autobiographical or not, is always about an interaction between the reader and author. Thus the interaction becomes the subject of the text; the writer of the autobiography is both the reader and the author. To find out about the author then, is also to investigate the reader in the act of reading.

One of Richardson's methods of disrupting generic and other expectations is consistent with her notion of time as vertical accumulation rather than horizontal progression. Miriam (who both does and doesn't speak for Richardson here) insists that "everything is a side issue," rendering absurd, in the realm of *Pilgrimage*, a desire to make unity, to mark a beginning or end, to assume any one life or text to be a linear progression of events. Many of Richardson's critics wish to cast *Pilgrimage* in one of the above lights—to extrapolate from the assumed parallel between Richardson's and Miriam's lives that *Pilgrimage* can and should be conceived of as "a whole," and that in doing so we will be better able to glean its meaning.[6] However, wholeness, I think, is not the aim of *Pilgrimage*.

Further disrupting generic and gender expectations, Richardson makes the main character, Miriam Henderson, a woman not merely because the writing of *Pilgrimage* is autobiographical, but equally because Richardson wishes to equate the pilgrimage, or inward travel of this psyche, with a unique kind of writing that she calls "feminine." In this sense, autobiography was also a particularly appropriate form for the illustration of what Richardson called "the feminine sentence," her version of Woolf's "psychological sentence of the feminine gender."[7] Thus, it is important to note that while this study is not biographical, in Richardson's case, biographical background can serve an important dual purpose. It supplies the skeleton of "real" thoughts and events on which *Pilgrimage* hangs, and by implying a process of transforming and selecting biographical material from her life, it also helps to shed light on the kind of aesthetic statement she wished to make.[8]

In *Pilgrimage*, Richardson attempts to manifest, as she put it, "a sense of time as vertical rather than horizontal."[9] For Miriam Henderson, the future, the present, the past, and fictive time all exist simultaneously in various vertical palimpsestic arrangements. Just as Miriam's life follows, foreshadows and precedes Richardson's, this "vertical" sense of time pervades Richardson's view of her own life. It is largely responsible for her interest in film, and guides all of her writing—not only that of *Pilgrimage.*[10]

As Fromm, one of Richardson's biographers, states, one of her "ultimate aims was [in Richardson's words] to be in 'current possession, from a single point of consciousness,' of [her] whole experience intact and consequently—from the vast synthesis in her mind—to be able to arrange 'the immediate future.'"[11] Though Richardson's life, like anyone's, can be described as a sequence of events during which she grew older and at the end of which she died, Richardson herself probably did not experience her life or her work as stories strictly beginning in the past and leading to the future. Instead, she "read" her life in a manner parallel to that in which Miriam reads books in *Pilgrimage*—as an adventure into side issues.

> Their adventure took them away from their subject into what Miriam knew 'clever' people would call 'side issues.' 'Nothing is a side issue,' she told herself passionately with her eyes on the green glare beyond the window (*Backwater*, 249).

Through the writing of *Pilgrimage* Richardson was able to construct time as vertical and to acutely experience her life as both hers and someone else's (Miriam's)—as both already having happened and not yet realized. It is not possible to untangle the intricate interweaving of her life and her work, particularly in *Pilgrimage*, and this, it seems, is what she intended. As she wrote in 1938 in a letter to Edward West,

> Isn't life the plot? Is what is "artistically" wrong with my work produced by a sense of the iniquity [hand-written word, unclear in manuscript] of monkeying with this plot? I have never wanted to be an "artist," nothing has more greatly astonished me than the being hailed as one.[12]

Miriam's life, as a vertical collation of "side issues" culminating in her becoming a writer, directly parallels that of Richardson and is the "plot" of *Pilgrimage.* Most of the events and the intellectual, spiritual, and psychic conflicts depicted in *Pilgrimage* have parallels in Richardson's life. To discuss *Pilgrimage* and the main characters in it therefore is also to discuss Richardson's life and to meet some of its primary inhabitants. Almost everything that occurs in *Pilgrimage* also happened in some form in Richardson's life, and yet some significant actual events were left out of, or altered in, *Pilgrimage.* Of the missing events, the two that are most prominent in their absence are Richardson's marriage and her mother's suicide.

PART I
The Novel and Film Writing Through the Lens of the Foreword

In the foreword to *Pilgrimage* Dorothy Richardson demonstrates and points to the impact that film had on her novelistic writing. Since the subject of this study is the ways in which Richardson's filmic and novelistic writings implicate one another, her Foreword, with its antenna in both worlds, provides a natural bridge between Parts II and III of this book and is the work on which most of Part I will dwell.

Written after the bulk of *Pilgrimage* and much of her other work had been published, the four-page foreword is also a rich source of Richardson's retrospective views on the development of her writing and the obsessions and concerns to which she returned throughout her life. Having grown up in the nineteenth century and become a writer in the twentieth, Richardson and her work are linked to many traditions at once. The Foreword shows that the version of realism she practices ties her strongly to a romantic tradition of pilgrimage and quest narratives; to the realist tradition of Balzac; to the tradition of modernist departures from Balzac, whom she calls in the Foreword "the father of realism"; to the embracing of what she calls the "feminine prose" of Dickens and James; as well as to the more avant-garde strains of modernism found in film, poetry and music (Foreword, 9. Note: In Part I numbers by themselves in parentheses will refer to pages in the Foreward.).[13]

Richardson wrote the Foreword on the occasion of the 1938 publication, in four volumes, of twelve of the "novel-chapters" comprising *Pilgrimage*. She states that its writing provided an "opportunity . . . of assembling the scattered chapters of *Pilgrimage* in their proper relationship"(12). The thirteenth and final novel-chapter, *March Moonlight*, published posthumously in 1967, presents the experimental aesthetic principles articulated in the Foreword in a more sustained way than any of the previous novel-chapters.

The Foreword, written before the twelfth volume was finished, was thus an apology in the sense of providing a retrospective explanation of the writing completed to that point, as well as a foreshadowing of what was to come. [14]

Richardson was troubled by the request of Dent, her publisher, for a preface or foreword to accompany the new edition. She interpreted it as indicative of the difficulty the public consistently had with her work. A foreword, she supposed, was to serve the purpose of making *Pilgrimage* easier to read. Believing that the difficulties encountered in reading *Pilgrimage* had their important and evident purposes, Richardson had hoped it would be unnecessary to explain them. But like her publisher, Richardson considered the four-volume edition to be the last chance for *Pilgrimage* to be published as a collected edition. To ensure exposure and sales, the publisher required a foreword. Richardson, in a half-similar spirit, agreed to provide one.

In placing my discussion of Richardson's writings on the early silent cinema next to my reading of *Pilgrimage*, I hope to reveal the way in which the articles on the film and the novelistic writings are the ulterior lives of each other and illuminate one another when read side-by-side. In addition to investigating the ways that these writings speak to and about one another, I hope that these parallel readings will also reveal the ways in which Richardson's articles on the film and her novels were necessary trajectories of the same curiosity and aesthetic investigation.

The Not Really Real: Towards A Filmic Poetics[15]

> Dorothy Richardson seems to express, more than any other writer, the English spirit. Her books are the best history yet written of the slow progression from the Victorian period to the modern age. She is the English Proust and like him, has written for the few . . . .
>
> What a film her books could make. The real English film for which so many are waiting. Apart from Miriam herself, the pages are filled with people, men and women who resume their whole thought and vocabulary in a few phrases or a few actions, immediately to be recognized for they are to be met everyday. *Dawn's Left Hand* begins (as perhaps films should) in a railway carriage (Winifred Bryher, in a review of *Dawn's Left Hand*, 1931). [16]

Between 1927 and 1933, Richardson wrote twenty-three articles on the early cinema.[17] All of these articles were published in the film journal *Close Up*, twenty of them under the column title "Continuous Performance." As a plotless, epical, written performance of Miriam Henderson's subjectivity in process *Pilgrimage* never formally ends, and is also in many senses a continuous performance. In keeping with her interests in the *Pilrimage* novels, in the *Close Up* pieces Richardson almost never focuses discussion on the plot or on specific features of a particular film. Instead, her main concerns parallel those she outlines in the foreword to *Pilgrimage*: problems of space, time, and narrative; disruptive reading and writing practices; the miracle (Richardson's word) of transfiguration that can occur in the cinema through the transgression of social and written formalities; the notion that some forms of representation are "feminine" and others "masculine" and the idea that "feminine" writing is a spiritual and transformative exercise. These writerly concerns converge for Richardson in the cinema, where a story is projected from a beam of light.

The cinema provided Richardson with a spatialized model, a spectacle, of the reading and writing technique that she employs in the novels.[18] As Benjamin states,

> The shooting of a film . . . affords a spectacle unimaginable anywhere at any time before this. It presents a process in which it is impossible to assign to a spectator a viewpoint which would exclude from the actual scene such extraneous accessories as camera equipment, lighting machinery, staff assistants, etc.—unless his eye were on a parallel with the lens.[19]

This spatial cinematic model adapted to the novel has the effect of putting the reader's eye on a line parallel with the camera lens, requiring, as Richardson enacts in the Foreword, a reading of images and words in motion and thereby creating a sensation of travel and disrupted sequential time. The fact that no single fixed viewpoint can be assigned to the spectator or the camera duplicates the intended effects of Richardson's writing practice. As a spatial model, the cinema also posed, in terms of the viewer and the screen, some of the same questions about the relation between reader and writer that occupy Richardson in the context of the novel. For example, she is fascinated by what she calls "the miracle of form in movement" found in the cinema ("Continuous Performance," *Close Up*, June, 1933, 131), by the audience's experience of the film, and by the way in which various kinds of musical accompaniment can transform a film. She was also fascinated with the light of the projector, which she saw as both the source and ignition of filmic narrative and which she used as a main motif in the *Pilgrimage* novels. If she had ever made a film perhaps it would have been the one she imagines in the March 1928 column: a film "... that might be called *A Mirror of Audiences*, with many close-ups" ("CP8," *Close Up*, March, 1928). It is to this imagined film, and the idea of it, that she can be seen to repeatedly return, and that she repeatedly invokes, in the "Continuous Performance" writings.

With its power of presenting disparate images and times directly next to each other, and its ability to create vivid atmospheres through its spectacular proportions, the film also offered Richardson an arena in which her concerns with narrative sequence and form could be played out on a large scale. Richardson's concerns reflected a widespread modernist discomfort with the relationship between subjectivity and representation. As Richardson points out in the Foreword, this discomfort is quite different for female and male modernists. In the "Continuous Performance" columns she elaborates on her interest in the "feminine" form of writing she discusses in the Foreword. In her view the silent film enacts this kind of feminine writing—a kind of writing that she was practicing in *Pilgrimage* even as she wrote the columns. In her criticism, she contrasts the power of the "feminine" silent film with the weaknesses of the new "masculine" talkie.

Because cinema posed many of the same questions that she asked about reading and writing, the "Continuous Performance" columns can be read as a kind of gloss on *Pilgrimage*. Richardson's view of the cinema was summarized by Eisenstein, with whom she shared many ideas, who said, "cinema is an expansion from literature."[20] But for Richardson the cinema was more; it was also an ideal enlargement and enactment of what another *Close Up* writer, Robert Herring, called the "not really real, really."[21]

The Foreword to Pilgrimage As Apologia And Prologue

In November 1938 reviews of the collected *Pilgrimage* novel-chapters began to arrive. The statement that this collected edition represented the finished *Pilgrimage*, a statement Richard Church, the editor, had made in marketing it, was having the effect Richardson had feared and predicted. Critics who had been sympathetic to her work were confused and said nothing about *Dimple Hill*, the last novel in the collected set. "The rest," Richardson said, "were delighted to announce that they had been right all along: the endless chronicle had simply petered out." *Dimple Hill* was being misunderstood as the final volume and therefore it was being viewed, she felt, as "a cul-de-sac rather than a conclusion." [22]

There were only a handful of reviewers who did not regard *Pilgrimage* in this light. To Richardson, these unfortunate results were "the horrid fruit" of her publisher Dent's plan. *Pilgrimage* had never received due attention and appeared to Richardson to be now buried with finality. She was largely correct. Ford Maddox Ford was not to be alone in considering Richardson "the most abominably unread recent novelist." [23]

As an apologia for *Pilgrimage* the Foreword displays Richardson's sense of irony with regard to the apparent necessity, perceived by Church and Dent, of providing an explanation for her work. This ironic, nearly sarcastic tone is evident throughout the four pages of the Foreword but is most blatant in the last paragraph, in which Richardson thanks the publisher for the "opportunity" to write the Foreword and expresses "a heart-felt apology" for causing her readers so much trouble.

> For the opportunity, afforded by the present publisher, of eliminating this source of a reputation for creating avoidable difficulties, and of assembling the scattered chapters of *Pilgrimage* in their proper relationship, the author desires here to express her gratitude and, further, to offer to all those readers who have persisted in spite of every obstacle, a heart-felt apology (12).

This statement of gratitude is addressed to those critics and readers who believed that the difficulties in *Pilgrimage* could have been avoided if Richardson had not insisted on using what she earlier in the Foreword terms her "small innovation." By implication, Richardson suggests that her reputation for creating "avoidable difficulties" is an unfair one, not because she has not created difficulties—indeed she is aware that she has—but because the difficulties have been absolutely unavoidable. She must have hoped that it would be clear that her method was deliberate and inextricably entwined with the content of her work.

The statements about poetics in the Foreword frequently echo the statements about writing and narrative structure that are made throughout *Pilgrimage* and in Richardson's critical writings as well, especially those about film. These echoes occur in the way in which Miriam's statements and passages from the "Continuous Performance" columns are recalled and rearticulated in the Foreword. The resonance would be particularly strong for any reader of the Foreword who had already read the first twelve novel-chapters and had followed Richardson's critical writing. The film criticism, for example, contains comments on elements found in the novels and reviews, so that, when the work is read together, an at least three-way commentary can be heard. For example, near the end of the "Continuous Performance" column titled "The Front Rows," Richardson says, "In the film as in life, the what matters less than the how" (January, 1928). This statement parallels and underscores her concern registered in the Foreword for "small innovation" and "difficulties" that function to call attention to the form and technique, that is, to the "how," of the *Pilgrimage* writing. The "how" is evident visually in the often unusual profiles of many of the *Pilgrimage* pages. At the same time both of the above statements also echo many of those made by Miriam in which she emphasizes that the most important aspect of reading is also the "how." Again and again she describes the way in which for her, reading is more a viewing of, an interaction with books, like the imagined engagement through all senses that an audience member in a cinema might experience while watching or "reading" a film, than it is about reading for "what" happened:

> The book was open. Her eyes scanned unwillingly. Her words? No one had ever said *fabric* about anything. It made the page alive . . . a woven carpet, on one side a beautiful glowing pattern, on the other dull stringy harshness . . . 'there is a dangerous *looseness*'. . . her heart began beating apprehensively. The room was dead about her. She sat down tense, and read the sentence through (*Interim*, 407).

In the realm of the reading experience that Miriam describes here, the "glowing pattern" of the page and that of the film screen shimmer in close proximity to one another. In this context Richardson's statement from "The Front Rows," "In the film, as in life..." invites rephrasing: In Richardson's novel, as in film, the what matters less than the how.

Although the Foreword was ostensibly written to explain the development of her writing in *Pilgrimage*, Richardson displays her resistance to the project by concealing as much about herself and her work as she reveals. She makes the most direct and clear statements about the work of other authors and uses the most circuitous and densely figurative language to describe her own. However, in the realm of her poetics "clear" is a slippery term and she may have viewed the figurative and circuitous as more "realistic," more clear and direct than a simple explanation. Near the beginning of the Foreword, for example, she writes a description of her own process.

> Since all these novelists happened to be men, the present writer, proposing at this moment to write a novel and looking round for a contemporary pattern, was faced with the choice between following one of her regiments and attempting to produce a feminine equivalent of the current masculine realism. Choosing the latter alternative, she presently set aside, at the bidding of a dissatisfaction that revealed its nature without supplying any suggestion as to the removal of its cause, a considerable mass of manuscript. Aware, as she wrote, of the gradual falling away of the preoccupations that for a while had dictated the briskly moving script, and of the substitution, for these inspiring preoccupations, of a stranger in the form of contemplated reality having for the first time in her experience its own say, and apparently justifying those who acclaim writing as the surest means of discovering the truth about one's own thoughts and beliefs, she had been at the same time increasingly tormented, not only by the failure, of this now so independently assertive reality, adequately to appear within the text, but by its revelation, whencesoever focused, of a hundred faces, any one of which, the moment it was entrapped in the close mesh of direct statement, summoned its fellows to disqualify it (9-10).

This complex explanation, densely layered with clauses elaborating on previous clauses, is in sharp contrast to the more direct description several paragraphs later of Henry James' technique. At the end of a typical paragraph-length sentence, she states that James has "evolved"

> a prose style demanding, upon the first reading, a perfection of sustained concentration akin to that which brought it forth, and bestowing, again upon the first reading, the recreative delights peculiar to this form of spiritual exercise (11).

Richardson provides this description of James' technique because she considers him to be a "pathfinder" for those turn-of-the-century writers, especially herself, experimenting with the form of the novel. The description of "this form of spiritual exercise" that his work "demands" sheds as much light on Richardson's own work and intentions as does her description of her own process.

The phrase from the Foreword, "Since all of these novelists happened to be men" (9) makes clear the context—that of a woman writing within a predominately male tradition in relation to which all of her decisions about how to write had to be made. Richardson's writing quest has also been aimed at a better understanding of how this context and these complex issues have shaped her aesthetic. The relationship between Miriam and Richardson embodies the problematic and complex issues of identity and authorship that Richardson considered to be embedded in the conditions of women writers at her historical moment.[24] In this vein, as both an autobiography and an epic journey, one of *Pilgrimage's* most important unannounced focuses is the slippery, mirror relation between Miriam and Richardson. As Heath suggests, Richardson's choice of words and names is too precise for it to be accidental, that embedded in the name "Miriam" is the possibility of "Mirror I am" and that it is linked by sound to the word *myriad*.[25]

The name reflects Richardson's preoccupation with the themes of feminine subjectivity present in all of her writing. In addition, Miriam's fluid, plural character, which merges with one environment after another, manifests a spiritual attitude or way of being that Richardson called "feminine" in the Foreword, the novels and the film writing.

As Richardson reveals in the Foreword, her preoccupation with issues of subjectivity is also manifest as a concern with the relationship between herself and her readers. And yet, perhaps as another strategy of disruption, she both names her work a "pilgrimage" and veers away from naming the genre in which she sees the work to fit—hoping not to pin any definite generic expectations on the project. At stake in naming the genre into which *Pilgrimage* fits is the set of "reading protocols" that accompanies any generic label.[26] In keeping with her ironic attitude and equivocation about naming the genre of *Pilgrimage*, or explaining any other aspect of the novels, she seems to have written the Foreword as a provocation: an explanation that would raise as many questions as it answered.

Remaking The Quest

Throughout the Foreword Richardson allegorizes the process of writing as that of a quest. Her concern with writing as quest is evident in her interest in remaking traditional pilgrimage and epic forms by placing a woman in the role of the traditionally male hero. At the same time, she grafts on to this altered genre the intact nineteenth-century bildungsroman, exemplified by such works as Charlotte Bronte's *Villette*, George Eliot's *Daniel Deronda*, and Jane Austen's *Emma*, which characteristically took the education and development of a young, middle-class woman as its subject. She further alters the traditional male genre by making masculine the dangerous and alien geography that must traditionally be traversed in order for the questing hero to return home changed and having made a discovery.

In the traditional quest myth, the landscape is feminized and the male hero traverses it in order to discover and construct his own subjectivity.[27] Usually the discovery with which the hero returns is that of an adult male subjectivity—a discovery arrived at through the transformative act of leaving home, the experiences and subsequent knowledge derived from the journey, and the authoritative and publicly legitimizing act of returning home with foreign adventures and a knowledge of "others," previously unknown, to relate. It is this possession of a story and the ability to tell it that are of particular significance. For Richardson, the film is also the realm of journey and spiritual quest. In closing the "Continuous Performance" column titled "Captions" she writes, "...the film has an unrivalled opportunity of presenting the life of the spirit directly.... The test of the film on whatever level is that the wayfaring man, though a fool, shall not err therein, though each will take a different journey" ("CP3: Captions," *Close Up*, September, 1927).

In her choice of the bildungsroman—the quest novel of formation or development—as one model for *Pilgrimage*, Richardson situates herself in a tradition of narrative which accommodates historical, cultural, and psychological considerations as part of the complexity of its structure. As the bildungsroman has its origins in Goethe's *Wilhelm Meister's Apprenticeship*, it is not surprising that Richardson refers in the Foreword to finding, with "a sense of relief," a "manifesto" for the writing of the novel in *Wilhelm Meister* (11). *Wilhelm Meister* also presents quest as a process of inward, as well as external, travel. As a hero whose goal is to "develop myself just as I am," Meister invites the kind of intervention in the male tradition typical of novels of female development that trace the movement of the main character from the internal to the external world.[28] Signaling the direction of her travel in *Pilgrimage*, Miriam says, "There's more space within than without."

Just as Richardson forges a way of writing that is, as she calls it "a feminine equivalent to the current masculine realism," Miriam's adventure is the making of a life that is a feminine equivalent to the current form of masculine independence (9). The obstacles to be overcome and the heroic feats that Miriam performs in *Pilgrimage* are private and internal rather than public and visibly monumental. As Labovitz describes,

> Without taking any short-cuts or glossing of the truth, Richardson structures this *Bildungsroman* to encompass Miriam's growth into her craft, from the first conviction born early in life that she "wanted to 'write a book'"(I, 80), to Miriam's passage toward a final goal, which despite its desperate "graspings and droppings" (III, 134), sees her restored to her original self and center.... From early defeat to final victory, the reader is made privy to one of the most intimate accounts of a female heroine's passage—that of the artist in the *Kunstlerroman*, the variant of the *Bildungsroman.*[29]

Richardson frames her departure from the male and female literary tradition as a departure from the "regiments." Miriam, too, chooses not to follow the traditional social expectations for a young, turn-of-the-century woman. Instead, like the male quest hero, she leaves home in order to become psychically and economically independent of her father. She chooses to live alone and instead of devoting her life to the care of others, she spends her shreds of spare time reading and eventually writing. She does not marry (as Richardson does within the time span of *Pilgrimage*) or have children.

Through her idiosyncratic way of living, Miriam personifies Richardson's formal departure in writing, "confessed to" in the Foreword as "an early habit of ignoring, while writing, the lesser of the stereotyped system of signs . . . and . . . [as] a small unconscious departure from current usage" (12). Miriam, for her part, in her many long walks through London, ignores the city's literal and figurative "stereotyped system of signs." She punctuates with her presence neighborhoods and streets defined as male territory and transgresses "stereotyped systems," entering places traditionally forbidden to a white middle-class woman.

Richardson indicates her concern with the link between formal narrative and syntactic structures of motion or travel and with internal attitudes regarding writing as spiritual process or quest. In both the Foreword and within the text of *Pilgrimage* she emphasizes that she chose a pilgrimage as the mode of quest because spiritual development is the aim of the journey that best describes her view of her own life and of Miriam's life, as well as her view of writing. Like writing, the film is also a destination for pilgrimage and a realm of spiritual development. The column titled "There's No Place Like Home" begins,

> Short of taking pilgrimages we remain in ignorance of new films until they become cheap classics....But these films coming soon or late find us ready to give our best here where we have served our apprenticeship and the screen has made in us its deepest furrows ("CP5: There's No Place Like Home," *Close Up*, November, 1927).

Echoing the title of a pilgrimage narrative that likely had much impact on Richardson, *Wilhelm Meister's Apprenticeship*, she suggests that as apprentices the film and film screen are our guides. For Richardson, the notion of development in any medium is complexly imbricated with elements such as class, social history, and gender.[30]

Since pilgrimages typically have circular itineraries—that is, a pilgrim leaves home, stops at minor shrine sites and at one or more major shrine sites, and then returns, hopefully altered by the journey—the shape of travel by pilgrimage also provides a formal map of how to read (travel through) the novels. In the context of the film, the shape and layout of the cinema become map and itinerary to Richardson and are therefore also of extreme interest. In "There's No Place Like Home," she says,

> For the local, or any, cinema the garage shape is the right shape because in it the faithful are side by side confronting the screen and not as in some super-cinemas in a semi-circle whose sides confront each other and get the screen sideways. The screen should dominate. That is the prime necessity. It should fill the vista save for the doorways on either side whose reassuring "Emergency Exit" beams an intermittent moonlight" ("CP5: There's No Place Like Home," *Close Up*, November, 1927, 46-7).

In the same spirit Richardson hopes to confront the reader with the visual page of *Pilgrimage* and to invite a circling back and rereading like the return pilgrimage to the film invoked in "There's No Place Like Home," or like the traditional seasonal return to Canterbury or Lourdes. In the fiction and the Foreword, the framing of reading and writing as allegorical pilgrimages points to a double purpose, indicating that, as in a dream account or a bildungsroman, all of the external events are to be read also as internal markers in the development of the subjectivity of the hero. This concern with the relation between meaning and the formal, syntactical structures with which it is constructed is typically modernist. However, the emphasis on writing and reading as kinds of travel and as spiritual acts, and the attention to the architecture of the cinema and the novel as formal models of a reading journey, are Richardson's peculiar focus.

Mirroring the emphasis on metaphoric and linguistic motion present in *Pilgrimage*, the Foreword ventures on what Richardson calls "the lonely track [that] had turned out to be a populous highway" (10). As in *Pilgrimage*, travel themes and languorously long sentences work together to demonstrate the importance of the structure/content relation. In the Foreword, Richardson calls the process by which she arrived at a "feminine equivalent to the current masculine realism" an "adventure." Displaying her link with the cinema, her array of active verbs and metaphors of motion give an almost filmic sense of a tangible person moving through physical space and time. To the writer who speaks in the Foreword (and who represents one of her many personas) Richardson gives a dramatic distance by referring to her in the third person, or by referring to herself as "the present writer." She describes her writing life as her "adventure" and herself as an "adventurer." This third-person "She" is a heroic character courageously choosing between the more traditional military route of "following one of her regiments" or the more dangerous uncharted route of "following the briskly moving script." "She"—the Foreword's heroine—valiantly chooses the latter, more dangerous route.

The reader is invited to participate in this literary drama of mythic proportions through a vehicle that Richardson implies is equally dramatic—that of active writing and reading—as a counterpart to active viewing and participation in the film. The invitation and the action of writing and reading is signaled by the many figures of motion, particularly those embodiments of writers as pilgrims stepping dramatically onto a "populous highway." The woman pilgrim, whose name Richardson does not mention, is "mounted upon a magnificently caparisoned charger" and is most likely Virginia Woolf; an unnamed "man walking, with eyes devoutly closed, weaving as he went a rich garment of new words wherewith to clothe the antique dark material of his rich engrossment," is probably Joyce. Proust is called the "earliest adventurer" and James is given "the role of pathfinder." At first, Richardson calls the route that "She" sets out upon "a fresh pathway," and a "lonely track," which then becomes—with the discovery that Woolf, Joyce, Proust, and

James are also on it—a "populous highway." The ghost of a proper, more regimented path which is presented in the opening of the Foreword as the path "She" did not choose, haunts her entire text. Near the end of the Foreword, Richardson implies that this proper path is the path of "current [proper grammatical] usage" from which she has made a "departure."

Nothing happens in the Foreword without motion. Although the Foreword's primary subjects are the invisible thought-events that led Richardson to innovations in technique and that shaped her attitude toward writing, she reveals these events through metaphors of motion, the same technique by which she allegorizes and makes visible Miriam's mental life throughout *Pilgrimage.* Her arrival at "feminine prose," involved a process in which "phrases began to appear" and "the Stream of Consciousness lyrically led the way." This personified stream of consciousness now takes over the lead from James, the first "pathfinder," who was an earlier leader. The most significant statements made describing feminine prose are related to motion: "feminine prose should properly move from point to point without formal obstruction" (12). In other words, without movement feminine prose would not be itself. Even the formal and classic complaints of the critics are ironically depicted as "the critic's continuous ballet." These critics do not simply criticize her work; rather they "dance upon it for being unpunctuated and therefore unreadable" (12). In the realm of feminine prose the word is *animated.*

Richardson has also structured the sentences and fifteen paragraphs of the Foreword so that they call attention to their own linguistic motion and hence to reading and writing as kinds of quests. As both actions and acts of construction, a writer or reader can leave home, or leave the comfort of familiar linguistic territory, pass through grammatical perils of unfamiliarly marked passages, and then return with a reordered sense of him- or herself and the world. The first paragraph of the Foreword is a good example of this method of structuring, which is repeated in every other paragraph as well. It consists of one sentence, eight-and-a-half lines long. The subject of the sentence is referred to in each line, modified and described in clause after clause, but not named until the last line. The references to the subject move from "his," "his," "him," "his," to the directly named subject, "Balzac . . . father of realism," as follows:

> Although the translation of the impulse behind his youthful plan for a tremendous essay on *Les Forces humaine* makes for the population of his great cluster of novels with types rather than with

> individuals, the power of a sympathetic imagination, uniting him with each character in turn, gives to every portrait the quality of a faithful self-portrait, and his treatment of backgrounds, contemplated with an equally passionate interest and themselves, indeed, individual and unique, would alone qualify Balzac to be called the father of realism (9).

This technique of deferring the subject until the end of a long paragraph produces first a suspended and anticipatory reading and second a circular rereading—the reader must go back and start again—which in turn highlights the processive motion. Thus, a reader's habitual notions about where she or he is heading while reading are disrupted. The direction of the reading is not directly or exclusively forward, nor does the end of a paragraph indicate a stop before proceeding, as readers have been taught to expect. Instead the end signals the time to perform another reading of the paragraph just read. On second and subsequent readings the reader has more information, and in bringing this knowledge back to what has been read before, renews the passage, even though the words remain the same on the page. On a second reading of the first paragraph of the Foreword, the most literal new information with which the reader now returns is the identity of the subject who has been referred to throughout. This idiosyncratic structure reveals something about the author's identity as well.

In other ways too, by requiring return readings, Richardson forces a sense of motion associated with the idea of a quest and with the moving pictures of the cinema. One device that particularly has this effect is that of giving a passage a strong aural resonance that is related to, or echoes, the meaning or content of the passage. This resonance arises from the poetic effect of the language, and, as does poetry or music, it remains in the ear after the passage has been read, motivating a curious second reading. In addition, Richardson often layers and complicates references, slowing down a first reading and making a second reading necessary in order to decipher the content. Simultaneously, this forced slow-down causes a closer contact with the texture of the language—a more attentive listening, touching, consideration of "the page alive . . . a woven carpet . . . a glowing pattern." Richardson's view of the ideal effect of musical accompaniment in the silent cinema was also the aim of her use of lyric in the novels: "...an orchestra that has rehearsed, with the film, music written or arranged for that film until the two are one, is the ideal" ("CP2: Musical Accompaniment," *Close Up*, August, 1927). It is towards this ideal union of sound, image and movement that she strives in the novels.

Sustained Concentration: Readers, Writers, Viewers and Participants

The importance of reader/writer and form/meaning relationships in Richardson's work, addressed in the Foreword, is reflected on a larger scale in the relation between, and structure of, the chapter and novel-volume units of *Pilgrimage.* Just as these smaller sentence and paragraph units invite and even require rereading or reordering, the larger chapter and novel units beckon the reader not only to read and reread, but also to dip randomly into the text, beginning and ending at whim. Richardson's deliberate invitation to this type of reading practice comes as a formal signal to the reader to transgress sentence, paragraph, and chapter demarcations—to read these demarcations as signs of definite starting or stopping places that need not be respected as such. Consistent with Richardson's belief that form and meaning are intimately entwined, and that it is artificial to speak of them as a duality, the narrative structure of the Foreword manifests what she calls a "spiritual exercise" and philosophy, which are epitomized in her statement that writing is the "surest means of discovering the truth about one's own thoughts and beliefs"(10).

Writing, then, is itself also a form of inner quest or pilgrimage. If Miriam reads books, as she states in *Pilgrimage*, as a "psychological study of the author," then Richardson writes *Pilgrimage,* in part, as a means of psychological discovery, or study, of her writing self— and also as the study of a feminine subject, Miriam—coming to writing.

Necessary to the practice of this kind of writing and reading is what Richardson calls in the Foreword an attitude of "sustained concentration," a term she attributes to Henry James. The motion of the internal and physical quest that Richardson wishes to express in the language of the Foreword is, in her view, fully addressed as a literary technique and mental state by James. Believing that James' work embodied this attitude, Richardson pays homage to him in the Foreword as "a charmed and charming high priest"(11), whose work provided her a "sense of relief," also perhaps a sense of being less alone on the "populous highway" occupied by writers experimenting with the novel. She indicates that James' work was instrumental in helping her discover her "feminine equivalent to the current masculine realism." His influence on her was, she writes, "far from inconsiderable"(11).

Richardson's descriptions of James' work have important implications for her own work as well. She explains that she aims for a feminine form of the "spiritual exercise" that she believes James practices. To Richardson, the spiritual exercise of James' technique is a function of the attention James pays to the relationship between reader and writer. As she puts it, his prose style demands, "upon the first reading, a perfection of sustained concentration akin to that which brought it forth" (11). This is also the nature of the demand that Richardson makes on her readers. If sustained concentration is attained, then James' technique "bestow[s], again upon the first reading, the recreative delights peculiar to this form of spiritual exercise." To "bestow again" is Richardson's aim as well. Her use of the word "recreative" is key. By "recreative" she wishes to invoke both the re-creation of the original sustained concentration experienced in the act of writing and the recreational "delights"—that is, the pleasure—experienced initially and then over again by the reader.

In using James and the film to help find and articulate her own form of spiritual exercise, she reveals both her view of the act of writing, and the way in which she wished her work to be read. Her cinema also held sacred and transformative properties. In the "Continuous Performance 4" column "A Thousand Pities," she says, "The film is a spirit and they that worship it must worship it in spirit and in truth" (*Close Up*, October, 1927). In terms of writing, this view is manifest in the novels through Miriam's increasingly frequent visitation to moments of pleasurable unity with the world—a unity often arrived at through the synesthetic merging of the world and words. These moments, which I liken to shrine sites to be visited along the road to a sacred destination, are the epiphanic moments generated from Miriam's critical and sensual perceptions of books, people, and places. Her approach evolves into a spiritual attitude toward language and comes to fruition in *Deadlock*, the sixth novel-chapter, when Miriam begins to write. Miriam describes the scene of "that first moment" of writing as the source from which everything would subsequently issue and to which everything else in the world would thereafter return.

> The years that had passed were a single short interval leading to the restoration of that first moment. Everything they contained centered there; her passage through them, the desperate graspings and droppings, had been a coming back. Nothing would matter now that the paper-scattered lamplit circle was established as the

> centre of life. Everything would be an everlastingly various joyful coming back. Held up by this secret place, drawing her energy from it, any sort of life would do that left this room and its little table free and untouched (*Deadlock*, 134).

This passage exemplifies the attitude of reverence that Miriam has developed for the act of writing. It is the fictional expression of the homage paid to writing—as internal subjective journey—in the Foreword.

In *The Tunnel*, the fourth novel-chapter, this idea again appears in a passage in which Miriam distinguishes between two kinds of reading, that which is a habit "like most men's reading" and that which is a quest (*The Tunnel*, 279). The distinction applies equally to writing, and it is clearly writing-as-quest that interests Richardson. What Miriam calls the "secret place" of writing and the "lamplit circle" is, like the beam of light cast from a film projector, the center of this practice. As earlier discussed, in both Richardson's and James' practice, this aesthetic spirituality is also imbued with the psychoanalytic overtones of the word "consciousness" as well as psychoanalytic notions of the subject. After describing James' technique, Richardson states that these notions about consciousness and its relation to the novel are technically manifest in her work through the use of "Stream of Consciousness" and "Interior Monologue" and the influence of what might be a written version of "Slow Motion Photography"(11).

Methods Of Disruption

According to Richardson, in order for writing or reading to be a quest, to serve as a means of discovery, or to engage the reader, one's habits must be disturbed. The larger context for Miriam's statement about the two kinds of reading, reading as habit and as quest, occurs after a discussion about novels with a clergyman in *The Tunnel.* Miriam addresses him silently, saying to herself, "Your reading is a habit, like most men's reading, not a quest. You don't want it disturbed" (*The Tunnel*, 279). She is surprised to find herself uninterested in this well-read man's ideas about what he has read. Richardson's use of idiosyncratic punctuation, or her lack of punctuation, is an attempt to produce a disturbance in the reader's habits that echoes the disturbance of habit that Miriam desires and that Richardson herself must have experienced when reading in the mode of quest.

Richardson uses the word "disturb" in the above passage, and elsewhere, in a positive sense to imply a change that turns a comfortably mundane act, such as reading, into an unpredictable adventure. This shift in reading habit and attitude also marks the shift into the realm of feminine prose. For, as Richardson states in the Foreword, "feminine prose, as Charles Dickens and James Joyce have delightfully shown themselves to be aware, should properly be unpunctuated, moving from point to point without formal obstructions" (12). This uninterrupted motion is the disturbance Richardson wishes to effect through the use of her "small innovation." As she is well aware, however, the other sense of "disturb" also applies. For example, her "small innovation" disturbs the critics, or those whom she calls the "official readers," and makes their reading of *Pilgrimage* negative and uncomfortable (12).

The emphasis on a "feminine" narrative technique that disrupts conventional narrative forms is everywhere evident in the novel-chapters and the "Continuous Performance" columns. In the columns, Richardson repeatedly distinguishes between the talkie and what she sees as the far-superior silent film. She calls the silent film "feminine," and attributes to it many of the capacities for disruption that "feminine" narrative possesses. She derides the talkie as being a conventional form that prevents audience inspiration and participation.

Parallel to the interactive viewing experience invoked by the silent film, and repeatedly described in the columns, there is throughout *Pilgrimage* both a playing of language—as though it were a musical instrument—and a playing with language—a disturbing of its order—as if it were a toy or an object to be handled. This practice is exemplified in the way in which Miriam and other women repeatedly appear after dinner or at tea to play the piano for guests. The issue of how they play is lingered over, both by the guests and by Richardson. Miriam often plays without following the proper rules of etiquette, that is, without restraint and gentility and without following the rules of musical notation. Sometimes she speeds up and pounds passionately on the piano keys, ignoring what the music indicates. These kinds of scenes appear often enough to gain an emblematic status, amounting to a precedent for Richardson's own departure from tradition. Like Miriam, Richardson plays with the sounds of language through her altered use of punctuation. She joins Miriam in refusing the traditional female role of obliging hostess, not inviting the reader into a comfortable setting but instead playing with the telling of a story. And like Miriam she follows her ear instead of convention and ends up telling a story so unrecognizable as such that the critics reproach her for being a feminist, just as the guests listening to the music, and Miriam herself, often worry over Miriam's femininity.

A classic example of Miriam's piano playing occurs in her sister and brother-in-law's parlor at tea time in the beginning of *The Tunnel.* Richardson analyzes in ironic detail the relation between the proper attitude of Miriam's body at the piano, her social role as a woman, and the way these aspects are manifest in her mode of piano playing. The passage deserves a lengthy excerpt.

> Opening a volume of Mendelssohn she played, from his point of view, one of the Songs without Words quietly into the conversation. The room grew still. She felt herself and Mr. Tremayne as duplicates of Harriett and Gerald, only that she was a very religious and womanly woman, the ideal wife and mother and he was a bad fast man who wanted to be saved. It was such an easy part to play. She could go on playing it to the end of her life, if he went on in business and made enough money, being a "gracious silence," taking an interest in his affairs, ordering all things well, quietly training the servants, never losing her temper or raising her voice, making the home a sanctuary of rest and refreshment and religious aspiration, going to church. . . . She felt all these things expressing themselves in her bearing. . . . Any interest in generalities, any argument or criticism or opposition would turn him into a towering bully. All men were like that in some way. . . . He would like one or two more Mendelssohns and then supper. . . . Harriett had felt her response to the chords and knew she was getting away from Mendelssohn. Mr. Tremayne had moved to a chair quite close to the piano just behind her. She found the Beethoven and played the first movement of a sonata. It leapt about the piano breaking up her pose, using her body as the instrument of its gay wild shapeliness, spreading her arms inelegantly, swaying her, lifting her from the stool with the crash and vibration of its chords. . . . The Largo came with a single voice, deep and broad and quiet; the great truth behind the fuss of things. She felt her hearers grow weary of its reiterations and dashed on alone recklessly into the storm of the last movement. Through its tuneless raging, she could hear the steady voice and see the steady shining of the broad clear light. Daylight and gaiety and night and storm and a great song and truth, the great truth that was bigger than anything. Beethoven. She got up, charged to the fingertips with a glow that transfigured all the inanimate things in the room.[31] The party was wreck-ed . . . a young lady who banged the piano till her hair nearly came down. . . Mr. Tremayne had heard nothing but noise. . . . His eyes smiled, and his uneasy mouth felt for compliments (*The Tunnel*, 27-28).

It is no accident that the first piece Miriam chooses to play is from a volume titled "Songs without Words." The impact of the lyrical passages in *Pilgrimage* often derives from a flood of words that operates in the same way as the flood of Beethoven in the above passage. It becomes a means to move beyond words, beyond specific narrative meaning or musical composition into "daylight and gaiety and night and storm and a great song and truth, the great truth that was bigger than anything"—especially bigger than any particular words. From the flood of words, therefore, it is possible to move beyond words into "songs without words." Language turns into music, and the reader travels through this music to a moment of transfiguration parallel to the one that Miriam experiences: "She got up, charged to the fingertips with a glow that transfigured all the inanimate things in the room." This sentence exactly describes one of the main characteristics of the transfigurative moments that occur throughout *Pilgrimage* in which inanimate things—from landscapes to buildings to objects—become animate and are infused with light.

In the realm of the film, Richardson refers to this kind of transfigurative moment, infused with the light of the projector, as "the revelation of the miraculous commonplace" ("CP11: Slow Motion," *Close Up*, June, 1928). This kind of revelation is catalyzed by the film because it, like some kinds of narrative, "is arranged and focussed at the distance exactly fitting the contemplative state" ("CP: Narcissus," *Close Up*, September, 1931).

Richardson suggests that Miriam's experience of transfiguration becomes possible when Miriam shifts from playing "from his point of view" as she does in the beginning, to playing Beethoven from her own point of view—playing, as she puts it, according to "her response to the chords." Two kinds of playing are implied here: the literal playing of the piano keys and the role playing she initially experimented with when "she felt herself and Mr. Tremayne as duplicates of Harriett and Gerald." Her subsequent shift from his point of view to her own, and from imagining herself as her sister Harriett, a proper married woman, to behaving as an improper woman guest in a parlor, is an allegory for Richardson's search for a feminine equivalent. This passage also allegorizes Richardson's own arrival, described in the Foreword in equally elated terms, at the technique of feminine prose—that is, at her own response to language and her way of playing it.

The technique of feminine prose is manifest in the shape and motion of Miriam's body as she plays, as well as in the palpable changes in atmosphere that occur during and immediately after the playing. Feminine prose is also evident in the passage's idiosyncratic punctuation, including the many ellipses and phrase fragments. On a larger scale it is manifest in the shapes and arrangements of words on the pages of *Pilgrimage* and in the bodily shape or "pose" of the chapters and volumes in relation to one another. When the Beethoven leaps "about the piano breaking up her pose," it is significant that "pose" can so easily be misread, or also read, as prose. The prose in *Pilgrimage* is broken up; like Miriam's body, it is the instrument of a "gay wild shapeliness." [32]

What Miriam experienced also looms as allegorical possibility and invitation to the reader throughout *Pilgrimage.* Richardson intends for Miriam's transfiguration and the various responses to it, to be a model that illustrates the two kinds of reading suggested in the Foreword: "official" and the implied unofficial, which are also two kinds of listening. To read, or write, or play in this third sense, as in a playful approach, is to desire not to know exactly what will come next but to listen for the current of a transfiguring moment which may be underway at any time. Reading as playing is quest rather than habit. Through the use of feminine prose, Richardson intends for the reader to follow Miriam's example and be transfigured by "this form of spiritual [reading] exercise." She also intends to imply that play can be serious: the serious play of a woman with the proper forms of language is not the frivolous play of a child, or of a hostess hoping to entertain guests or critics in her parlor.

Echoing the Foreword and framed significantly in musical terms, Miriam makes one of many paradigmatic statements regarding Richardson's methods of narrative disruption and her belief in the necessity of activating the reader/writer relation. This statement comes in *Deadlock*, the novel-chapter in which Miriam begins to write, and is made during a conversation about the symphony.

> Have you ever heard that the Shah preferred of a whole concert, only the tuning of the orchestra?
>
> I know. [Miriam answers] That's always supposed to be a joke. But the tuning of an orchestra, if there is enough of it at once, is, wonderful. Why not both? It's appalling the way people have of liking only one thing. Liking "good" music and disapproving of waltzes (*Deadlock*, 123).

In Miriam's complaint about people's conventional ways of listening to the tuning-up of an orchestra, a whole concert, or waltzes, Richardson emphasizes again her concern with writing that instigates a participatory reading—a listening participation in the process of tuning-up as well as in the carefully rehearsed spectacle of the symphony. She implies that like a participating member of the symphony audience who has departed from conventional listening, a participating reader would be as interested in the process of writing that produced the texture of a completed book as in the completed book itself. In order to become engaged in the tuning-up or the writing process, the reader must also do "both," as Miriam says. In approaching a book, one must *both* read by ear and follow the sound of language, *and* read by eye. Through this technique, Richardson suggests, the reading itself becomes a kind of writing. In drawing a parallel between herself and the Shah who, being from another culture, has not learned conventional western tastes and therefore likes the tuning-up of an orchestra as much as a whole concert, Miriam indicates how foreign her own tastes are to her culture—so odd, in fact, that they, like the Shah's, could be material for a joke.

In the Foreword Richardson discusses the 1913 completion of the first chapter of *Pilgrimage* as having been "written to the *accompaniment* [my emphasis] of a sense of being upon a fresh pathway, an adventure so searching and, sometimes, so joyous as to produce a longing for participation; not quite the same as a longing for publication" (10). For Richardson, writing is a means of participating in a sense of adventure, of producing a "joy" that can then be reproduced in the reader, and by the reader. This "longing for participation" makes essential all of the means she can employ to engage the reader in both the tuning-up process, or the sense of "being upon a fresh pathway," and the orchestral spectacle of the novel-chapters working together as an epic concert.

In the Foreword Richardson describes this participatory experience in the writing process involving "a stranger in the form of contemplated reality [who] has for the first time its own say" (10). The stranger guides the writing, but only, she explains, after the preoccupations with her "regiments" fall away. Just as a stranger guides the writing of *Pilgrimage*, so too, in writing it, Richardson hopes to guide the estranged reader. In making the act of reading strange—in syntax, sentence, and paragraph structure—she also wants to make the reader strange to her or himself. The purpose of this "making strange" is to present writing as an action and a process, rather than in its usual guise of an invisible and omnisciently produced object. By this means Richardson also hopes to compel the reader to perceive her or his reading as a process in which certain choices are available—choices that are minimized if reading is considered to be an invisible mechanical act always the same for everyone. In addition, if writer and reader are both "adventurers" on a "journey," then a relationship exists between them that parallels that of "the stranger that guides" and Richardson's writing which follows. Reflecting on this kind of reading experience, Miriam asks while reading *A Human Document*, "Why did this strange book come so near, nearer than any others, so that you felt the writing, felt the sentences as if you were writing them your-self?" (*Honeycomb*, 384-85).

In the following passage from the Foreword Richardson describes the exact nature of her relation with this stranger and the way she is guided while writing.

> Aware, as she wrote, of the gradual falling away of the preoccupations that for a while had dictated the briskly moving script, and of the substitution, for the inspiring preoccupations, of a stranger in the form of contemplated reality having for the first time in her experience its own say, and apparently justifying those who acclaim writing as the surest means of discovering the truth about one's own thoughts and beliefs, she had been at the same time increasingly tormented, not only by the failure, of this now so independently assertive reality, adequately to appear within the text, but by its revelation, whencesoever focused, of a hundred faces, any one of which, the moment it was entrapped within the close mesh of direct statement, summoned its fellows to disqualify it (10).

The stranger is able to speak only because Richardson's previous "preoccupations"—that is, her concern with her male and female predecessors or the early "regiments," including figures such as Balzac and Bennett—have "fallen away" as she writes. She wishes to make this stranger or "independently assertive reality . . . appear within the text," but discovers that this is not an easy effect to create. One of the reasons the stranger is so illusive in writing is that its "revelation," or the moments in which it reveals itself, are manifest through "one hundred faces"—a hundred kinds of image, speech, and word-music—and the moment she attempts to make a direct statement, to reduce this myriad hoard into one descriptive statement, the stranger "summons its fellows to disqualify it."

For Richardson, then, writing in the form of direct statement is like wrestling with Proteus: the moment the stranger is touched, or directly approached, it changes form and is no longer static enough to be described. Unlike Proteus, the stranger is able to present all of its forms simultaneously, thereby taking on the sense, as Richardson calls it, of a "revelation" which is not dependent on embodiment for its manifestation. To be manifest in writing, therefore, the stranger requires an abandonment of direct statement. It requires the positing and immediate dissolving of direct statement or the discovery of a technique free of direct statement that will be simultaneously suggestive of multiple faces, of many possibilities at once. And to this end the hieroglyphic film, simultaneously presenting word, image and sound on its screen/page, provides an ideal model for Richardson. Richardson's cinema could also be seen as a palace of substitution, the ultimate place in which the stranger comes alive, as one "contemplated reality" is swiftly substituted and accompanied by others.

The stranger appears most strongly in *Pilgrimage* in those moments in which the most formal disruption occurs on the page. At these points, distinctions between prose, pose, and poem collapse entirely and acute attention is drawn to the syntax and cadence of the prose line-turned-lyric, the presence of Miriam's body, senses and consciousness, and the motion and visual arrangement of words on the page. These "shrine site" moments are often ignited through the act of Miriam reading. But this is reading elevated to a sacrament, a concentration on reality requiring a "contemplative state" that—to echo Richardson—transforms reality. These sacramental passages serve as signals to readers of *Pilgrimage*, who, in the act of reading about reading, are reminded of what they are doing. An example of one such passage appears in *The Tunnel* as Miriam returns in a state of great joy to the room in which she lives:

> The room was white and blue lit, with a sweet morning of moonlight. She had a momentary impulse towards prayer, and glanced at the bed. To get so far and cast herself on her knees and hide her face in her hands . . . [my ellipses] her face praying to her hands, her hands praying to her face, both throbbing separately with their secret, would drive something away.

And a few lines later,

> *Prayer*. Being so weighed down and free with happiness was the time. . . *sacrifice* . . . the evening sacrifice of praise and prayer. . . .
> Why am I so happy and free?

And a paragraph later, the explanation:

> To *see* the earth whirling slowly round, coloured, its waters catching the light. She stood in the middle of the floor hurriedly discarding her clothes. They were old and worn, friendly and alive with the fresh strength of her body. Other clothes would be got somehow; just by going on and working . . . there's so much—eternally. It's stupendous. I've no right to be in it; but I'm in. Someone means me to be in. I can't help it. Fancy people being alive. You would think everyone would go mad. She found herself in bed, sitting up in her flannellette dressing jacket. The stagnant air beneath the sharp downward slope of the ceiling was warmed by the gas. The gaslight glared beautifully over her shoulder down on to the page . . . (*The Tunnel*, 98-99).

This paragraph ends exactly as quoted here and is followed by a large space before the last paragraph in the chapter begins. In the last paragraph the narrative shifts from Miriam's first-person account to Richardson's third-person interjection, which occurs at the moment in which Miriam, after having literally lost her discrete self in the joy of being alive and becoming myriad, "found herself in bed" reading. Thus Miriam and Richardson together, the first and third person, enact the presence of the stranger and the hundred faces of revelation as well as the attitude of sustained concentration that Richardson strove to realize.

The "stranger in the form of contemplated reality" guides and is at the heart of Richardson's concerns in the writing of *Pilgrimage*, her essays, and her film reviews. She arrives at her techniques of narrative disruption out of necessity, finding them to be the only means by which the revelation of the stranger may be caught. Engagement and estrangement are thus closely linked as technique and experience for both Richardson and her readers. Construing the silent cinema as also provoking states of engagement and estrangement, it took on fascinating and fantasized properties for Richardson as a three-dimensional scene of the stranger's revelation.

NOTES: Monkeying With the Plot and PART I

1. The order of the *Pilgrimage* novel-chapters and the dates of publication are as follows:

Volume I:	*Pointed Roofs*, London, Duckworth, 1915.
	Backwater, London, Duckworth, 1916.
	Honeycomb, London, Duckworth, 1917.
Volume II:	*The Tunnel*, London, Duckworth, [Feb.] 1919.
	Interim, London, Duckworth, [Dec.] 1919.
Volume III:	*Deadlock*, London, Duckworth, 1921.
	Revolving Lights, London, Duckworth, 1923.
	The Trap, London, Duckworth, 1925.
Volume IV:	*Oberland*, London, Duckworth, 1927.
	Dawn's Left Hand, London, Duckworth, 1931.
	Clear Horizon, London, J. M. Dent & Cresset Press, 1935.
	Dimple Hill, vol. I-IV, London, J.M. Dent & Cresset Press; New York: Alfred A. Knopf, 1938. First collected edition of *Pilgrimage*.
	March Moonlight, published in the 1967 edition that Dent reissued.

For information on later editions, foreign-language editions, translations and numerous other publications by Dorothy Richardson please see the bibliography. Richardson considered each of the novels to be a chapter in the overall epic of *Pilgrimage*. *Pilgrimage* covers the time between 1891 and 1915; from Miriam's eighteenth to her forty-second year. The novel-volumes are not divided equally between these eighteen years. For example, *Pointed Roofs*, the first chapter, covers only five months; *Revolving Lights* consists of fragments of a few non-consecutive days and *Oberland* covers two weeks.

2. John Rosenberg, *Dorothy Richardson: The Genius They Forgot* (London: Duckworth, 1973), 155.

3. As Rose states in a related discussion, "Her [Richardson's] views on the permutations effected by time on life and artistic endeavor may be found throughout her work, in discursive form, in essays, as well as in *Pilgrimage* where theories become narrative." Shirley Rose, "Dorothy Richardson's Focus on Time," *English Literature in Transition*, vol. XVII, no. 3 (1974), 163.

4. The easy-to-make, but by itself erroneous, conflation of Dorothy Richardson and Miriam Henderson is discussed at greater length in notes 24, 25 and 32, as well as in the "Skyey Apparition, White Searchlight" section of Part II. Few of

Richardson's critics have made the distinction between Richardson's and Henderson's points of view, or between the complicated and deliberate alternation between third and first person narration in *Pilgrimage*. One excellent discussion of this issue occurs in Gloria Fromm's "What Are Men to Dorothy Richardson?" in *Men by Women*, ed. Janet Todd (New York & London: Holmes and Meier Publishers, 1981). See especially pages 169-70. In footnote 4 of "What Are Men to Dorothy Richardson?" Fromm provides a highly useful account of previous critical work on Richardson that conflates the narrator, author, and Miriam. Fromm says,

> A fairly representative formulation is Thomas F. Staley's in *Dorothy Richardson* (Boston: G. K. Hall, 1976), 14: "Miss Richardson is surely Miriam Henderson from the first moments of *Pointed Roofs* . . . to the last nuances of *March Moonlight* . . ."; and Horace Gregory refers to "Dorothy-Miriam" throughout his book, *Dorothy Richardson: An Adventure in Self Discovery* (New York: Holt, Rinehart and Winston, 1967). Most recently, however, Gillian Hanscombe, in her introduction to the Virago edition of *Pilgrimage* (London, 1979), suggests that Miriam is Dorothy Richardson's "fictional alter ego," implying relationship or at least supplementarity rather than identification. But at the same time, in an otherwise important essay, "Male and Female Consciousness in Dorothy Richardson's *Pilgrimage*" (*Journal of Women's Studies in Literature*, 1979), Suzette Henke alludes to *Pilgrimage* as "thirteen volumes of thinly-veiled autobiography."

5. In *The Art of Life* (26), Hanscombe formulates and elaborates on this problem as well.

6. For example, in *Dorothy M. Richardson*, Caesar Blake states,

> Reading *Pilgrimage* analytically as a single book, we may be able to define its meaning as a criticism of life, describe the structure which supports that meaning, and relate the book's style to the design of the whole (8).

7. Virginia Woolf, "Dorothy Richardson" in *Virginia Woolf, Women and Writing*, ed. Michele Barrett (New York and London: Harcourt, Brace, Jovanovich, 1979), 191. Originally published in *Times Literary Supplement*, (May, 1923).

8. For a brief summary of Richardson's biographical background see the Appendix. For biographical studies see the work of Fromm, Rosenberg, Gregory and Blake, to name only the most extensive.

9. Gloria G. Fromm, *Dorothy Richardson, A Biography* (Urbana, Chicago, and London: University of Illinois Press, 1977), 63. Unless otherwise stated, all bio-

graphical information is derived from Fromm's biography.

10. For an excellent discussion of the relation between Richardson's view of time and memory and its relation to her narrative technique, see Shirley Rose, "Dorothy Richardson's Focus On Time." In this essay Rose quotes a particularly relevant statement of Richardson's:

> It is the characteristic vice of the intellect to see the past as a straight line stretching out behind humanity like a sort of infinite tail. In actual experience it is much more like an agglomeration, a vital process of crystallization grouped in and about the human consciousness, confirming and enriching human experience, living unconsciously in individual nerve cells . . . and consciously in individual intelligence, thanks and thanks only to Records . . . . The ideal human type is perhaps he in whom action and contemplation are perfectly blended (Rose, 165; from "Comments by a Layman," *Dental Record*, vol. XXXVIII, August, 1918, 351).

11. Fromm, *Dorothy Richardson, A Biography*, 173-74.

12. Dorothy Richardson to Edward West (Vita Sackville's husband), November 23, 1938, Berg Collection, New York Public Library.

13. In Part I numbers by themselves in parentheses refer to pages in the Foreword to *Pilgrimage.* Richardson refered to the novels that compose *Pilgrimage* as "Chapters" and to the "Chapters" that she grouped together as "novel-volumes."

14. Elizabeth W. Bruss, *Autobiographical Acts, The Changing Situation of a Literary Genre* (Baltimore and London: Johns Hopkins University Press, 1976), 9. As Bruss States,

> Of course autobiography has appropriated forms and techniques from other types of discourse. The apology, for example, is a form now almost exclusively associated with autobiography, its original and nonliterary functions all but forgotten.

15. I am using the word "filmic" in the same sense as Barthes, for whom it is not equivalent with the film:

> Forced to develop in a civilization of the signified, it is not surprising that (despite the incalculable number of films in the world) the filmic should still be rare . . . so much so that it could be said that as yet the film does not exist (any more than does the text); there is only 'cinema,' language, narrative, poetry, sometimes extremely 'modern,' 'translated' into 'images' said to be

> 'animated.' Nor is it surprising that the filmic can only be located after having—analytically—gone across the 'essential,' the 'depth' and the 'complexity' of the cinematic work; all those riches which are merely those of articulated language, with which we constitute the work and believe we exhaust it. The filmic is not the same as the film, is as far removed from the film as the novelistic is from the novel (I can write in the novelistic without ever writing novels) (Roland Barthes, *Image Music Text*, trans. Stephen Heath, New York: Noonday Press, 1977, 65).

It is in this sense that Richardson wrote her novels and wrote about the film in a "filmic," far more than a novelistic, register—without ever having made a film, and rarely discussing any specific film in her "film" writings.

For a detailed discussion of the "filmic" see Stephen Heath, *Questions of Cinema* (Bloomington: Indiana University Press, 1981) 40. And for a discussion of the cinema's relation to language and the distinction between the cinema and the film see Heath's Chapter 9, "Language, Sight and Sound." All of this work has contributed significantly to my thinking about Richardson's relation to the cinema and the filmic.

16. Winifred Bryher, "*Dawn's Left Hand*, by Dorothy M. Richardson," in *Close Up*, vol. 1. VIII, no. 4 (December, 1931) 337. *Dawn's Left Hand* was first published by Duckworth, London, in 1931.

Although Bryher states in this review that as a film *Pilgrimage* would be "the real English film for which so many are waiting," what she then describes as the structure of the narrative that lends itself to being filmed, is more a description of that which is filmic rather than that which is actually filmable. For example, it is Richardson's use of the railway carriage in the opening of *Dawn's Left Hand* that particularly led Bryher to envision *Pilgrimage* as a film. Many of the other *Pilgrimage* novels, and chapters within novels, open with the presence of either a railway carriage or the beginning or end of a journey. (See Part III for further discussion of this.) Bryher's response to these figures of travel and motion through space can thus be seen as a tribute to the success of Richardson's attempt to use a narrative technique that would trigger a filmic experience for the reader.

In addition, Bryher is responding here to the documentary, ethnographic element of *Pilgrimage*; the way in which it "expresses the English spirit" and is a "history." It is also partly in response to this notion of *Pilgrimage* as realistic documentation and Miriam as ethnographer par excellence that Bryher thinks the novels would make a good film.

17. For a complete list of the titles of the "Continuous Performance" articles see the Bibliography.

18. In his essay, "A Comparative Approach to the Form and Function of Novel and Film: Dorothy Richardson's Theory of Art," Paul Tiessen also takes this view:

> Richardson's description of the experience of a person actually watching a film provided her with a graphic, operational model illustrating what was for her the function of all art. At the same time the formal characteristics which she saw as inherent in the film medium helped her to determine the conventions which in another medium, such as literature, would contribute most to the fulfillment of the function. The themes and techniques of her own fiction were her creative culmination of her theory of art, and as a critical approach to these the formal and experiential aspects of film provide the model (*Literature Film Quarterly*, vol. III, no. 1, Winter, 1975, 83-90).

19. Walter Benjamin, "The Work of Art in the Age of Mechanical Reproduction," in *Illuminations* (New York: Schocken Books, 1969) 232-33.

20. Sergei Eisenstein, "Achievement," in *Film Form*, ed. and trans. Jay Leyda (New York: Harcourt, Brace and Company, 1949) 182.

21. Robert Herring, "A New Cinema, Magic and the Avant Garde," in *Close Up*, vol. IV, no. 4 (April, 1929) 52.

22. Fromm, 312.

23. Ford Maddox Ford, *The March of Literature* (London: Allen and Unwin, 1939), 148. As quoted in Rosenberg.

24. Stephen Heath presents and elaborates on this idea in "Writing For Silence: Dorothy Richardson and the Novel," in *Teaching the Text*, eds., Kappler and Bryson, (London: Routledge & Kegan Paul, 1983). Relevant and useful discussions of the female "I" as used in the bildungsroman authored by women and as used by modernist women poets occur in *The Voyage In, Fictions of Female Development*, eds. Abel, Hirsch and Langland (Hanover and London: University Press of New England, for Dartmouth College, 1983), 9-11; and in Carolyn Burke's "Supposed Persons: Modernist Poetry and the Female Subject," *Feminist Studies*, vol. 11, no. 1 (Summer, 1985).

In *The Voyage In*, a different account of Freudian psychosexual difference is presented based on the theories of Chodorow, Dinnerstein, Miller, Flax and Gilligan. This account is resonant with the story of Miriam's development as well as with the notion of her as a myriad subject. It presents the possibility of an "I," an ego, who comes to know itself in relation with, rather than through separation from, others and the world. As elaborated by the editors in the Introduction:

> A distinctive female "I" implies a distinctive value system and unorthodox developmental goals, defined in terms of community and empathy rather than achievement and autonomy. The fully realized and individuated self who caps the journey of the *Bildungsroman* may not represent the developmental goals of women, or of women characters. Female fictions of development reflect the tensions between the assumptions of a genre that embodies male norms and the values of its female protagonists. The heroine's developmental course is more conflicted, less direct: separation tugs against the longing for fusion and the heroine encounters the conviction that identity resides in intimate relationships, especially those of early childhood. The deaths in which these fictions so often culminate represent less developmental failures than refusals to accept an adulthood that denies profound convictions and desires (10-11).

And as Burke elaborates in "Supposed Persons," this plural "I" that signals the personae of a fictional or poetic presence does not necessarily represent the author. In the context of this differently construed female subject the act of representation for a woman writer can, as it does with Richardson and Miriam, become imbricated with immense complications. Psychological/phenomenological questions are raised such as, Who is the mirror of whom? And, What technique of writing can indicate the stability and instability of a constantly questioning subject?

These are certainly some of the questions with which Richardson wrestles, which guide her choices of narrative technique and her explanations in the Foreword.

25. In "Writing For Silence: Dorothy Richardson and the Novel," Stephen Heath states that one of *Pilgrimage's* most important and unannounced focuses is the slippery, mirror relation between Miriam and Richardson. He suggests that Richardson's choice of words and names is too precise for it to be accidental, that embedded in the name Miriam is the possibility of "mirror I am," and that it is linked by sound to the word *myriad.* In *Teaching the Text*, ed. Kappler and Bryson, (London: Routledge & Kegan Paul, 1983).

26. In his article "Generic Protocols: Science Fiction and Mundane," Samuel R. Delany investigates the question of "why genres are not rigorously definable." He describes the problem as a "taxonomical dilemma [which is] simply this: as soon as we would take a group of texts, a recognizable type of writing, say, till now considered simply 'a local form,' and argue that it is really a genre, we are in the odd position of having to describe in a formal way why these texts can no

longer be formally described, and then go on to describe them informally in such a way that their processes, operations, functions, and general workings are still clearly recognizable." Samuel R. Delany, "Generic Protocols: Science Fiction and Mundane," in *The Technical Imagination: Theories and Fictions*, ed. Teresa de Lauretis, Andreas Huyssen, Kathleen Woodward (Madison, Wisconsin: Coda Press, 1980) 176.

27. For further discussion of the pilgrimage and epic as traditional male genres refer to the "Monstrosity and Impurity" section of Part III.

Also see: Page duBois, *Centaurs & Amazons: Women and the Prehistory of the Great Chain of Being* (Ann Arbor: The University of Michigan Press, 1982); and duBois, "Sappho and Helen," in *Women in the Ancient World, The Arethusa Papers*, ed. Peradotto and Sullivan (Albany: State University of New York Press, 1984) 95-105.

> Echoing this idea, Simone de Beauvoir states, Woman is the Sleeping Beauty, Cinderella, Snow White, she who receives and submits. In song and story the young man is seen departing adventurously in search of a woman; he slays the dragon, he battles giants; she is locked in a tower, a palace, a garden, a cave, she is chained to a rock, a captive, sound asleep; she waits (Simone de Beauvoir, *The Second Sex*, trans. Parshley, New York, Vintage Books, 1970, 271-72).

28. For a far more detailed discussion of this issue in connection with Richardson refer to Part III.

For an excellent and more detailed discussion of these issues see *The Voyage In, Fictions of Female Development*, ed. Abel, Hirsch and Langland, (Hanover and London: published for Dartmouth College by University Press of New England, 1983) 4-45. Also see *A New Mythos, The Novel of the Artist as Heroine 1877-1977.*

Consistent with this use of *Wilhelm Meister* as a model is the fact that Miriam's first journey, in the first novel-chapter *Pointed Roofs,* is to Germany. Miriam continues to investigate, and in the earlier novels to idealize, German culture throughout *Pilgrimage.*

29. Esther Labovitz, *The Myth of the Heroine The Female Bildungsroman in the Twentieth Century* (New York: Peter Lang, 1986) 58. This rich and unprecedented study is an excellent source for a detailed discussion of *Pilgrimage* and the female bildungsroman.

I am also grateful to Esther Labovitz for her deep interest in and respect for the work of Dorothy Richardson, and for the conversations we have had about Richardson's work that have yielded many insights. It is her integrity and expansive approach that have allowed *this* book to take a shape that I would wish for it.

30. Racist and colonial discourses are inscribed in the *Pilgrimage* novels and in the "Continuous Performance" columns. Richardson's poetics, of course, also inscribe elements of these discourses in the form of aesthetic concerns. The ways in which this inscription occurs is complex and in need of critical attention. While highly problematic, a recent essay by Rebecca Egger, "Deaf Ears and Dark Continents: Dorothy Richardson's Cinematic Epistemology," is useful in addressing some of these issues. Egger in *Camera Obscura, A Journal of Feminism and Film Theory*, No. 30 (Indiana University Press, for the University of California, Santa Barbara, May, 1992).

31. Up to this point in the citation, the ellipses are mine. After this point they are Richardson's. Because she uses ellipses often and in an idiosyncratic manner I will indicate when I have introduced my own ellipses into her text. Otherwise it can be assumed that the ellipses are hers.

32. For an excellent analysis of the same passage from *The Tunnel* see Gloria Fromm's "What Are Men to Dorothy Richardson?" in *Men by Women*, edited by Janet Todd (New York and London: Holmes and Meier Publishers, 1981), 168-70. Fromm also states that Miriam presents herself to Tremayne through her playing of the music, but Fromm's analysis focuses on the persons of narration Richardson employs. Fromm sees this passage as particularly susceptible to what she sees as the common confusion between and conflation of Miriam and Richardson (discussed in notes 4, 24 and 25). I agree with Fromm that the way in which this often occurs is that the third-person form of narration is mistaken for the first person. As Fromm states,

> Indeed, although the third-person form of narration in *Pilgrimage* has been taken, in effect, for the first person, none of the potentially useful distinctions that have evolved from studying the techniques of fictional autobiography have been applied to Dorothy Richardson's novel.
>
> For better or worse, author and heroine have scarcely been distinguished one from the other. While it is certainly true that Miriam's consciousness—as motor—operates the novel, Dorothy Richardson as certainly holds the key. She chose to narrate as though through Miriam's consciousness primarily because of her conviction that no other method of presentation would convey an accurate enough psychological reality, or, as she herself put it, "a feminine equivalent of the current masculine realism."

PART II
Filmic Poetics

Film: The New Modernist Art Form

> In life, we contemplate a landscape from one point, or, walking through it, break it into bits. The film, by setting the landscape in motion and keeping us still, allows it to walk through us (Dorothy Richardson, "CP: Narcissus," *Close Up*, September, 1931, 185).

As Eisenstein suggested, the modernist novel and the film had more in common with one another than perhaps any other written text has ever had with a visual medium. The film, the new art form of the twentieth century, manifested the conditions and was the expression of modernism. It provided a spatial and mental allegory for the kind of modernist experience Henry James described as "never limited, and . . . never complete"—the state of most nonrepresentational modernist art forms.[1] Benjamin observed that

> around 1900 technical reproduction had reached a standard that not only permitted it to reproduce all transmitted works of art and thus to cause the most profound change in their impact upon the public; it also had captured a place of its own among the artistic processes. For the study of this standard nothing is more revealing than the nature of the repercussions that these two different manifestations—the reproduction of works of art and the art of the film—have had on its traditional form.[2]

In order to trace one of the repercussions that the art of film had on "its traditional form," it is necessary to look beyond film. Unlike other art forms—book production and sculpture casting, for example—film at the turn of the century did not have its own tradition of technical reproduction; its technical predecessors were the diorama, the daguerreotype, and the photograph. Instead, early film found its roots in the novel. It is therefore no surprise that film was initially both a vehicle through which to scrutinize the form of the novel (as well as other social forms of representation) and a medium that suggested and reflected new forms of writing.

An example of this can be seen in Woolf's essay "The Cinema," in which she speaks of the novel as "prey" to and "unfortunate victim" of the film and calls their alliance "unnatural." While Woolf is both disturbed and intrigued by the novel/silent cinema alliance, Richardson is only intrigued. However, their interests intersect in Woolf's question, "But what, then, are its [the cinema's] devices?" It is in the devices of the cinema that Woolf sees hope for the film to move out of its "parasitic" relation to the novel. And it is partly a fascination with the potential use of these devices in the novel that fixes Richardson's attention on the film. In "The Cinema," Woolf strikes the nerve of some of the main devices of the cinema which repeatedly fascinate Richardson in the "Continuous Performance" columns. Richardson and Woolf echo one another more closely and profoundly perhaps here in Woolf's discussion of the cinema's promise as located in its devices than anywhere else. There are many instances of this resonance in "The Cinema," but some of the most striking can be heard in the following statements and questions: "For a moment it seemed as if thought could be conveyed by shape more effectively than by words."—"Is there, we ask, some secret language which we feel and see, but never speak, and, if so, could this be made visible to the eye?"—"The likeness of the thought is for some reason more beautiful, more comprehensible, more available, than the thought itself." And finally, "Yet if so much of our thinking and feeling is connected with seeing, some residue of visual emotion which is of no use either to the painter or poet may still await the cinema." It is in relation to this last statement that Richardson may have departed from Woolf. While Woolf imagines that the "visual emotion" of the cinema is useless to the painter and poet, Richardson imagines a backwards commerce in which "shape rather than words," a "secret language," manifest in "the likeness of the thought rather than the thought itself," as well as other devices of the cinema might be put to use in the poetic modernist novel.[3]

The advent of modernism, coinciding with that of the film, can be marked by the shift from the belief that it is possible to report subjective states, to the belief that it is possible only to render them. Viewed as a rendering machine the modernist film was redolent with the suggestion of technical and conceptual innovation for many mediums. In the realm of psychology, William James characterized this shift in his *Principles of Psychology*, published in 1890, in which he named the "stream of consciousness." Consciousness, he said, is an amalgam of all that we have experienced and continue to experience. We are selective in our thoughts, selectively attentive or inattentive, zeroing in on certain objects and thoughts and blocking others out entirely. No thought occurs in the mind in exactly the way it did before. "Experience," he said, "is remoulding us every moment, and our mental reaction on every given thing is really a resultant of our experience of the whole world up to that date." According to James, thought has rhythm, tempo, and pace; it involves a "clearly lighted centre of experience" surrounded by a twilight region—a "fringe" or "halo" of other thoughts.[4]

Debating about the novel in the 1880s, Henry James extended the definition of experience and of fiction to include the subjective world.

> It is equally excellent and inconclusive to say that one must write from experience; to our suppositious aspirant such a declaration might savour of mockery. What kind of experience is intended, and where does it begin and end? Experience is never limited, and it is never complete; it is an immense sensibility, a kind of huge spider-web of the finest silken threads suspended in the chamber of consciousness, and catching every airborne particle in its tissue. It is the very atmosphere of the mind; and when the mind is imaginative—much more when it happens to be that of a man of genius—it takes to itself the faintest hints of life, it converts the very pulses of the air into revelations.[5]

The attempt to define experience and to extend the definition of fiction to include the new category of experience called "consciousness" is manifest in the modernist novel. As James questions what it might be like to write out of this amorphous event called "experience," his descriptive terms and metaphors proliferate: "never limited . . . never complete," "an immense sensibility," "a huge spider-web," a "chamber," an "atmosphere," the conversion of the "pulses of air into revelation." The proliferation is symptomatic of the difficulty of naming something that appears to be new. James' terms point to the transition from the apparently literal social-realistic novel of the nineteenth century in which the author was viewed as a kind of reporter or witness of a knowable "reality," to the early twentieth century and its questioning of what constituted reality or experience.

These peculiarly modernist descriptions of consciousness were echoed in almost every turn-of-the-century technological and cultural realm. The artistic and technological inventions of the day had in common their ability to, or desire to, create the experience of a simultaneous "convergence" of disparate elements that would then give way to a "revelation," or a new understanding of the relation between time, space, and the human organs of perception. In Henry James' words, these innovations made disparate elements "converge" to suggest "an atmosphere of the mind." Among myriad examples of this turn-of-the-century mode in the realm of technical invention are the phonograph, the telephone, the wireless, major increases in train travel, and of course the film—all of which had considerable impact and are thus especially emblematic of the consciousness of the time. Technical innovations influenced the concerns and formal techniques of much of the writing and art of the period. In 1906, for example, G. S. Lee wrote, in his "rapturous eulogy of technology" titled *The Voice of the Machines,* that the new phonograph made it possible to "speak forward in time to the unborn and listen backwards to the dead."[6] Thanks to the invention of the telephone (in 1876) and the wireless (in 1897), large numbers of people became able to experience many different and distant events at the same time. The cinema recorded events and shaped a vision of the past. The detail and accuracy of millions of memories were increased by the newsreels of recent history regularly shown in the early cinema houses.[7] It was now possible to be in two places at once.

Theories of simultaneity proliferated in writing and art. Many of these were modeled on the ideal simultaneous nature of counterpoint in music. Henri-Martin Barzun, Blaise Cendrars, and Guillaume Apollinaire worked in various modes to create a poetry of simultaneity. In 1912 Barzun founded a journal to present his theory of simultaneity and to publish works that conformed to it. Barzun was interested in achieving polyphonic effects in poetry, and thought that a "multiple lyricism must render the multiplicity of modern life."[8] In 1913 Cendrars published, in collaboration with painter Sonia Delaunay, *La prose du Transsibérien et de la petite Jehanne de France,* which was announced as "the first simultaneous book." This work was a formal manifestation of the new simultaneous experiences of convergence and fragmentation characteristic of the turn of the century.

> Printed on a sheet two meters long, it was meant to be seen all at once so that the spatial limitations of one page after another would not chop up its wholeness. It was illustrated down the left side with Sonia Delaunay's *couleurs simultanées.* The poem describes

> Cendrars' journey from Moscow to Harbin on the Trans-Siberian railway in 1904, and above the text he reproduced a map to show the route at a glance. Thus the reader saw "simultaneous" colors, a map of the trip and a poem about it at the same time.[9]

The equation of writing as a kind of travel by rail, indicated by the map hovering above the words and images, and illustrating that travel through space could also rearrange time, signals the emergence of a new aesthetic. There was widespread interest in the notion that a formal spatial arrangement of words on a page, or of visual images, could produce in a reader or viewer a sense of collapsed time (all "times" seen on the map being experienced at once).[10] Cendrars' piece is characteristic of much modernist art in that it calls attention to its production as a reproduction. Benjamin's observation about the Dadaists applies to this and many other modernist pieces as well.

> What they intended and achieved was a relentless destruction of the aura of their creations, which they branded as reproductions with the very means of production.[11]

This statement also applies to *Pilgrimage*, which doubles itself and calls attention to its production as a reproduction by constantly discussing Miriam's process of arriving at the writing of a book that would have characteristics much like *Pilgrimage* itself. A doubling is also effected by Richardson's refusal to allow the reader to forget that he or she is producing the book, as a projector produces a film, through the lens of his or her reading practices. In addition, by posing as autobiography, *Pilgrimage* gestures toward something "real" and in the past, that the writing both is and isn't about. These methods engage the viewer or reader in active participation; as Benjamin says, "At any moment the reader is ready to turn into a writer."[12]

The invention of the cinema in the last decade of the nineteenth century contributed to an altered sense of the present. The experience of simultanaeity could be synthesized with the filmic techniques of cutting between non-sequential events or repetitions of the same event from different perspectives.[13] Contrast editing and intercutting were among the first techniques used to render simultaneity in film. They made it possible to splice open a moment and insert other perspectives or to insert the actions leading up to that point as if occurring simultaneously. These techniques had their parallel uses in the novel. For example, Richardson duplicated the close-up, which expanded time and space, in *Oberland*, the ninth novel-chapter of *Pilgrimage*, which covers two weeks in 120 pages; *Pointed Roofs* (the first), which covers five months in 157 pages; and especially *Revolving Lights* (the seventh), which covers only parts of a few nonconsecutive days in 66 pages. As in Joyce's *Ulysses* or Woolf's *Mrs. Dalloway*, depictions of a moment in time were often extended over many pages in *Pilgrimage*. In 1916 the Futurists lauded the ability of the cinema to "give the intelligence a prodigious sense of simultaneity and omnipresence" and "a fleeting synthesis of life in the world."[14]

Film also had great economic appeal.

> Resting on an industrializable technological base, cinema, different to theatre, offers the possibility of an industry of spectacle. And spectacle is then evidently crucial with its introduction of the hold of meaning and vision and representation into, as a fact of, the industry itself. The series is not a chronology but a constant interlock: projection, for instance, which is at once 'early' (projecting devices were experimented in the mid-seventeenth century, Kircher's famous magic lantern) and 'late' (intensive work on projectors between 1893 and 1896, from the phantascope to the biograph), cannot but engage at one and the same time, and determiningly, commerce and spectacle and the relation of the two (the possibility of a new theatre-novel-image industry, the possibility of a new theatre of the subject, representing, positioning, fixing: a veritable speculation).[15]

It is where projection and spectacle coincide (the "interlock") that the "theatre of the subject" is performed in the novel of speculation—the stream-of-consciousness novel. There was much commerce at this time between writers of novels and producers of films. However, those in the business of film production were buying novels for their "story" value, while writers interested in the film had become less concerned with plot and were captured instead by the film's powers of evocation. Ironically those novels purchased in great quantities for adaptation by the film industry (and often never actually adapted) were not the novels experimenting with notions of "consciousness."[16]

The "three areas of technical understanding"—"photography, persistence of vision, projection"—on which the creation of commercial cinema hinged, have their parallels in turn-of-the-century technical innovations in the novel.[17] The possibility of accurately depicting a character or capturing a "realistic" representative image by way of the photograph gave way to the possibility of capturing motion itself on the film or recording the movement of consciousness. The "persistence of vision" that dominated the film called into question many of the same issues regarding the relation between sight, memory, and narrative that were being explored by such figures as Proust, Joyce, Woolf, Bergson, and Freud in the context of the novel, philosophy, and the new field of psychoanalysis. As Benjamin states, "The camera introduces us to unconscious optics as does psychoanalysis to unconscious impulses." In similar fashion, the stream-of-consciousness novel introduces us to the texture and motion of the conscious and unconscious in daily life.[18] Concerned technically, philosophically, and psychologically with "representing, positioning, fixing" that which is impossible absolutely to represent, position, or fix, film posed at once many of the burning questions of modernism regarding space, time, and narrative.

In the realm of the novel the experiments of Proust, Joyce, Woolf, James, and Richardson were all attempts to render in prose the experience of what James called an "amalgam of consciousness." As Stephen Heath describes, the nineteenth-century novel, like the photograph, was seen as a mirror, and the task of the novelist was to create an apt reflection.[19] This was no longer the task of the twentieth-century novel.

Having questioned what constitutes a "realistic" reflection, or account, the assumption of an easy parallel between an author and his or her text, and a text and the nineteenth-century "real world," also became problematic for many early twentieth-century writers. It was at this moment when categories such as author, text, and reality were called into question that one-to-one mirror-like correspondences between a represented and a "real" world were no longer possible to draw. Consequently, the belief in the ability to report on subjective states and an objective world changed to the problematic of how to render various states of consciousness. The late nineteenth- and early twentieth-century moment of this shift consisted of the recognition that "reality" was not an absolute conception but a social representation. As such, it was governed by social formalities and genres and a montage of codes of behavior. This recognition, as Heath describes, threatened to undo the mirroring function of the novel—a function that in turn served to uphold and reproduce the very norms outside of itself in a "real" world that it seemed to reflect and confirm. As Heath says, "For a particular society, in fact, the work that is realistic is that which repeats the received forms of

'Reality.' It is a question of reiterating the society's system of intelligibility."[20]

Those European modernist writers, whose work reflected the turn-of-the-century shift away from the attempt to repeat society's systems of intelligibility and toward an attempt to render them, risked being unreadable.

> What founds the text in part, and to an extent that has grown steadily since the beginning of the nineteenth century, is the novel and what assures this foundation is its readability ("unreadable" being a term with which we trace the horizon of our sense, of our desire not to read our limits). This readability is relayed by a series of codes and conventions, by the text of the already known and written: that work is readable therefore, which is cast within their horizon, which repeats them in their naturalized transparence.[21]

To move from the belief that subjective states are possible to report to the conviction that they can only be rendered requires a shift in the horizon of sense. Horizon is the appropriate word here because, in its evocation of a large space delimited by a horizontal line beyond which it is not possible to see, it suggests the place where the light disappears. As a line of type, or a sentence, at the edge of visibility or legibility, the "unreadable" invokes the formal concerns with spatial arrangement, projection, and illumination so characteristic of the kind of "unreadability" common to the work of many modernists.

If the foundation of the novel is assured by its readability, which is relayed by a series of codes and conventions, then the text that is not already known will have a different physical shape and look on the page. Because of its different use, or lack of use, of codes and conventions, the "not-already-known" text maps an enigmatic terrain. Here the unreadable and the unrepeated meet where what has come to appear natural to them does not reappear. Such a text will also have a different and possibly unrecognizable horizon line. This shift—from recognizable to not—occurs when a profoundly different experience of language and form takes place, so that mirroring or representing is no longer relevant to the task that writing has become.

> This shift is not to be understood in the traditional terms of a change from "social realism" to "psychological realism"..., but in terms of the deconstruction of the very "innocence" of realism. Its foundation is a profound experience of language and form and the demonstration of that experience in the writing of the novel

> which, transgressed, is no longer repetition and self-effacement but work and self-presentation as text.[22]

The shift to "work and self-presentation" as the text and motivation of writing describes exactly Richardson's project of autobiographical epic. The writing of *Pilgrimage* arose out of a belief that "life [was] the plot"—a belief that dramatically disrupted the nineteenth-century distinction between life and art, between the plot that is a microcosm of "life" and the story that is now conceived of as the plotless unfolding of life. In a letter to Vita Sackville-West dated November 23, 1938, Richardson asked,

> Isn't life the plot? Is what is "artistically" wrong with my work produced by a sense of the iniquity of monkeying with this plot?

In *Pilgrimage*, the shift to "work and self-presentation as text" is manifest in Miriam, whose life is the plot and whose consciousness is the subject of the epic novel. Always preoccupied with the blend of consciously noticed and unconsciously perceived things, Miriam exclaims as she sits at her writing table,

> But this was life! These strange unconsciously noticed things, living on in one, coming together at the right moment, part of a reality. . . (*Deadlock*, 133).

This thought leads Miriam to rise from her desk, look around, and find her familiar room "strange." She recalls, as if it were an epiphany, the first time, years ago, that she saw the ink stains on her desk.

> The years that had passed were a single short interval leading to the restoration of that first moment. Everything they contained centred there; her passage through them, the desperate graspings and droppings, had been a coming back. Nothing would matter now that the paper-scattered lamplit circle was established as the centre of life. Everything would be an everlastingly various joyful coming back. Held up by this secret place, drawing her energy from it, any sort of life would do that left this room and its little table free and untouched (*Deadlock*, 133-34).

The familiar room was made strange by the collapse in time ("the years were a single short interval") which is one of the methods of cutting and collapsing that attracted Richardson to the cinema, where the familiar and quotidian are also made strange. Miriam's "paper-scattered lamplit circle" and Henry James' "clearly lighted centre of experience" invoke the issues of selective attention and inattention; the relation of thought to space and to asynchronic time; the notion that thought has rhythm, tempo, and pace; and the shared impulse to render these experiences through metaphors of light surrounded by darkness. Just as Miriam "draws her energy" from the "paper-scattered lamplit circle"—the original scene of writing—Richardson draws her energy from, and is fascinated by, the lamplit circle of the film projector which for her is also a secret place, a circle scattered with paper—a scene always about writing and always provoking writing about writing. The "Continuous Performance" columns exist in the interstices where the novel and the early film overlap. In the columns she spins out a poetics of the "experience" that William James invoked in *Principles of Psychology.*

Close Up and The Turn-Of-The-Century Context

Close Up and Pool Publishing were founded in 1927 in Territet, Switzerland by Kenneth Macpherson, Winifred Bryher and the poet H.D. (Hilda Doolittle).[23] *Close Up* was published for six-and-a-half years, from July 1927 to December 1933. Pool's list of publications included

> several volumes of prose by Bryher and Macpherson, an essay by Hanns Sachs against the death penalty, three monographs on cinema, and a film review, *Close Up,* which joined the still-young tradition of literary "little magazines." In addition, Pool undertook the production of films.
>
> *Close Up* . . . represented the critical and promotional pole of Pool's activities. Publication was assured with admirable regularity by a minimal team; the consistently high aesthetic quality of the magazine culminated in a larger and more ambitious format in March 1931. Editorial duties were shared in order to cover the whole field.[24]

The regulars in what came to be called "the *Close Up* group" included Bryher, Macpherson, Robert Herring, H. D., Richardson, and Oswell Blakeston. The writers who regularly appeared in *Close Up* shared common concerns in regard to the cinema, but did not actually constitute a "group" in any formal sense. Many of them had never met and knew each other only through their published work in *Close Up.* Still, they were linked by their common and unusual interests in the unique terrain of concerns that *Close Up* represented. As Friedberg states, some of the recurrent themes in their writing included

> 1) the idea of a British cinema, its problems and potentials, 2) the impact of Soviet filmmaking and film theory, 3) the problem of censorship, 4) the encouragement of alternative distribution and exhibition networks (cineclubs and film societies) and of alternative production circumstances (especially the amateur movement), 5) the relation of still photography and film stills to cinematic form, 6) the role of theory and criticism itself.[25]

Other themes can also be traced, though they were not as passionately debated: psychoanalysis, the role of the film spectator, representation and racism, the development of, among others, Czech, Japanese, and the Portuguese cinema. There was also a continuous critical and theoretical discussion within *Close Up* investigating the act of writing about the cinema.

Richardson's contributions ranged from practical concerns with censorship to speculative articles on the gendered position of the spectator, film as narrative, the impact of the filmic form of representation on the other arts and on other aspects of society, and film as an ideal form. Her concerns were almost never with specific films but rather with the film as a medium or experience. Just as the form of the *Pilgrimage* novels mimed the shape of Miriam's consciousness, the "Continuous Performance" columns mimed, to some extent, the filmic experience as she believed it occurred. Richardson's columns were theoretical in that they provided a reflective gloss on the film experience, a kind of meta-narrative about the narrativity of film. Simultaneously they pointed to the mechanics of their own writing, thereby raising questions regarding the function of writing about cinema and the kinds of writing that might be appropriate to the subject of cinema.

A unique aspect of *Close Up's* editorial policy was the variety of writing related to film that Bryher, Macpherson, and H. D. thought appropriate to publish under one cover. Many issues of *Close Up* contained a selection ranging from poetry by, for example, Stein, Marianne Moore, or H. D. to theoretical essays by Eisenstein, Pudovkin, or Hanns Sachs.

The common vocabulary and concerns of the *Close Up* writers mirrored many of the events of the time. The dissemination of psychoanalytic theory, along with many other new articulations of subjectivity, shattered any remaining enlightenment and romantic notions about the intact individual who has obvious and easily describable motivations. Crises in subjectivity reflected crises surrounding issues of representation. The fragmentation of the modernist subject was also inherent in the demands of and confusions about the "new woman." The uncertain gender of the new woman, in turn, implied a reexamination of what it meant to be male. In the same vein, the early-century crisis in colonization and the experience of World War I altered the British and European sense of their dominant position in the world. All of these changes, both causing and coinciding with the breakdown of the Victorian family, posited new subjectivities which were played out and explored through the convenient commodification and widespread distribution of the film. Against this backdrop, *Close Up* occupied a typical avant-garde position, providing a cosmopolitan reflection and a critique of issues that were being acted out in the popular realm of the cinema.

Much of the work in *Close Up* was written to address the closely linked issues of representation, psychoanalysis, and new constructions of gender or negotiations around problems raised by "the woman question." Richardson's writing on film grappled with all of these issues—most often through the lens of, and in response to, this "question." Richardson was concerned specifically with the ways in which the woman question affected women writers and artists. Female writers occupied the complexly gendered role of the subject actively creating a representation—a traditionally male position. In *Close Up,* Richardson and many of the other writers responded to a matrix of historically received issues concerning women writers and artists. Among these questions were definitions of mental illness and health, and the proper sexuality and agency for a woman. These issues arose, in part, because of the increasing public presence and publication of women writers from the mid-nineteenth century on. One, among a number of hotly contested issues from the mid-nineteenth into the early twentieth-century, was whether or not a woman should write.

Some brief background on the historical development of these issues will set *Close Up* and the concerns of its writers in context. Whereas in the mid-nineteenth century the issues surrounding the woman question focused on the rise of the woman writer, in the early twentieth century many of the same issues were raised in relation to women and the cinema.

From the mid to late Victorian period there was a remarkable increase of madness, of women committed to institutions, and of publication among women. Also at this time, hysteria was named and defined as an illness. Writing about the famous Dora case Freud said,

> It still strikes me myself as strange that the case histories I write should read like short stories, and that, as one might say they lack the serious stamp of science.

And later,

> The mechanism of poetry is the same as that of hysterical phantasies.[26]

Freud may have been worried that, in writing up the Dora case, he was beginning to slide away from science to the other side—the side of short stories, poetry, or "hysterical phantasies." His discomfort in reflecting on the ways in which his own subjectivity ("it strikes me myself as strange") was manifest in the unscientific form of his writing—a sign of lack of seriousness, a sign, that is, of gender—is indicative of the kind of unease raised by the woman question. When the sides don't remain in place, the confusing of the categories—male and female, science and short stories, poetry and hysterical phantasy—generates enormous anxiety. As Freud also said, hysteria is often manifest in bisexuality—the "illness" that embodies slippage as confusion of categories.

Early twentieth-century British and American women writers inherited the predominantly white and middle-class nineteenth-century debate on the woman question. The term "woman writers" itself embodied gender slippage as confusion of categories. With the major increase of women writing in the nineteenth century, one of the main issues around which the woman question debates revolved was the proper relation of women to writing and literature, and the links between sexuality and art.

> In [mid-nineteenth-century] discussions of women and literature, the sexually laden language suggests two theories. According to one, female imagination is a volatile and highly erotic force that must be repressed, or at least controlled; according to the other, women's writing is a sign of sexual and emotional frustration. Both must be seen against the prevailing assumption that artistic creation is, like the sexual act, a male activity in which women have only an extremely restricted part. As the *Saturday Review* reminds readers in 1865, "Female nature, mental as well as physical, is essentially receptive and not creative."[27]

From the late Victorian period on into the early twentieth century, the conflicting demands on women to signify "feminine" orderliness and purity in the midst of a growing industrial society, and to perfectly control their behavior as well as demonstrate their domestic managerial skills, coincided with a growing fear of female sexuality.[28]

In comparing the fiction and poetry written by many modernist women with Freud's late Victorian analyses of female hysterics, it is striking to see the emergence of what could be called a poetics of hysteria. For "hysterics" this was a grammar of subversion spoken through the body and in words, but not written—at least not by Freud's hysterics, although perhaps by Freud himself. For the women writers it is a subversion of grammar and other given rules of ordering words on the page. This refusal to follow rules of composition led to the production of written pieces that were diagnosed by critics as abnormal and unhealthy in a peculiarly feminine way—one that is related to abnormal feminine sexuality. This same diagnosis was applied to much modernist writing by men. As Dowling has outlined, the decadent and the "new woman" were closely associated in late Victorian British criticism and reviews, and often in *Punch.* The decadent became a repository for anxiety about the increasingly slippery category of the "feminine," and in turn, the "new woman," along with new forms of writing, was often seen as decadent. The association of decadent with feminine, and of modernist forms of writing with decadence, explains the defensive behavior of many male modernist writers toward female modernists and in regard to their own work. Because of their subversions of grammar and traditional form, male modernists were quite likely to be considered "effeminate" by critics—if not they themselves, then their work—and fear of this judgment was high.[29]

Keohane and Bernheimer suggest that hysteria can be viewed as an expression of the desire to escape the strangulating demands of repressive, patriarchal, bourgeois family and social expectations. All of the classic symptoms of hysteria can be seen as attempts to break out of social roles by exaggerated identification with what was, or is, considered to be "feminine," or through exploration of alternative modes of experiencing and describing the world. Poems, novels, and films that were healthy and made sense, like hysterics when recovered and normal, shared this trait: they told linear narratives proceeding along logical sequences of thought, rather than falling in their telling through a steep kilter of association, fragmentation, mute spaces on the page, palimpsestic memory overlays, hostile harangues, or hallucinatory lapses. These concerns with sequence and form reflect a modernist discomfort with the relationship between subjectivity and representation—a discomfort quite different, as Richardson has pointed out, for female modernist writers than for male.

Consistent with the dominant ideology of the time, female modernist writers were often seen by such contemporaries as Pound and Eliot as receptacle-like muses rather than active agents. Thus the kinds of subjectivity and poetics presented by many modernist women writers—women who are already unnatural by virtue of writing—are posed against dominant notions of what is properly and naturally feminine.[30] One of the traits that often distinguishes women's work from that of experimenting male modernists is an exploration of gender constructions within and through the structure of the novel or poem. As Burke states,

> Modernism implies a thoroughgoing critique of attention. The female modernist poets' "I" may help us to understand what actually precedes and underlies the attempt to speak "in a woman's voice" or to talk "(just) like a woman."[31]

Virginia Woolf and Dorothy Richardson were among the first to experiment with altering the form of the novel by writing from the point of view of "a woman's consciousness." Many other modernist female novelists and poets, too, have featured the dismantling of feminine essences, as well as "a critique of attention," in their critical, poetic, and fictive writing. In fiction and poetry this critique of attention can be witnessed by looking at the arrangements of language on the page.

Richardson's concern with a processual subject, language, and content, and her alertness to the subtle dependencies between form and content, were shared by many other contemporaries, some of whom were male and many of whom were working in other mediums, especially film. These concerns were expressed through a number of techniques, including that of continuous inner monologue, a mix of broken and endlessly trailing-off syntax, and a drastic move away from linear narrative. These techniques were used by Richardson and by many other modernists in strikingly different ways—all in order to achieve their versions of Heath's "unreadable." Stein's poetics of a "continuous present," her move away from linear storytelling, and her emphasis on the materiality of language, are echoed in this statement by Eisenstein regarding film: "In 1924 I wrote, with intense zeal: 'Down with the story and the plot!'"[32]

Film, and in turn *Close Up*, were not only repositories for anxieties but were also receptacles of various kinds of early-century idealism. Richardson's "Continuous Performance" columns are riddled with an idealism that Bryher articulates in a discussion of the unique merits of the film.

> We felt we could state our convictions honorably in this twentieth-century form of art and it appealed to the popular internationalism of those so few years because "the silents" offered a single language across Europe.[33]

The notion that film is an "honorable" rather than dishonorable form in which to state convictions implies that there is an inherent integrity between "this twentieth-century form of art" and the content of these twentieth-century ideals or "convictions." Bryher suggests here, as Richardson and others suggest elsewhere, a moral elevation of film over other forms of art; film is better because it represents modernist experiences more accurately. Part of its ideal nature lies in the notion that film provides, in Bryher's words, "a single language across Europe." Bryher frames film as a linguistic medium of communication, a visual language that, like Esperanto (invented out of the same impulse in 1887 by L. L. Zamenhof, a Russian philologist) provided an ideal medium through which one could be everywhere and nowhere at once—a perfect vehicle of a perfect cosmopolitanism.

Some of the elements of ideal modernist experience reenacted by film included the experience of fragmentation and the post-colonial fantasy of knowing the other (whether the "other" be woman or native) not through language, but through the privileging of sight—through an acquisitive overlay of image and technology that could be coded as exchange. The idealized cinema provided a link between a late nineteenth-century cosmopolitanism, present in the novels and thought of many writers including Eliot and Sand, and a turn-of-the-century "popular internationalism."

For a certain class of people and for many associated with *Close Up*, cosmopolitanism, travel, and the cinema became linked by the necessity to travel in order to see.

> Travel became equated with the work, study and exploration of the worldwide status of cinema, demanding pilgrimages to, not cities, but screens. Travel also implied, for all those who could afford it, a freedom from the restraints of social fixity, from the family, and for a woman, from the Father.[34]

In *Pilgrimage*, Miriam illustrates the importance and widespread presence of then-current notions of cosmopolitanism when she argues with Bernard Mendizabal, a Spanish Jew and significant figure in *Pilgrimage*, for the validity of her theory of cosmopolis. Later, she muses on the word "cosmopolis" and the turn-of-the-century discussion surrounding it.

> Cosmopolis, she scribbled in her note-book. The world of science and art is the true cosmopolis. Those were not the words in Cosmopolis but it was the idea. Perhaps no one had thought of it before the man who thought of having a magazine in three languages. It would be one of the new ideas. Tearing off the page she laid it on the sofa-head and sat contemplating an imagined map of Europe, with London, Paris and Berlin joined by a triangle, the globe rounding vaguely off on either side. All over the globe, dotted here and there, were people who read and thought, making a network of unanimous culture. It was a tiring reflection; but it brought a comfortable assurance. . . . People arrived independently at the same conclusions in different languages, and in the world of science they communicated with each other. That made cosmopolis. Yet it was an awful thought that the world might gradually become all one piece; perhaps with one language; perhaps English if those people were right who talked about Anglo-Saxon supremacy. "England and America together could rule the world." It sounded secure and comforting, like a police station (*Interim*, 342-43).

It is significant that this quote comes from *Interim*, the novel-chapter that was being written in 1919 when European supremacy could be defined as including those dots around the globe where "people who read and thought" lived. The "primitive" places surrounding the dots of European colonies were those areas where people didn't read and think in a way recognizable to Europeans. Miriam's simultaneous attraction to the "comfortable assurance" of this "unanimous" world and her critique of this "awful" unifying imperialistic fantasy in which the whole world becomes a "police station" appears repeatedly in the film columns and throughout *Pilgrimage*. It is also mirrored in her ambivalence for the Jewish Mendizabal, who, as his name implies, is associated with the shadowy caverns of mastication and articulation. He is the diabolical mandible—threshold into unrecognizable regions of utterance and unexplored neighborhoods of London and of thought. As Sephardic Jew he is symbolically and also (likely) literally a dark figure—cosmopolitan but not Anglo-Saxon, so at the same time a perpetrater of and a foil to the "police station" potential of "cosmopolis."

Miriam's work as a dental assistant kept her gazing into the dark mouths of many Anglo-Saxons. Her attention to the mouth, its hygiene, correction and mechanics is matched by Richardson's constant attention to and interrogation of the proper rules of grammar, speech and writing and their potential to colonize, to universally correct and police behavior.

It is in keeping with the turn-of-the-century context that the argument that triggered Miriam's musing is with a Jew. In the work of Richardson, Joyce, and many other modernist writers, Jewish characters became emblematic of the cosmopolitan displaced urban "other"—the one who belongs to no country and must travel, or who lives in a foreign place, in order to survive. The Jew personifies the cosmopolitan ideal: he or she needs to learn to be at home in any country, but is without the luxury of those who traveled to see—making "pilgrimages" to screens. The Jew is foreign to the Christian world but came before it, as the Old Testament precedes the New. The Jewish male also embodies the slippage of gender categories: as an immigrant to Britain he is foreign, and like the colonized native or the British turn-of-the-century woman, he cannot be a full legal citizen in his new home country. The Jew, the native, and the woman live at home under foreign rule. Freud, though a full citizen for most of his life and not an immigrant, presents another example of a Jew who, due to his Jewishness, is more foreign than many other modernist male writers, and worries with them over maintaining the legitimacy and authority of his own position. This position owes its ambiguous status partly to Freud's and some other modernist writers' many registers of foreignness and thus their ability to be confused with, or to occupy the slippery and suspicious category of the turn-of-the-century woman writer. In line with this early-century connection between the Jew and the woman writer, Richardson offers another significant figure in *Pilgrimage*: Michael Shatov, a Russian Jew, who, like Mendizabal, acts as a guide helping Miriam venture into previously unknown or forbidden modes of thought and areas of London.

In a spirit of cosmopolitanism more utopian and less suspicious than that of Richardson's "police station," a spirit consistent with Bryher's dream of a "popular internationalism" fueled by the silents which "offered a single language across Europe," one of the first advertisements for *Close Up* read:

> The first review to approach films from the angles of art, experiment, possibility . . . *Close Up* will be in touch with all progressive and developmental work achieved in every country, and will

> represent the views of the foremost in thought and letters throughout the world. All followers of film should have it in their possession. Its invaluable information and criticism will be equally appreciated by the technician, the film enthusiast, literary world and the general public.[35]

This advertisement manifests *Close Up's* sense of itself as uniting through its existence "art, experiment and possibility," its desire for global mass appeal and total inclusion of "all followers of film" and "all progressive and developmental work." These desires speak to the grandiose avant-garde impulse to synthesize the fragments of modernist experience into the kind of mysterious trans-time and space communication that the Esperanto-like film provided. It is easy to see in this desire a repetition of the same unifying imperialist colonial gesture in the realm of art that some of these same modernists critiqued in the political arena. In this spirit a film journal that could extend the experience of the film back into writing, as well as providing a forum in which to critique the new experience, did the work of the projector's ability to both zoom in close up and to pan a vista, that is, to unify the (conceptually and geographically) distant and near. Many modernists working in areas other than the film identified with the projector's ability to join "art, experiment and possibility" and wrote of their fields in these terms.

Close Up was the perfect place for these modernists to meet and publish. As Richardson states in a 1928 "Continuous Performance" column titled "The Cinema in Arcady," in which she discusses the one-year-old presence of the film in a small town and the changes it affected,

> One clearly visible incidental result of this intensive cultivation [of the film] is to be noted: these people, and particularly the younger generation, have no longer quite the local quality they had even a year ago. They are amplified, aware of resources whose extent is unknown to them and have a joyful half-conscious preoccupation with this new world that has been brought into their midst. . . . The "yokel" is less of a lout than he was wont to be and the dairymaid even on workdays is indistinguishable from her urban counterpart. . . . These youths and maidens in becoming world citizens, in getting into communication with the unknown, become also recruits available, as their earth-and-cottage-bound forbears never could have been for the world-wide conversations now increasingly upon us in which the cinema may play, amongst its numerous other roles, so powerful a part ("CP 12: The Cinema in Arcady," *Close Up*, July, 1928, 57).

SKYEY APPARITION, WHITE SEARCHLIGHT:
In the Interstices—The Continuous Performance

> It was the first hint of the Film's power of tackling aspects of reality that no other art can adequately handle. But the power of the Film, of Film drama, filmed realities, filmed uplift and education, all its achievements in the realm of the Good, the True and the Beautiful, appealing to the many, and in the realm of the abstract, appealing only to the few, rests alike for the uninstructed, purblind onlooker and the sophisticated kinist, upon the direct relationship, mystic, joyous, wonderful, between the observer a continuous miracle of form in movement, of light and shadow in movement, the continuous performance going on behind all invitations to focus upon this or that, of the film itself ("Continuous Performance," *Close Up*, June, 1933, 131).

In this last paragraph of the last "Continuous Performance" column, Richardson reveals some of her reasons for naming the column as she did and, with regard to subject, her purpose for dwelling "*behind* all invitations to focus upon this or that, of the film itself" (my emphasis). The filmic object that Richardson invented was ideal, had surface, depth, mystery, acted on the viewer in surprising and unpredictable ways, and therefore, like the Bible or other mysterious or unpredictable texts or experiences, required exegesis. It was both a concealing and revealing mechanism. Richardson's ideal film came into being through the writing of the "Continuous Performance" columns, a writing viewed as exegetical in itself. With this writing she could create foreground, reenact and place the "miracle" (her word) "behind" the surface, the miracle that, to her, was the epiphany and main purpose of the cinema.

Behind "this or that, of the film itself" was the "direct relationship" which was "a continuous miracle of form in movement . . . the continuous performance." It is characteristic of Richardson's hermeneutic approach to believe in and to invent a "something" or someplace located behind the film to be discussed and focused upon, and also to believe in something between the observer and the "film itself." Motivated by a similar approach to film viewing as to fiction writing, she wrote about film in order to discover and illuminate that which was interstitial—the "behind and between" evoked by the cinema.

Fueled by this behind/in front, or surface/depth, interpretative apparatus, Richardson viewed the event of the cinema, like the circumstances surrounding a revelation, as manifoldly symbolic. Her own continuous performance, which made a place for itself in *Close Up* between a supposed author's continuing "presence" in the magazine—a presence authenticated by repeated columnar appearances—and the written text of *Close Up*, as well as between readers and that text, was also many-layered. This supposedly real presence in *Close Up*, as an author having been to the cinema and now writing about her experience, mirrors the complex relationship in *Pilgrimage* between Richardson, whose writing is both autobiographical and not, and Miriam, whose consciousness, rather than the particular events of her life, is the written performance of the text. In *Pilgrimage* and the columns, the writing is structured in such a way that the subjectivity and identifications of the reader, and the positions of author and subject—whether it be Miriam's consciousness or the consciousness associated with the silent film—are many-layered and deliberately unstable.

Richardson's continuous performance was written from various imaginary positions, one of which was that of a viewer of a silent film in a cinema theater, the writing appearing not as subtitles on a screen but as a silent private inner speech running in counterpoint to a simultaneous reading of subtitles and images. Behind the layers presented in the writings that appeared in *Close Up* continually ran an imaginary idea of film and The Film. This idea served as the page or screen on which the continuous symbolic writing moved.

Simultaneously, Richardson's persistent writing on the scene or screen of an imaginary film posited the notion that the "real" film being written about and viewed by others might also partake of an imaginary construction whose investigation would be an appropriate and useful subject for film criticism. After drawing a distinction between FILM (her capitalization) and the movies in the January 1929 "Continuous Performance" column titled "Pictures and Films," Richardson implies that film is "guilty" because it is more complicated than the snapshot and the movie, and unlike them does not go "straight to the imagination of the onlooker" but enters the onlooker's consciousness by a more surreptitious and circuitous route. As she states in "Pictures and Films,"

> The film as a work of art is subject to the condition ruling all great art: that it shall be a collaboration between the conscious and the unconscious, between talent and genius. . . .The film, therefore, runs enormous risks. . . . But the snapshot, and the movie . . . is

> food for all. It can't go wrong. It is innocent, and its results go straight to the imagination of the onlooker, the collaborator, the other half of the game (55).

Since snapshots and movies are not, in Richardson's view, "work[s] of art," they are capable of "going straight to the imagination of the onlooker," whereas the film, as potential "great art," is dependent on a different kind of collaboration for its success. It is this imaginary notion of and standard for the successful film residing somewhere between "the conscious and the unconscious, between talent and genius" that makes film guilty whereas snapshots and movies are innocent. While implying with the word "guilty" that film is the more powerful medium, Richardson states that it is a mistake to attribute a moral superiority to film over snapshots or movies. Rather, it must be recognized that a different kind of collaboration is invoked through the different mediums. This collaboration, dependent on the notion that there is something more than meets the eye behind the film, is the object of Richardson's investigation.

In the "Continuous Performance" column of September 1931 titled "Narcissus," she elaborates on the difference between the collaboration that film demands of its onlookers and that of other mediums.

> Every imaginable kind of film, talkies included in their utmost nearness to or distance from stage-plays, reduces or raises, as you please, the onlooker to a varying intensity of contemplation, that is, in a way that cannot be over-estimated, different from the contemplation induced by a stage-play just because, whatever the ostensible interest of the film, it is arranged and focussed at the distance exactly fitting the contemplative state ("CP: Narcissus," *Close Up*, September, 1931, 184).

The exact distance that "fits" the contemplative state is also the distance that invokes the collaboration of the conscious and the unconscious in a "game" peculiar to the guilty film. In describing, investigating, and duplicating the mechanics of this game in the "Continuous Performance" columns, Richardson explores a composite of certain recurring themes: images of women in cinema; the function of the audience; a critique of the function of sound and an account of the reasons for the superiority of the silent cinema; the function of subtitles; the cinema as local parish or shrine, a place to go on pilgrimage; faith in art as salvation (film being art); film as a vehicle for revealing "that which is unbounded in man"; the narrative function of film, with discussions of "the worst criminal of all: the good ending"; the politics of cinema, including censorship and films for children; "the miraculous commonplace" that occurs on the screen; the cosmopolitan role of the cinema "to bring people into worldwide conversations"; the role of musical accompaniment in the cinema; the advent of the talkies; feminine and masculine cinema with the silents as feminine; and problems of the physical shape of the film theater as related to the arrangements of seating and the screen.

Many of the concerns of the "Continuous Performance" columns are so closely related that, as is also true for Richardson in the columns themselves, to discuss one is often to immediately invoke the others.[36] One idea that Richardson returns to repeatedly and that guides many of her other concerns has to do with film as "a small ceremonial prepared for a group." In a June 1929 column titled "Almost Persuaded," she writes,

> The film is a social art, a show, something for collective seeing, and even in the day that finds us all owning projectors and rolls of film from the circulating filmery it still will be so, a small ceremonial prepared for a group, all of whom must adjust their sensibilities at a given moment and at the film's pace. Reading, all but reading aloud, is a solitary art—is this why it has been called the unpunished vice, and ought we to scrap these pages and swear only that we hope Wells may be right about the alleged competitor?—and the film can no more replace it than the Mass can replace private devotions. The film is skyey apparition, white searchlight, [sic] The book remains the intimate, domestic friend, the golden lamp at the elbow ("CP: Almost Pesuaded," *Close Up*, June, 1929, 34).

As writings framed in a journal which is sent out to many subscribers, the "Continuous Performance" columns bridge the gap between the private devotion of reading and the public film "Mass." The anxiety about the possibility of the film replacing the novel is manifest in the "white searchlight" of the projector, which not only signals the public realm but also gives the scene of the cinema an ominous slant. The searchlight is an apparition in the sky above the spectator that is able to see more than the spectator can see unaided. Can the film see more than the novel? Can the reader of the novel be seen by the film? Can reading be seen in the film? The projector operates like a searchlight at night, illuminating areas that are usually cloaked in darkness. Its search is sometimes a surveillance—an attempt by the police to uncover criminals or a means to reveal hidden dangers such as icebergs at sea. Similarly, Richardson's film as "skyey apparition" and "white searchlight" may reveal something dangerous or ominous to those in the dark of the cinema that they otherwise may not see. It may expose something of the audience to itself. If a member of the audience turns her or his head away from the screen, the white searchlight will reveal the spectacle of spectators in the act of viewing.[37] This gesture of turning away marks the starting point for the writing of the continuous performance—a writing that takes the "social" scene of "collective seeing" and recasts it as "intimate," transforming the harsh white of the searchlight into a soft "golden" and "domestic friend."

Richardson's film is unfriendly partly because of its omniscient powers: "all of . . . [the audience] must adjust their sensibilities at a given moment and at the film's pace." Through the act of writing, some of the film's power can be domesticated, taken back, or imitated; the author and reader, like the beam of the white searchlight, can decide how to adjust their own sensibilities and at what pace to proceed. In the cinema, Benjamin states, "the audience's identification with the actor is really an identification with the camera."[38] This negotiation with omniscient power, and the suggestion that revelations may arrive through the film, turns the film that Richardson constructs into a sacred experience, a "small ceremonial prepared for a group."

When read side-by-side, the novel-volumes and the "Continuous Performance" columns serve as critical articulations of, and performances of, the ideas each contain. Just as the novels are not "pure" fiction and contain many long sections of social/literary critique, the "Continuous Performance" columns, in the guise of critique, invent a filmic object that is often used for entirely other purposes. The "film" produced and critiqued in these columns is a third thing, existing somewhere between the writing of the novels and the writing "about" film. In the *Close Up* columns, Richardson invents film as an extra-literary object that provokes her into a continuous writing performance about the desire to write. For her, the film and the experience of viewing it repeatedly posed the question, How to write the desire to write? Richardson, who saw questions about the formal and phenomenological terms of gendered identity everywhere, used this new medium to investigate the nuances and mechanics of her own and other women's desire to see and be seen—to either have agency or to "suffer" as an agent of the male gaze.[39] Believing that men and women speak different languages and that women are taught from the beginning to speak "his," Richardson thought that it was only through the writing of "feminine prose"—a kind of silent speech—that women could speak their own language. As Miriam says in *Pilgrimage*,

> In speech with a man a woman is at a disadvantage—because they speak different languages. She may understand his. Hers he will never speak or understand. In pity, or from other motives, she must therefore, stammeringly, speak his. He listens and is flattered and thinks he has her mental measure when he has not touched even the fringe of her consciousness (*The Tunnel*, 210).

For Richardson the silent film is rich with possibility because it is feminine writing incarnate, an animate silent speech that does not leave women at a disadvantage. In addition, it offers the possibility that men may understand, without recognizing that the means of their understanding is the "other" language. Thus, as a "small ceremonial," Richardson's film is focused at the right distance for the contemplative state. It echoes her view of James' prose, demanding "upon the first reading [viewing], a perfection of sustained concentration akin to that which brought it forth, and bestowing, again upon the first reading, the recreative delights peculiar to this form of spiritual exercise" (Foreword, 11).[40]

MAGIC FINGERS WRITING: The Structures of Richardson's Film

For Eisenstein, as for Richardson, cinema is "an expansion from literature,"

> an expansion from the strict diction achieved by poetry and prose into a new realm where the desired image is directly materialized in audio-visual perceptions. And finally, it is only in cinema that are fused into a real unity all those separate elements of the spectacle once inseparable in the dawn of culture, and which the theatre for centuries has vainly striven to amalgamate anew.[41]

Eisenstein's "desired image" is enacted through the "not really real, really" of Richardson's cinema. Like Richardson, Eisenstein published in *Close Up*, and the two held many parallel ideas regarding the compositional and structural similarities between film and literature. As Eisenstein states, "Why should the cinema follow the forms of theatre and painting rather than the new methodology of language? . . . language is much closer to film than painting is."[42]

Richardson, too, observed the ways in which film followed "the new methodology of language," particularly in her own work. In this sense, film critique provided her an avenue for investigating and articulating her "new methodology" and her views on language. To read the "Continuous Performance" columns is to be repeatedly sent back to the novels and at the same time sent out to the actual viewing experience of the early silent cinema. Eisenstein works from the other end: he refers to literature in order to explicate his theories about film. "The pages of literature offer us models of completely unexpected compositional structures, in which are presented phenomena that 'in themselves' are quite ordinary."[43] Eisenstein understood and wrote more about the links between literature and the film than any other filmmaker contemporary to Richardson. Although the cinema "materializes images in audio-visual terms" (Eisenstein), for Richardson and to some extent for Eisenstein as well, it simultaneously evokes a desire similar to that which is present in and produced by writing—a desire for images that are immaterial, though perhaps also audio-visual. For both Richardson and Eisenstein, the scene of cinema is a spectacle of writing.

Richardson often describes the cinema in terms of metaphors about writing. This analogy was drawn by many early modernists writing about the cinema. In the following passage from Robert Herring's *Close Up* article "A New Cinema, Magic and the Avant Garde," for example, the projector is personified as having fingers that write with light. This passage could easily have been written by Richardson. It echoes many of her statements in the Foreword to *Pilgrimage* and in the "Continuous Performance" columns in its implication that the spatial arrangement of projector, screen, and audience is also an arrangement of knowledge and desire—an arrangement that for Richardson is also gendered.

> There is the screen, and you know the projector is at the back of you. Overhead is the beam of light which links the two. Look up. See it spread out. It is wider and thinner. Its fingers twitch, they spread in blessing or they convulse in terror. They tap you lightly or they drag you in. Magic fingers writing on the wall, and able to become at will (a qualified statement of course, for at whose will?) a sword or an acetylene drill, a plume or waterfall. But most of all they are an Aaron's rod flowering on the wall opposite, black glass and crystal flowers (just the kind of remark that does not

> help) . . . . One strand of the beam widens, a white finger detaches itself, goes off over the screen, while the others wait, continue, keep the thing going, confident that it will return. The finger is a cowboy's hat. It went off when he took his hat off and flung it on a table. . . . Those people who saunter so haughtily, who fight for their ends with such abandon, who hail taxis and dismiss servants with one imperious gesture, they are all slaves of that lamp in the projector. They are not really real, really. . . . They need the lamp to bring them to life and their life is one of movement and light which is not determined by them (Robert Herring, "A New Cinema, Magic and the Avant Garde," *Close Up*, April, 1929, 52).

Herring locates the spectator in a precise spatial arrangement: there is a screen that can be described as simply "there" because it is facing the audience. From the point of view of the spectator, the source of knowledge and volition is known but unseen: "you *know* the projector is at the back of you" (my emphasis) although you don't see it. That which is known without being seen has a different status from that which can be seen. The "materialization of an image in audio-visual perceptions"—Eisenstein's definition of the desire that is met in the cinema—is a desire that also has its source in the unseen action behind. The arrangement of knowledge is also an arrangement of desire, "the *desired* image is directly materialized in audio-visual perceptions" (my emphasis). In this spatial arrangement, desire is located behind the screen and overhead as it travels on "the beam of light which links the two" (the projector and the screen). "Magic fingers" write on a screen that becomes "the wall"—a wall that by the implication of being written on is easily replaced in imagination by a page.[44]

These fingers of light have the volition of a terrible god-like author as they "twitch," "spread in blessing," or "convulse in terror." They are "magic" and can transform into various shapes "at will." But, in complicating the positions and possible identifications available for author, subject, and reader, Richardson might also ask, At whose will? She implies in the "Continuous Performance" columns that there is no clear answer, even beyond the context of the Herring article, to this question. The impossibility of supplying a clear answer indicates the instability of viewer identification with the mechanism of projection and the images being projected—the "audio-visual perceptions"—an identification that may shift or blur. In Herring's article, "Whose will?" is the question that activates the "fingers of light" and it is also the question that locates the mystery and desire peculiar to Richardson's silent cinema. The mystery is the "blessing and terror" bestowed by the light, the images, the sound, another unknown power, or all of these in unity.[45]

This imagined unity with the motion of the projector's writing light, signals the kind of ancient, immediate, pre-Oedipal realm that the film is able to invoke. The film's power to call up an ancient time or a state of preverbal memory—a time before differentiation from the Mother occurs—is particularly significant to the filmic cosmology Richardson spins out in the "Continuous Performance" columns and to the important role the film played for many modernists. Its importance to Richardson is due to its close connections to the formation of the subject in relation to language. In psychoanalytic terms, the infant's intense attachment to the mother's body is the earliest, most complete, and thus most ancient memory or experience of unity that the subject will ever have. Embodying this experience, Richardson's early cinema is characterized by the same elements present in the original pre-Oedipal experience of merging. Specifically, the silent film is "in close alliance with the unconscious" and it expresses itself through "the resources of rhythm, intonation, gesture and melody."

It is important to the merging effect of the early cinema that the only language present was in printed subtitles on the screen, leaving intact the pre-Oedipal realm of unity, while displacing the usually dominant symbolic "magisterial" speech of the Father. For Richardson, Kristeva, and Irigaray, the Father's speech and mode of thought is allied with the male entrance into, and disruption of, the pre-Oedipal merging between mother and infant. Kristeva calls the Father's speech "the speech of the Logos" because it represents a logical or more linear mode of consciousness, much less allied with the unconscious than the semiotic.

Viewing all social phenomena as symbolic, Kristeva, like many other feminist theorists, situates the issues of "the female speaker" (or the question, How does a woman speak?) within her general analysis of the process of signification.[46] As processes of signification, both film and language can be seen to embody important stages of subject formation. In Kristeva's terms, the symbolic and semiotic combine to effect the communicative function of the film and of language.

> The symbolic and semiotic are two closely related modalities of signification, which in our cultures, tend to be related as master and slave. That is, the symbolic plays the role of the Logos, or magisterial discourse, and the semiotic speaks through nonsense

or "childish" language. This theory has important implications for feminist thought because, in Kristeva's view, the semiotic derives its energy from the realm of the presymbolic, or the pre-Oedipal. It first occurs in the phase of the infant's intense attachment to the mother's body. The semiotic then, is in close alliance with the unconscious and expresses itself as the organization of instinctual drives through the resources of rhythm, intonation, gesture and melody.[47]

The order of the relation between Mother, infant, and (later) Father, presents to the infant a need to deal with "absence, representation and abstraction; that is, with the uses of language."[48] It is in this sense that the silent film, due to its ability to invoke pre-Oedipal unity and its simultaneous presence in the symbolic realm as narrative, was able to serve as a spectacle of writing for Richardson. As representations, film and the photograph invoke for Richardson (and for Miriam) that which is absent—what Richardson calls "something else in things as they stood, blinding." That which is absent includes memories of events and feelings that, although seen, are not literally captured in a given representation. Richardson returns repeatedly throughout *Pilgrimage* and the "Continuous Performance" columns to the blindness that the sight of the "although seen" but not "literally captured" produces. For Richardson, the visible representation of the film itself generates an invisible excess so bright that it sheds a blinding light on the cultural economy in which the representation is produced. It is this blindness, this seeing the (usually hidden) dark and seeing in the dark, that provides her with a point of intervention and investigation into the mechanisms of representation. Thus in their display of the workings of absence, representation and abstraction, the film and photograph are able to serve as a spectacle of writing, and at the same time to suggest a way of writing about the predicament and conditions they present. These elements—absence, representation and abstraction—presented to the infant in the pre-Oedipal stage as a need to deal with language, is a need that is never entirely resolved. And so the performance of them is both continuous and continuously fascinating.

The attempt to meet or resolve this need is complicated for women who can identify with the Father when he enters the pre-Oedipal realm in the guise of language, but whose identification with him will then be thwarted. This "being thwarted" occurs due to the cultural coding of the feminine as "naturally" allied with the semiotic. Thus, continued identification with the symbolic will be discouraged in a girl. By extension, it is considered "unnatural" for a woman to write since by doing so she allies herself with the symbolic. These early negotiations around the construction of identity in relation to language use and gender are also manifest in syntactical and grammatical constructions.

> Although the symbolic functions never entirely displace the semiotic, they come to dominate in speech, as in writing. When we learn what we call sentence structure, we absorb a concept of identity as defined by syntax, which posits as a given the subject and its objects.[49]

Richardson recognized that identity, particularly gendered identity in writing and speech, was learned and reinscribed at the level of sentence structure and syntax. In order to invent feminine prose, therefore, she developed an "early habit of ignoring, while writing, the lesser of the stereotyped system of signs, and, further, when finally sprinkling in what appeared to be necessary, to a small unconscious departure from current usage" (Foreword, 12). In a sense, the silent film also radically departed from current usage. As did Richardson in *Pilgrimage*, the film was able to convey a pre-Oedipal atmosphere of semiotic undifferentiated experience that wavered, as did the novels, on the edge of the symbolic, on the edge of telling a story.[50]

In referring to the elements that form the "real unity" of the filmic "spectacle," Eisenstein speaks of them as "once inseparable in the dawn of culture." It is as if the film had gone back to recreate a unity that existed before collectively recorded or individual conscious time. This invocation of unity and of a time before conscious memory echoes the cinematic spatial arrangement that produces the possibilities for awe and belittlement in Richardson's cinema. This is exemplified by Herring's phrase, "They are all slaves of that lamp in the projector" (Herring, "A New Cinema, Magic and the Avant Garde," April, 1992, 52). Discussing the nature of the merging that occurs in the cinema, Eisenstein says,

> In a single cinematographic act, the film fuses people and a single individual, town and country. It fuses them with dizzying change and transfer. With an all-embracing compass of whole countries or of any single character. With its ability to follow watchfully not only the clouds gathering in the hills, but also the swelling of a tear from beneath an eyelash.[51]

This experience of fusion created by the cinema—of an intimacy with that which is close up, "the swelling of a tear," and that which is far away, "the clouds gathering in the hills"—is also present in the statement "Overhead is the beam of light that links the two." It is also manifest throughout the "Continuous Performance" columns in Richardson's reiteration of the necessity of "stillness and concentration [that] depend in part upon the undisturbed continuity of surrounding conditions, the musical accompaniment [that] should be both continuous and flexible. By whatever means, the aim is to unify" ("CP 2: Musical Accompaniment," *Close Up*, August, 1927, 61). The sense of fusion can be extended from the screen and projector, the moving images and the music, to links between other couples as well, particularly the pre-Oedipal infant and mother, the dreamer and the dream, the slave viewer and the master projector. The pre-Oedipal necessity of dealing with language is implied by the presence of the beam of light that "links the two." This linkage through space is a point of conversion for narrative: "life enters cinema as movement, that movement brings with it nevertheless its problems of composition in frame."[52] These problems are narrative ones involving the effective use of elements similar to those present in the semiotic realm—the manipulation of rhythm, intonation, gesture, melody, and image. Simultaneously these problems trigger the desire for, deep ambivalence towards, and complexity for women involved in entry into the symbolic. The spatial problems of film editing, framing, and making are also narrative ones because

> frame space is constructed as narrative space. It is narrative significance that at any moment sets the space of the frame to be followed and "read," and that determines the development of the filmic cues in their contributions to the definition of space in frame (focus pull, for example, or back-lighting). Narrative contains the mobility that could threaten the clarity of vision in a constant renewal of perspective; space becomes place—narrative as the taking place of film.[53]

Filmic narrative, then, is the taking of space by the film and the transformation, through its movements, of that taken space into place. Through this taking and linking motion, both the screen and the viewer are transformed into places. It is the film's dreamlike and pre-Oedipal character that is responsible for transforming the viewing subject into a "place" traversed by image, light, and movement.

> Psychoanalysis . . . has come to stress the dream as itself projected on a screen: the dream screen, blank surface present in dreams though mostly "unseen," covered by the manifest content of the

> projected dream; a screen that represents the breast (infinitely extensive centre of the baby's visual space) and then also sleep (the desire for sleep) as an original ground of pleasure "before" difference, "before" identity, "before" symbolization. In cinema, the images pass (twenty-four per second), the screen remains; covered but there, specified—the images of this or that film—but the same—the satisfying projection of a basic oneness.[54]

The cinema as "dream screen" and the viewer as dreamer is the place "before." Since Richardson is primarily interested in this place "before" of the film—and its ability to reenact "an original ground of pleasure 'before' difference . . . identity . . . symbolization" it makes sense that she rarely speaks about specific films. Instead she dwells on the elements that are necessary to maintain "the satisfying projection of a basic oneness."

As mentioned, one of these elements is musical accompaniment. Throughout the *Close Up* pieces, the necessity of the right kind of musical accompaniment is frequently discussed in relation to the merging that the cinema can evoke. As a parallel to novel writing, Richardson implies that words, like musical notes, can also evoke rather than merely accompany moving images in the mind of the reader. Some of the elements present in a successful linguistic evocation are also the "projection of a basic oneness" between reader, text, and imagined author, as well as, in terms of the film, "undisturbed continuity." This notion of "basic oneness" strikes the chord again of what Richardson calls in the Foreword a "longing for participation; not quite the same as a *longing* for publication" (my emphasis; Foreword, 10).[55]

In the column "Musical Accompaniment," Richardson describes not only the function of music in creating "undisturbed continuity," but the danger that arises if music and film are out of sync.

> If film and music proceed at cross purposes the audience is distracted by a half-conscious effort to unite them ("CP: Musical Accompaniment," *Close Up*, August, 1927, 61).

Richardson aims to create a similar "undisturbed continuity of surrounding conditions" through the musical accompaniment of words in the novels. Elaborating on the way in which the ideal musical accompaniment for film is "as continuous as the performance and blending with it" she simultaneously articulates the function of the piano playing that recurs throughout *Pilgrimage*, the play with formal modes in which to read notations on a page, and the significance of the sound of words, which operates in the novels, as does music in the film, as "connective tissue."

> The music is not an alien sound if it be as continuous as the performance and blending with it. That is why, though a good orchestra can heighten and deepen effects, a piano played by one able to improvise connective tissue for his varying themes is preferable to most orchestral accompaniments. Music is essential. Without it the film is a moving photograph and the audience mere onlookers. Without music there is neither light nor color, and the test of this is that one remembers musically accompanied films in colour and those unaccompanied by music as colourless ("Continuous Performance," *Close Up*, July, 1927, 37).

The continuity of the performance and the transformation of the audience from "mere onlookers" into "participants" is essential for Richardson and is dependent on music.[56] Significantly, the kind of playing that best serves as "connective tissue" is that which is "played by one able to improvise." In *The Tunnel,* when Miriam plays the piano at tea time, she transgresses the proper parlor etiquette by improvising. When she finishes playing she gets up from the piano "charged to the fingertips with a glow that transfigured all the inanimate things in the room" (*The Tunnel,* 28). Miriam's reading of the music and her playing, and Richardson's reading of the film and her poetics as practiced in the novels, overlap. This overlap suggests that the merging that Richardson sees as possible in the cinema is a state to aim for in the novels and in daily life—a state of transformation from "mere onlookers" into "participants." This merging, with its transfiguring result, recalls once again Richardson's description of James' technique which, through a perfection of sustained concentration, bestowed the transforming "recreative delights" inherent in writing that is also spiritual practice.

Two elements are equally important to Richardson's project of transfiguration: a sense of merging and a sense of play, or improvisation—as in playing the piano differently, or departing from current proper syntactical usages in order to achieve "a perfection of sustained concentration." She suggests that departure from the symbolic, that is, the grammatical or formal law of the Father, is necessary to feminine transfiguration.

It is useful to recall another scene of pre-Oedipal fusion—also dependent on light and a spectacle of writing and reading, also a kind of "spiritual exercise"—Miriam's "paper-scattered lamplit circle . . . established as the centre of life. . . . [a] secret place." This "circle" operates by a constellation of "feminine" desire similar to that which propelled the invention of "the feminine equivalent of the current masculine realism" (Foreword, 9) and that of Richardson's silent cinema. As a written (as opposed to filmed) spectacle of writing, its spatial arrangements and configurations of knowledge are different from but overlap with those of the film. To arrive at the "paper-scattered lamplit circle" also requires a retrieval—a going back to the ancient in order to intensely occupy the present. As Miriam says, "The years that had passed were a single short interval leading to the restoration of that first moment. Everything . . . had been a coming back . . . Everything would be an everlastingly joyful coming back." Richardson realizes that the "restoration of that first moment" is a journey back to a different imagined origin for a female than for a male spectator. In this sense, as in many others, she anticipates the thought of many later feminist film critics and literary theorists in her attempt to render, mime, and critique the desire and position of a female spectator.

The viewer of the film is caught while the film moves. This notion of the film traveling through the space of the spectator reverses what de Lauretis has pointed to as the gendering of narrative space. In conventional narrative practice, she says, women are the objects or landscape, and landscape is marked as a feminine space through which a masculine subject travels. In the cinema, the spectators occupy narrative space and thus all are put in the feminine position of landscape, that which is still and traversed.[57] The cinema's reverse spectatorial and reading arrangement is for Richardson also an allegory for the kind of narrative disruption she practices in *Pilgrimage*, in which the explorer of the wilderness frontier (London, in this case) is feminine and moves through a landscape that is not static but is simultaneously in motion. The question of who a static spectator identifies with on the screen determines the kind of doubleness with which that spectator will view her or his own position in relation to the action. It is this juncture of doubleness that makes the cinema so useful as a site for describing the workings of gender identification in visual narrative as parallel to the identification that is operative in the novel.

The choices of sites with which to identify can be divided along the axis of male (active agent—powerful—traveler through, and spectator of, passive landscape) and female (passive agent—powerless—the looked at—the body of passive landscape). Thus, even if caught while viewing, a male spectator has the option of identifying with the male position framed on the screen, that of the one who is engineering the action. A male spectator can be both catching and caught. In contrast, if the female spectator identifies with the female position she is doubly caught, as she is if she identifies with the male, since she is able to move through the landscape but only in disguise through her identification with the male position. These tensions between who is caught and who catches, who is traveled through and who travels, are the same tensions that Richardson features in her modernist attempt to render consciousness rather than report "reality." In so doing she alters the conventional position of the author and the author function, providing alternative sites for reader and writer identification.

Before Richardson analyzed the feminine and masculine film in *Close Up*, Miriam had analyzed the idea of the "feminine" as "an effect, a trick" and "an advertising manner" in *The Tunnel.* The fourth of the novel-chapters, *The Tunnel* was published in February 1919, nine years before *Close Up* began publication and before Richardson began writing the "Continuous Performance" columns. Since Miriam's analysis takes place while she watches a woman and watches and listens to a lecture on photography, it serves as an illuminating counterpoint to Richardson's later analysis in the "Continuous Performance" columns of the relation between images of women on the screen and feminine speech.

At one point, Miriam's male "companion" in the lecture hall turns to her and comments about a woman nearby.

> 'There's a pretty lady,' said Mr. Hancock, conversationally, just as the light was lowered. Miriam glanced across the half-circle of faintly shining faces and saw an effect, a smoothly coiffured head and smooth neck and shoulders.

As Miriam contemplates the "effect" that she has just seen, the following words break into her reverie about women and the feminine—a reverie sparked by the entrance of the "pretty lady" in the doorway of the lecture hall, an entrance that took her attention away from the lecturer, just as the French lecturer was saying,

> 'Development-in-thee-method-of-intaircepting-thee-light.'
> 'Daguerre' . . . a little Frenchman, stopping the sunlight, breaking it up, making it paint faces in filmy black and white on a glass. . . .'

> . . . [Miriam] sat through the first minutes of the lecture, recalling the bearing and manner of the figure, with sad fierce bitterness. Mr. Hancock admired "feminine" women . . . or at any rate he was bored by her own heavy silence, and driven into random speech by the sudden dip and sweep of the lace appearing in the light of the doorway . . . . But anyhow he, even he, was one of those men who do not know that an effect like that was just an effect, a deliberate "charming" feminine effect. But if he did not know that, did not know that it was a trick and the whole advertising manner, the delicate, plunging fall of the feet down the steps—"I am late; look how nicely and quietly I am doing it; look at me being late and apologetic and interested"—out of place in the circumstances, then what was he doing here at all?

Miriam continues in this train of thought, going on to consider men's contribution to women's desire to be "effect," to be looked at being late, being nice, quiet, interested, or apologetic.

> Then men mustn't stare at them and treat them as works of art. It was entirely the fault of men . . . perfectly reasonable that the women who got that sort of admiration from men should assert themselves in the presence of other works of art. The thing men called the noblest work of God must be bigger than the work by a man. Men plumed themselves and talked in a clever expert way about women and never thought of their own share in the way those women went on . . . unfair, unfair; men were stupid complacent idiots. But they were wonderful with their brains. The life and air and fresh breath coming up from the platform amongst the miseries and uncertainties lurking in the audience, was a man . . . waves of light which would rush through the film at an enormous speed and get away into space without leaving any impression, were stopped by some special kind of film and went surging up and down in confinement—making strata . . . " supairposeetion of strata" . . . no Englishman could move his hands with that smoothness, making you see. "Violet subchloride of silver."

Miriam glances at Mr. Hancock—he is asleep. She attributes this to the earlier entrance of "the frilled lady . . . patronizing the lecture" and "exhibiting" her "interest." Miriam's attention is next captured by the exhibit of some color photographs.

> When the colour photographs came, Miriam was too happy for thought. Pictures of stained glass, hard crude clear brilliant opaque flat colour, stood in miraculous squares on the screen, and pieces of gardens, grass and flowers and trees, shining with a

> shadeless blinding brilliance. . . .
>
> Miriam sat silent, busily searching for something to express the effect she felt. But she could not tell him what she felt. There was something in this intense hard rich colour like something one sometimes saw when it wasn't there, a sudden brightening and brightening of all colours till you felt something must break if they grew any brighter—or in the dark, or in one's mind, suddenly, at any time, unearthly brilliance. He would laugh and think one a little insane; but it was the real certain thing; the one real certain happy thing. And he would not have patience to try to hear her explain; and by that he robbed her of the power of trying to explain (*The Tunnel*, 105-7).

In the "Continuous Performance" columns, Richardson attempts to steal back, for Miriam, "the power of trying to explain" the "effect" of what she saw. Richardson, like Miriam, distinguishes between kinds of effect: there is the feminine effect signaled by appearances like that of the "frilled lady" framed by the doorway and bathed in light, and there are kinds of effect that may be perceivable only to a "feminine" consciousness. In the columns, feminine effect is discussed in terms of its various incarnations in the context of the cinema: the frilled lady, and other figments of light and lace like her, appear on the film screen or they inhabit the audience, cloaked in shadow, some of them whispering and gossiping. Miriam in *Pilgrimage* and Richardson in *Close Up* both investigate and attempt to articulate the "effect" of the power of the photographic image and the filmic medium itself. Like the color photographs shown in the lecture, images in the film "stand in miraculous squares on the screen" and are capable of making the viewer "too happy for thought."

Although Richardson used the term "feminine" in a positive sense to indicate a mode in which she chose to work, her description of the feminine in the passages from *The Tunnel* illustrates all that to her is negative and petty about women—all of the pandering and self-objectifying that women perform for men. Miriam calls men "stupid complacent idiots" but acknowledges that it is from the man on the platform that "life and air and fresh breath" issue. This ambivalence about the masculine and the feminine, and the positive value of each, led her to treat both words as markers for, or signs of, kinds of consciousness. Neither Miriam nor Richardson have any doubt about which of these modes is the most socially recognized and powerful. Miriam knows that she, for example, could never rob him of the power of trying to explain, as he is able to rob her. Even in his silence Mr. Hancock is protected by science. He is in control of the whole procedure of projecting and intercepting light. Richardson and Miriam recognized that the seemingly neutral and "scientific" descriptions of the mechanics of photography, like those of film, were also spatializations of structures of knowledge and power, and thus were gendered—as was their reception in the lecture hall.

> . . . waves of light which would rush through the film at an enormous speed and get away into space without leaving any impression, were stopped by some special kind of film and went surging up and down in confinement—making strata.

And later,

> Miriam felt that he understood, as her ignorance could not do, exactly what it all meant scientifically; but there was something else in the things as they stood, blinding, there, that he did not see.

The "something else in things as they stood, blinding" that Miriam perceived and Mr. Hancock saw but did not see, was the spectacle of the feminine effect standing in the back of the lecture hall and the masculine performance it made possible in front. The unscientific "something else" that Miriam knows is lodged in the language of the "scientific" description: "these waves of light stopped by some special kind of film and surging up and down in confinement" are related to the confinement of the frilled woman entering the lecture hall framed by the door "unable," as Miriam says, "to escape Mr. Hancock's gaze."[58] As Miriam says earlier, "men mustn't stare at them [women] and treat them as works of art." Women who are intercepted by the male gaze and treated as "works of art . . . surg[ing] up and down in confinement" are caught in the frame of the doorway—or the photographic frame—or the film frame.[59]

Hancock's gaze on the frilled woman in the doorway is his signature, his Hancock written on her. While he gazes upon her she is his "work of art." Richardson describes the way the lady is reduced to a gesture: "a sweep of lace appearing in the light of the doorway," representing to Hancock his power over her. Hancock is doubly authorized to take credit for inventing her: first by being male and second by the "scientific" speech of the male lecturer with whom he is allied. Except for Hancock, the lady would escape making an "impression" just as the "waves of light" would escape if the scientist did not "intercept" them "by the introduction of some special kind of film." The film surface receives the imprint of this economics of staring—an economy that Richardson perceives to be at work in even grander proportions when the lecture hall becomes a movie house and the light in the doorway behind the audience becomes the light of the film projector casting the frilled lady onto the screen in front of them.

In addition to the spectacle of the gaze that Miriam sees, she also sees another "something else in things as they stood," "something one sometimes *saw* [my emphasis] when it wasn't there, a sudden brightening . . . of all colours" into an "unearthly brilliance." This second "something else" is the effect caused by the color photographs which gesture in their brilliance toward an unseen something beyond them. This seeing of something not there recalls Herrings's description of the spatial arrangement of the cinema in which he compares the beam of light of the projector to "magic fingers writing on the wall." The images seen on the film screen and produced from the projector light "are not really real, really." That is, to see these images is also to see something that isn't there. Elaborating on the second effect that Miriam saw and on the idea of the "not really real, really," Herring, echoing Richardson, wrote in the same *Close Up* article that

> anything that is real, in however small a degree, is magical, in an equivalent degree, and behind the worst photoplays there is the reality of light and of movement, and so there is a little magic everywhere where you see a cinema. These people respond to the spell. They are not drugged by light, as is so often said. That's wrong. Only half-way. They are stimulated by it and able automatically to discount incident and player without noticing it, and accept instead without knowing it the drama of movement and pattern. Images, if you like, in which it doesn't matter essentially whether it's a woman or a chair there. It's the space they occupy, the light they make manifest by being there. That's what is got. It's abstract.[60]

The second effect occurs regardless of "incident and player" and is "magic" because it happens as "automatic stimulation." In other words, its mechanisms are invisible although its effects are powerful, and its power is compounded by the fact of its being invisible. The sensation is that of being "stimulated" by light, movement and pattern, an effect that images create simply through their occupying space and "the light they make manifest by being there." In regard to Herring's statement—"it doesn't matter essentially whether it's a woman or a chair there"—it is exactly the observation that if a framed woman replaces a framed chair it does matter, indeed everything is altered, that largely fuels Richardson and Miriam's investigations into the cinematic and photographic apparatus. However, whether it is a woman or a chair on screen, the mechanism of magic Herring describes still operates.

Another contributor to *Close Up,* the psychoanalyst Barbara Low, also says, writing of the film: "It's abstract." The image displays that aspect of the audience that is invisible to itself: it may be a representation of a chair or a color photograph, but through its occupation of light and space it also represents to the viewer the unconscious (the "half-drugged") as well as the consciousness of the viewer. The invisible "abstract" workings of consciousness and the unconscious can perhaps be best perceived by "what it makes manifest by being there" or, like an image, by what it is not. Low says that "the drama of movement, [and] the fact that light is of all things what we need most and respond to most; they meet in the cinema." The implication is that the workings of the unconscious and of consciousness are most directly represented by a "drama of movement" through light and space.[61] That this drama is "what we need most and respond to most" again gives cinema a primary and urgent status, akin to the pre-Oedipal significance of food or physical contact. In Low's and Richardson's cinema the basic and primary needs of the audience are met.

The mechanisms of Herring's "magic" cinema and the workings of the second effect that Miriam sees in the photographs are described in more detail in the analogous case of Freud's "Mystic Writing-Pad."

> Some time ago there came upon the market, under the name of the Mystic Writing-Pad, a small contrivance that promises to perform more than the sheet of paper or the slate. It claims to be nothing more than a writing-tablet from which notes can be erased by an easy movement of the hand. But if it is examined more closely it will be found that its construction shows a remarkable agreement with my hypothetical structure of our perceptual apparatus and that it can in fact provide both an ever-ready receptive surface and permanent traces of the notes that have been made upon it.[62]

Like the writing on the mystic pad, which uses a stylus that deposits no ink or carbon, the writing in light on the cinema screen is present and then is immediately erased, and the screen's surface has what Freud calls "an unlimited receptive capacity." However, fragments of this light-writing remain in the mind of the viewer, as on a writing surface that is able to retain permanent traces. It is most unusual for a surface that can retain traces, such as the mind or a piece of paper, to be found alongside one that is infinitely receptive but unable to retain permanent traces, such as the film screen. These properties are normally mutually exclusive. According to Freud, the unusual coincidence of the two in the Mystic Writing-Pad reproduces the conditions of consciousness, particularly the workings of the memory. In the cinema, where this coincidence of normally exclusive properties also occurs, an elsewhere or other time, a past or future, is evoked and imagined as an extremely immediate experience. In this sense also, the cinema combines "what we need most and respond to most."

As surfaces on which to write, the film screen, the photograph, and the lady bathed in light and framed by the doorway, all have "an unlimited receptive capacity." But, unlike a piece of paper, they are incapable of retaining permanent traces. Both kinds of surfaces—retentive and not—serve as "substitutes for our memory" so long as the right conditions are met: "either the receptive surface must be renewed or the note must be destroyed." The "magic fingers writing" constantly renew the screen, becoming "first a cowboy hat, then a person sauntering so haughtily," and producing what Miriam calls, in terms of the photograph, this second "effect," the seeing of "something else that wasn't there." The "something else" is a glimpse of her own mental apparatus in operation—her receptive capacity, unlimited like the light, combined with her own permanent memory traces, as specific as the space surrounding an image. Freud explains how this mental apparatus functions.

> All the forms of auxiliary apparatus which we have invented for the improvement or intensification of our sensory functions are built on the same model as the sense organs themselves or portions of them: for instance, spectacles, photographic cameras, ear trumpets. Measured by this standard, devices to aid our memory seem particularly imperfect, since our mental apparatus accomplishes precisely what they cannot: it has an unlimited receptive capacity for new perceptions and nevertheless lays down permanent—even though not unalterable—memory traces of them.[63]

As a "small ceremonial prepared for a group," Richardson's collective Mystic Writing-Pad, the cinema, is a perfect "device to aid our memory." In its ability to evoke memory, it is able to erase, renew, and invent individual and collective images and history. It imitates the sense organs in being able to perform both of Freud's functions: it is a surface that has unlimited receptive capacity for new perceptions, and it lays down "permanent though not unalterable memory traces" in the consciousness of the viewer and on the surface of the film. Richardson touched on this aspect of cinema in the 1928 "Continuous Performance" column titled "The Cinema in the Slums."

> Mankind's demand for pictures, like the child's demand, is much more than a childlike love for representation. There is in the picture that which emerges and captures him before details are registered and remains long after they are forgotten. And this influence . . . is exercised as potently by a photograph as by a "work of art" and by a moving photograph, if it be the work of an artist, much more potently. Imagination fails in attempting to realize all that is implied for cramped lives in the mere coming into communication with the general life, all that results from the extension of cramped consciousness ("CP 10: Cinema in the Slums," *Close Up*, May, 1928, 61).

As an auxiliary apparatus, the projector, even more than the "photographic camera," portrays and amplifies Richardson's two kinds of feminine effect. It is the "potence" of "that which emerges and captures . . . before details are registered and remains long after they are forgotten" that fascinates Richardson and makes her see the film as both a model of "the feminine equivalent to the current masculine realism" and a spectacle of writing.

INNER SPEECH AND UTTERED SPEECH: The Film Gone Male

In his essay "Film Form: New Problems," Eisenstein referred to inner speech and uttered speech and their distinctive syntaxes.

> Inner speech, the flow and sequence of thinking unformulated into the logical constructions in which uttered, formulated thoughts are expressed, has a special structure of its own. This structure is based on a quite distinct series of laws. What is remarkable therein, and why I am discussing it, is that the laws of the construction of inner speech turn out to be precisely those laws which lie at the foundation of the whole variety of laws governing the construction of the form and composition of art-works. And

> there is not one formal method that does not prove the spit and image of one or another law governing the construction of inner speech, as distinct from the logic of uttered speech. It could not be otherwise.[64]

These ideas are relevant to the scene in *The Tunnel* in which Miriam attends the photography lecture. Miriam's thought process as she considers the "feminine" and as she intervenes in Hancock's gaze, has the structure of Eisenstein's "inner speech." In *Pilgrimage,* inner speech can be recognized by its divergence from what Richardson describes as the "clever" speech of men—or from "uttered speech."

The kinds of "effect" that Miriam experiences in *Pilgrimage* can be more fully explicated in terms of Eisenstein's inner speech and uttered speech. Eisenstein described these two kinds of speech in relation to the operation of inner monologue in film. He then proceeded to elaborate on what constitutes the inner speech of artworks. This is where Richardson and Eisenstein again intersect. His description of inner speech in film as the location of the "construction of the form and the composition of artworks" could also serve to define what Richardson calls the "feminine," particularly in relation to the kind of inner monologue that she employs for the "construction of her artwork," that is, Miriam's inner speech as structure of the novels.

In the scene in the lecture hall, Richardson achieves a filmic effect in writing through the use of a spatialized juxtaposition of Miriam's inner monologue (operating like inner speech), uttered speech and moving image. The temporal, uttered speech of the lecturer is interrupted by the spatial intercut of Hancock's gaze on the frilled lady—a gaze that is fixed and atemporal. Although interrupted by inner monologue and Hancock's atemporal gaze, the lecture continues on the temporal level while in the spatial realm an intersecting of looks and inner speech occurs. As narrator, Richardson intervenes to interject Miriam's inner speech between the uttered speech of the lecturer and the gaze, or visual speech, of Hancock. Miriam cuts into Hancock's gaze by also seeing the frilled lady, but by seeing her differently. Her looking defamiliarizes the familiar sight of framed woman, providing an unfamiliar site for reader identification and an unfamiliar site of volition and authorship. Through Miriam's interjection Richardson posits another kind of feminine over and against the one authored and trapped in the doorway by Hancock or the one excluded by, as Eisenstein puts it, the "logical constructions" of the lecturer, the constructions of uttered speech, that which Miriam calls "scientific" and Richardson calls "male."

In his description of the "image-sensual" structure of inner speech, which he believes also structures the film, Eisenstein articulates the processes that Richardson took to be feminine.

> We know that at the basis of the creation of form lie sensual and imagist thought processes. Inner speech is precisely at the stage of image-sensual structure, not yet having attained that logical formulation with which speech clothes itself before stepping out into the open. It is noteworthy that, just as logic obeys a whole series of laws in its constructions, so, equally, this inner speech, this sensual thinking, is subject to no less clear-cut laws and structural peculiarities.[65]

In Eisenstein's formulation, inner speech is dressed differently and Miriam also is dressed differently from the frilled lady, and from the men who have "clothe[d] themselves" in uttered speech or the signs of uttered speech (lace to mark women's silence and men's speech) before "stepping out into the open."

The "sensual thinking" that film invokes for both Eisenstein and Richardson compels them to undertake what Eisenstein calls, "the task of mastering the 'mysteries' of the technique of form."[66] These mysteries hidden in a filmic object constructed as if in need of hermeneutic exegesis are for Richardson "mysteries" regarding the gendering of formal structures and the "mysterious" capacities of "sensual thinking" taken to be feminine technique. This technique can transmogrify writing into film, audience into projector, projector into writer, and light into memory. Because film has the capacity to proceed by means of "sensual and imagist" thought processes, as well as the capacity to transmogrify, it becomes, for Richardson, a "mass" or "ceremonial"—a communion with "what one saw when it wasn't there." What is not there is most materially evident in the cinema but is just as pervasively present in written narrative.

Eisenstein performs this "mystery of the technique of form" in the making of his films and investigates it in his many critical essays on the film. Richardson mixes the performative and the critical registers in the "Continuous Performance" columns and in *Pilgrimage*, where she is constantly performing and inquiring into the nature of the "mysteries" of "sensual thinking" as they are enacted in the film, the novel, and the film journal.

For Richardson, inner speech and uttered speech have their parallels in the silent film and the talkie. Because the power that Richardson sees in the silents is fueled by the same principles as those of inner speech, it would be disastrous to interrupt them with sound, or the logic of uttered speech. In the September 1929 "Continuous Performance" column "Dialogue in Dixie," Richardson, having just seen a talkie, discusses the different kinds of hearing required in a silent and in a talkie. She finds "the most destructive factor" of the talkie to be "the hold up, the funeral march of words, more distracting than the worst achievements of declamatory, fustian drama." This "destructive factor" can bring about "the diminution of the faculty of seeing," which is diminished by "the necessity of concentrating upon hearing the spoken word." This destruction does not occur in the silent film, where "music and song demand only a distributed hearing which works directly as enhancement rather than diminution of the faculty of seeing." Richardson distinguishes between the "distributed hearing" that occurs in the silent and the "concentrated listening" of the talkie, which "is immediately fatal to cinematography." Giving an example of the way in which the talkie robs the cinema of its power, Richardson says,

> Imagine, to take the crudest of examples—the loss of power suffered by representations of passionate volubility—the virago, the girl with a grievance, the puzzled foreigner—if these inimitable floods of verbiage could be heard. . . . In all its modes, pure-film talk is more moving than heard speech. Concentration upon spoken words reveals more clearly than anything else the hiatus between screen and stage. In becoming suddenly vocal, locally vocal amidst a surrounding silence, the photograph reveals its photographicality. In demanding for the films the peculiar attention necessary to spoken drama all, cinematographically, is lost; for no gain ("CP: Dialogue in Dixe," *Close Up*, September, 1929, 215).

For Richardson, the "sensual thinking" characteristic of inner speech is manifest in the "pure-film talk" of the silents, which does not diminish the faculty of seeing. In viewing a silent, the interaction of the visual elements must be carefully attended to and read in order to see or hear the sense of the film. In the statement, through "becoming suddenly vocal" the "photograph reveals its photographicality," Richardson implies that cinematographic representations that don't break into a "flood of verbiage" also don't reveal their cinematographicality. This concealment is desirable. It is due to this concealment of themselves as strictly cinematographic—or as only films and only in reference to the cinema—that "distributed hearing" can occur in the silents. Distributed hearing and the "enhancement of the faculty of seeing" are two of the elements necessary to formalizing Eisenstein's stage of "image-sensual structure," in which the perceptions have not yet "attained that logical formulation with which speech clothes itself before stepping out into the open." For the film to remain outside of the realm of "logical formulation," it must be kept from stepping into uttered speech. Thus, in order for film to remain a "small ceremonial," feminine in its ability to "create atmosphere" and invoke that which is not really there, its speech must be silent. Its effectiveness, then, is in not revealing or requiring that it is only a film. Instead, Richardson would prefer it to be experienced as a "real" dream or a "real" atmosphere of the mind and, as such, she says "No spoken film will ever be able to hold a candle to silent drama, will ever be so "speaking" ("CP: Dialogue in Dixe," *Close Up*, September, 1929, 215).[67]

In the March 1932 column "The Film Gone Male," Richardson explores in even greater depth the relation between women's talk, the appearance of women on the film screen, and the feminine silent film. She states that "in the day of its innocence" the film was regarded as "a medium of communication." This "communication," however, was not of the usually expected kind: rather than relaying a message or telling a story, "it provided a pathway to reality" through its "insistence on contemplation" ("CP: The Film Gone Male," hereafter "FGM," *Close Up*, March, 1932, 37). She decides in the same column that the silent film is a feminine medium of communication.

> The film . . . in the day of its innocence, in its quality of being nowhere and everywhere, nowhere in the sense of having more intention than direction and more purpose than plan, everywhere, by reason of its power to evoke, suggest, reflect, express from within its moving parts and in their totality of movement, something of the changeless being at the heart of all becoming, was essentially feminine ("FGM,"37).

Echoing her earlier statements in "Dialogue in Dixie," she goes on to say that the film could only retain these feminine qualities as long as it remained silent, speechless. For "in becoming audible and particularly in becoming a medium of propaganda, it is doubtless fulfilling its destiny. But it is a masculine destiny. The destiny of planful becoming rather than of purposeful being" ("FGM"37).

In *Pilgrimage,* as well as in other writings, Richardson divided masculine and feminine along these parallel axes of planful becoming and purposeful being. Developing these notions in her 1925 essay "Women In The Arts," she states that "short of sainthood, a man must do rather than be. . . . he is potent not so much in person as in relation to the things he achieves."[68]

The silent film, lacking "clear speech" and "the orderly thought of man" evoked a "purposeful being" Richardson called feminine. In "The Film Gone Male" she explains that women and men who do not question the value of "orderly, clear speech" represent to her "the men's camp and are distinguishable by their absolute faith in speech as a medium of communication" ("FGM," 36).

In pursuit of an aesthetic of purposeful being, Richardson studied the ways in which speech, or visual images, can break into "talk"—for, as she states in "The Film Gone Male," though many women chatter, gossip, or talk incessantly, "only one in a thousand can talk." This kind of talk is a mode of communication, but it is not the communication that simply relays information or meaning in such a way that a reader or viewer could expect a word or thought to represent and correspond to a single object or phenomenon. The kind of communication that interests Richardson does not occur through direct reference or one-to-one correspondence between a word and a thing. For women to really talk, she says—for them to communicate in the same mode as the "speaking" of the silent film—they must use speech so that it is not a facade, not the "gossip and chatter" resorted to in relation to men in order to cover up their embarrassment of what men might perceive as their "palpitating spiritual nakedness" ("FGM," 37). In addition to the possibility of being perceived as a sign of "nakedness" or lack, a woman's use of speech outside of the modes of gossip or chatter might (also or instead) be perceived by a male as a threat and thus lead to the same result: disenfranchisement of the female speaker.

In regard to the feminine facade, Doane says, "the masquerade doubles representation; it is constituted by a hyperbolisation of the accoutrements of femininity."[69] In the realm of Richardson's thinking, the feminine accoutrements being hyperbolically displayed would be chatter, gossip, or incessant talk—these are the lace and frills of the linguistic masquerade Richardson describes. The masquerade "doubles" representation because the feminine accoutrements represent femininity and so does the body of the woman who wears or speaks the accoutrements. This is hyperbolic representation because, like the Russian doll that contains a series of smaller identical figures, the feminine, in representing itself, repeats its representation of itself.

In the first paragraph of "The Film Gone Male," Richardson explains why the distinction between "talk" and "clever speech" matters. She sees in the two modes of communication two kinds of perception which have vast implications. Characteristically, she opens the paragraph with a declarative statement that she later uses as a straw man: "Memory, psychology is to-day declaring, is passive consciousness." She then goes on to distinguish between two kinds of memory: the kind she sees "this dictum" to propose, and a kind of memory that might exist if one did not accept "this dictum." Those who do accept it

> see the in-rolling future as living reality and the past as reality entombed. They also regard every human faculty as having an evolutionary history. For these straight-line thinkers memory is a mere glance over the shoulder along a past seen as a progression from the near end of which mankind goes forward.

Richardson next illustrates the way in which an apparently neutral view of the past, memory, or history often contains a set of powerfully gendered beliefs. Continuing to describe "these straight-line thinkers," she says,

> they are also, these characteristically occidental thinkers, usually found believing in the relative passivity of females. And since women excel in the matter of memory, the two beliefs admirably support each other.

Moving from ironic tone into illustrated example, she explains the ways in which a person's relation to memory is also a relation to language. If one does not think in terms of evolutionary progress, she suggests, there might be an alternative way of perceiving and thus articulating the passage of time. If "memory is passive consciousness," then memory will of necessity be associated with that which is feminine. But, she suggests, even this association is a product of "straight-line thinking," and though some women "never question the primacy of "clear speech" and are the "docile disciples of the orderly thought of man," others do not "abdicate" or become "a partisan, a representative that is to say of one only of the many sides of [the] question." These other women understand that though the "feminine" kind of memory is not manifest in "straight-line thought," it is also not necessarily passive. In fact, such women may be able to see "many sides of the question" regarding the feminine relation to memory and thus to language. Richardson concludes the paragraph by differentiating "memory proper," a "mere backward glance," and "prolonged contemplation of things . . . past and done with."

> But there is memory and memory. And memory proper, as distinct from a mere backward glance, as distinct even from prolonged contemplation of things regarded as past and done with, gathers, can gather, and pile up its wealth only round universals, unchanging, unevolving verities that move neither backwards nor forwards and have neither speech nor language ("FGM," 36).

To Richardson, "memory proper" exhibits feminine character, and yet it is not passive. Its "feminine" character is manifest in its "gathering" of its "wealth" only around "universal" and "unchanging" truths. The activity and volition of this feminine memory are embedded in the verbs Richardson uses—"gathering" and "piling up" of memory's wealth. This accumulation is not centered on that which is only personally past, but, possibly ignited by a certain cast of light or a personal memory, it also gathers and piles up around "unchanging, unevolving" truths that "mov[ing] neither backwards nor forwards," are neither progressive nor regressive.

Because "memory proper" does not move in succession as does straight-line thinking or the "diachronic" linguistic mode described by de Saussure, Richardson's Swiss contemporary, it belongs to what he calls the "synchronic" linguistic function. Many illuminating parallels can be drawn between de Saussure's descriptions of the synchronic and diachronic linguistic axis and Richardson's descriptions of the feminine silent and masculine talkie. Consistent with the character of the synchronic function, for example, the language of memory proper has no history; it is simultaneous experience, and its communication occurs in mediums such as those of music or poetry. Like the thing beyond the photographs or the film or, like the excess beyond representation that escapes representation, memory proper gathers and piles up to reveal, sometimes through words, the wordless "unevolving verities" beyond words that belong to the realm of the "synchronic." In de Saussure's terms, "Everything that relates to the static side of our science [science of language] is synchronic; everything that has to do with evolution is diachronic."[70]

It is the presence of memory proper and inner speech in the synchronic silent cinema that makes Richardson's silent film powerfully and poetically evocative and "feminine," and it is the lack of this that, in Richardson's view, makes the talkie, with its "uttered speech," hopelessly diachronic and thus masculine. Again striking a cosmopolitan note, Richardson returns near the end of "The Film Gone Male" to answer the question, What kind of communication is the film? She states that

> it is a medium, or a weapon, at the disposal of all parties and has, considered as a battlefield a grand advantage over those of the past. . . . The new film can, at need, assist Radio in turning the world into a vast council-chamber and do more than assist, for it is the free partner. And multitudinous within that vast chamber as within none of the preceding councils of mankind, is the unconquerable, unchangeable eternal feminine. Influential ("FGM," 38).

Thus, although the talkie fulfills the "masculine destiny" of the silents, the nature of the filmic medium is such that "the unchangeable eternal feminine" will also continue to maintain a "multitudinous" presence in the "vast council-chamber" of the talkie. This presence is "influential," and it has never before had a medium by which to remain so strongly present in the "council-chamber of mankind." Optimistic, even in the face of the disappearance of the silents, Richardson ends "The Film Gone Male" dramatically.

> Weeping therefore, if weep we must, over the departure of the old time film's gracious silence, we may rejoice in the prospect of a fair field and no favour. A field over which lies only the shadow of the censorship. And the censorship is getting an uneasy conscience ("FGM," 38).

In "The Film Gone Male," Richardson comes close to accusing women of using speech as an accoutrement in the kind of feminine masquerade about which her contemporary Joan Riviere, the British psychoanalyst, theorizes in her 1929 essay "Womanliness as a Masquerade."[71] Since Riviere's work illuminates Richardson's discussion of the many women who "chatter, gossip or talk incessantly" and the "only one in a thousand who can talk," it is worth dwelling on at some length. Riviere was in analysis with Ernest Jones from 1916 to 1920, and by 1919 had patients of her own. In 1921 Jones recommended that she enter psychoanalysis with Freud, which she did. Her psychoanalytic theory is strikingly similar to the theory that Richardson and Miriam, both believing they are unattractive to men because of their "masculine" talk and intelligence, spin out in fiction and critical writing. Witness Miriam after the episode in the lecture hall:

> If she had been the frilled lady, sitting forward with her, forward-falling frill, patronizing the lecture and "exhibiting" her interest, he would not have gone to sleep (*The Tunnel*, 107).

Instead, since she is not the frilled lady and Hancock did fall asleep, Miriam's thoughts "recoil" and "circle" on the "miserable" implications for her embedded in the spectacle she is witnessing. These "miserable implications" are spelled out in a letter that Ernest Jones wrote to Freud in which he says of Riviere what Miriam and Richardson imagined men said of them: "She is not the type that attracts me erotically though I certainly have the admiration for her intelligence that I would have with a man."[72] The assumption of a necessary separation between female erotic attraction and male intelligence is the axis on which Richardson's and Riviere's theories of masquerade pivot. In "Womanliness as a Masquerade," Riviere states her objective:

> I shall attempt to show that women who wish for masculinity may put on a mask of womanliness to avert anxiety and the retribution feared from men.
>
> It is with a particular type of intellectual woman that I have to deal. Not long ago intellectual pursuits for women were associated almost exclusively with an overtly masculine type of woman, who in pronounced cases made no secret of her wish or claim to be a man. This has now changed.[73]

Riviere describes some of the professional women with whom she has worked in an analytic context, and some that she knows outside of that context. In all of the examples the women show great intellectual capacity in public speech. This proficiency causes extreme anxiety, and for each the anxiety is in some way related to the

> reprisals she anticipated from the father-figures after her intellectual performance. The exhibition in public of her intellectual proficiency, which was in itself carried through successfully, signified an exhibition of herself in possession of the father's penis, having castrated him. . . . The display once over, she was seized by horrible dread of the retribution the father would then exact.[74]

This dread is dealt with in various ways after or during the women's performances. One woman, in spite of her excellent performance, would be "excited and apprehensive all night after, with misgivings whether she had done anything inappropriate and obsessed by a need for reassurance." Another dresses up in especially feminine attire to deliver her talks and afterwards begins "compulsive ogling and coquetting."[75] This last solution to the problem of symbolically castrating the father recalls the frilled lady whose silence, distance, and lacy attire served to reaffirm Hancock's masculine position—a reaffirmation that would have been disrupted if she had taken the podium. To avoid the "retribution" of the father, many women use the device that Richardson describes—"chatter, gossip or [incessant] talk." Those few who really "*talk*," however (Richardson's emphasis), risk retribution, and these few daring and perhaps secretly frightened women are also the focus of Riviere's investigation.

Riviere's discussion is particularly relevant to an understanding of "The Film Gone Male" because the anxiety she describes is located in women's speech and in the sight of woman in front of the audience (What will she wear while she talks in order to placate or attract?). As a result of her observations, Riviere is led to ask the same question Richardson explores:

> These conclusions compel one once more to face the question: what is the essential nature of fully developed femininity? What is *das ewig Weibliche*? The conception of womanliness as a mask, behind which man suspects some hidden danger, throws a little light on the enigma."[76]

Here again is the light that must be thrown on the woman—the enigma—so that she can better be seen. This light recalls once again the scene in *The Tunnel*—the lectern, the photograph, and its "intaircepted [sic] waves of light that would rush through if they weren't stopped by some special kind of film surging up and down in confinement." The confining on the film suggests the confinement of the otherwise dangerous woman, the exciting surging of this confinement and the "hidden" excess behind the scenes of the cinema.

Riviere never defines women's identity outside of the masquerade; in fact she suggests that genuine womanliness and the "masquerade" are the same thing. Richardson, however, believes that there is something that can be called feminine behind the facade of the masquerade. Indeed she believes that there is such a place as behind the masquerade. In Richardson's formulation of the masquerade in regard to speech, a woman who questions the function of "clear speech" is equivalent to a woman who questions her position in an economy of exchange in which women's talk serves to assure men of their dominant positions. For Richardson, the assumption that good speech is clear, orderly, and primarily a medium used to communicate information is an assumption that is complicit with a male economy.

To conceive of women's speech as masquerade is to evoke, simultaneously, the mechanism by which the spatial economy of the film operates. As Doane states,

> The viewer must not sit either too close or too far from the screen. The result would be the same—he would lose the image of his desire.[77]

As film theorist Burch also points out, spectatorial desire is aligned with a certain spatial configuration. The image of woman is seen at a distance, a distance that is necessary and must be maintained, just as the lack of an actual presence on the screen must be maintained. A woman who, in Richardson's description, either questions the function of clear speech, or talks in public in the second kind of way, destabilizes the spatial position of the image of herself and thereby disrupts the masculine structure of the look. In speech, the look is transcribed as possession of knowledge, or as the power to interpret meaning. Thus a woman who questions the function of "clear speech" moves too close or too far from the screen, or causes the viewer to move too close or too far away, thereby shifting the terms of distance and disrupting the position of the one who possesses knowledge. In moving herself she takes agency—becomes not just the image of intercepted light on the film but also the intercepter—and through that agency she destabilizes the structure of the "image of his desire." This description is equivalent to women's public speech, in which a woman takes the podium and threatens the man's position of knowledge by speaking in public. As Doane states in a discussion of the spatial economy that the masquerade maintains,

> The masquerade, in flaunting femininity, holds it at a distance. Womanliness is a mask which can be worn or removed. The masquerade's resistance to patriarchal positioning would therefore lie in its denial of the production of femininity as closeness, as presence-to-itself, as, precisely, imagistic. The transvestite adopts the sexuality of the other—the woman becomes a man in order to attain the necessary distance from the image. . . . In Montrelay's words, "the woman uses her own body as a disguise."[78]

Or, in Richardson's terms, she uses her own words, or the form of her own speech, as a disguise. In writing almost literally on the surface of the film and from within the element of the filmic experience, rather than about the film, or about a film that exists in a place distant from the scene of writing, Richardson also alters the terms of the film's spatial positioning. She writes close up: in the "Continuous Performance" columns as well as in *Pilgrimage* she produces femininity as "closeness, as presence-to-itself, as precisely imagistic." Through this writing, the film is brought up close as she becomes the projector's fingers of writing light. In *Close Up*, the film or the "small ceremonial prepared for a group" is also transcribed into a text to be read, or a "private devotion." It is "focussed at the distance of a book," the distance of private devotion. At the same time, Richardson's film is kept at the distance of an ideal object—always lost and always being retrieved—always restoring that impossible-to-restore "first moment." As she states in the "Continuous Performance" piece titled "Narcissus," "distance is enchantment. It is a perpetual focus" and "whatever the ostensible interest of the film, it is arranged and focussed at the distance exactly fitting the contemplative state" ("CP: Narcissus," *Close Up*, September, 1931). This is the distance of the "imagistic."

Through the simultaneous enactment of intimate close-up and panning from a distance in the *Close Up* columns, Richardson effects what Doane calls "a defamiliarisation of female iconography." She thereby disrupts the mechanisms by which the masquerade operates in film.[79] Just as Miriam improvises on the piano then rises "transfigured," thereby disrupting the Victorian icon of the controlled woman in the parlor entertaining guests, Richardson defamiliarizes the film and the female iconography in it by using the "Continuous Performance" columns as a site of "feminine" public speech and as a place from which to destabilize the spatial economy of the cinema.

In "The Film Gone Male," the something authentic, or beyond, the masquerade disguise of women's "chatter, gossip or incessant talk" is what she calls the "essentially feminine." This essential femininity is exemplified in the image that, in *Dimple Hill*, the second-to-last novel-chapter of *Pilgrimage*, becomes an icon: the image of the Quaker woman who gives testimony, speaks in a public place in which, as Richardson says, the "spiritual identity" of a woman was recognized and women were not "an appendage to be controlled, guided and managed by man" (*Dimple Hill*, 420). In other words, this is a utopic space outside of patriarchal structures, a femininity outside of the masquerade.

Richardson's investigation of women's talk in "The Film Gone Male" and in *Pilgrimage* parallels her exploration of the function of images of women on the film screen and the various relations of male and female viewers to those images throughout the "Continuous Performance" columns. It is in the cinema that she sees "womanliness" and fantasies of the feminine reiterated again and again. The cinema is an occasion for self-conscious and self-reflexive masquerade because it is the scene in which everyone acts, everyone seriously plays at being ultrafeminine, ultramasculine, an icon of anger, poverty, etc. "Playing at" or "acting like" is highlighted in the cinema, particularly for women, who, as Richardson notes, are able to detect effect, and see that other women, or they themselves, are in mask when men are often unable to detect it.[80]

By interjecting her own writing into the scene of the British movie house in the late twenties to early thirties, Richardson pursues that which the spectacle of woman on the screen makes visible—that something of her which has escaped discourse. She defines that something in "The Film Gone Male" as that which men perceive as women's "palpitating spiritual nakedness," and which Miriam describes in *Revolving Lights* as women's ability to

> hold all opinions at once, or any, or none. It's because they see the relations of things which don't change, more than things which are always changing, and mostly the importance to men of the things men believe. But behind it all their [women's] own lives are untouched (*Revolving Lights*, 259).

Again lining up the feminine with the syntagmatic axis and with the realm of inner speech, Miriam elaborates on the theme of the nature of women's consciousness in comparison to men's throughout *Pilgrimage.* Privileging again a particular kind of blindness, she inverts the gendered and power-laden metaphors of sight and the spatialized structures of knowledge embedded in the masquerade, making justice, for example, a blindfolded woman who sees that the shadows on the wall, like those in Plato's cave, are only appearances.

> Justice is a woman; blindfold; seeing from the inside and not led away by appearances; men invent systems of ethics, but they cannot weigh personality; they have no individuality, only conformity or nonconformity to abstract systems; yet it was impossible to acknowledge the power of a woman, of any woman she had ever known, without becoming a slave (*Deadlock*, 37).

Echoing Herring's statement "We are all slaves of the lamp in the projector," Richardson again invokes what Riviere calls "some hidden danger" that men suspect and that men and many women are afraid to acknowledge. The object of fear is what Richardson calls "the power of a woman." The nature of this power is that women can see from the inside—even blindfolded a woman can see—and thus a woman embodies justice since she can judge and weigh beyond the proscribed limits of an "abstract system."

Acknowledgment of this power is frightening because enslavement might follow. There is also fear of the possibility of being either castrated or castrating, of one's power being diminished as either a woman or a man. This is the same fear and fascination of "the lamp in the projector" that many modernists had of the power and light of the early cinema.

In her discussion of the fear of women's speech or image, Richardson echoes the work of many contemporary feminist theorists who have attempted to account for this something which has escaped, which is then a threat in its absence and which must yet remain absent in order to maintain the structures of gender it upholds. As Irigaray says,

> woman does not exist owing to the fact that language—a language—rules as master, and that she threatens—as a sort of "prediscursive reality—to disrupt its order. Moreover it is inasmuch as she does not exist that she sustains the desire of these "speaking beings" that are called men: "A man seeks a woman—this is going to strike you as odd—owing to something that is located only in discourse, since, if what I am suggesting is true, namely that woman is not-all, there is always something in her which escapes discourse."[81]

In the "Continuous Performance" columns, Richardson investigates "that something of her [that has] escaped," the evidence of which can be witnessed in women's presence and deceivingly present image on the screen. In her investigation of that which has escaped, she puts words in the place where there is nothing: nonexistent woman projected on a screen. Her interest in the rich possibility couched in this mechanism of projection is based in the simultaneous presence and absence that the cinema displays—the "escape" from discourse that the cinema frames. Though men are also present and absent as image, their doubleness does not reenact on a large scale women's cultural position in relation to the hierarchic structures of language and the resultant link between women's public speech and the sight of woman.

Richardson's fascination with the way in which meaning is generated through, then beyond, words and her fascination with the ideographic composition of sentences, paragraphs, letters, and punctuation on a page, was also played out in the visual arrangement of image and light on the screen. She used the "feminine" silent film to illustrate spatially and visually the kind of travel by inner speech that Miriam often embarks upon—a journey toward

> the strange thing for which there were no words. . . . It was the thing that was nothing. Yet it seemed the only thing that came near and meant anything at all (*Interim*, 344).

The *Close Up* columns were interstitial in the sense that they were written between the wordless desire for this "nothing" invoked by the silent film, and a simultaneous voluminous flood of words pouring into the *Pilgrimage* novel-volumes, between a presence that could be written about and an absence or excess that kept escaping. Explaining this "disruptive excess" that is the evidence of absence, the sign of that which has escaped, Irigaray says,

> the issue is not one of elaborating a new theory of which woman would be the subject or the object, but of jamming the theoretical machinery itself, of suspending its pretension to the production of a truth and of a meaning that are excessively univocal. Which presupposes that women do not aspire simply to be men's equals in knowledge. That they do not claim to be rivaling men in constructing a logic of the feminine that would still take onto-theologic as its model, but that they are rather attempting to wrest this question away from the economy of the logos. They should not put it, then, in the form "What is woman?" but rather, repeating/interpreting the way in which, within discourse, the feminine finds itself defined as lack, deficiency, or as imitation and negative image of the subject, they should signify that with respect to this logic a disruptive excess is possible on the feminine side.[82]

"Repeating" and "interpreting" the way in which the feminine finds itself defined as lack within discourse, Richardson devises a poetics of excess, a "sensual thinking" that carefully mimes the "feminine" qualities she finds inherent in the silent cinema. Even the excessive length of the unfinished thirteen-volume epic was produced in the face of "that strange thing for which there were no words"—produced, like the "Continuous Performance" columns, in part to disrupt the "onto-theo-logic" notion that a novel or film needs to be about anything. Instead the importance for Richardson lies in the "construction of the form and the composition" of inner speech—that is, the arrangement and focus of words and images so that they would speak a distance and atmosphere "exactly fitting the contemplative state" ("CP: Narcissus," *Close Up*, September, 1931, 184).[83]

Richardson's Aesthetic Mystification of the Cinema

Richardson's hermetic beliefs meet and are manifest as method and focus in her aesthetic mystification of the cinema. She was attracted to film's transferring of things through the music of words and its interplay between sound, silence, space, and especially light. The hermetic notion that the coming together of all of these elements is the condition for the union of the soul with life speaks to the "miracle" that occurs in Richardson's cinema. The notion that nothing, including the soul, is destructible also speaks to the "Continuous" part of the column title and to the aim of the film columns—to investigate the "direct relationship, mystic, joyous, wonderful, between the observer a *continuous* miracle of form in movement" ("Continuous Performance," *Close Up*, June, 1933, my emphasis).

She held this aesthetic-mystical project in common with the early to mid-twentieth-century hermetic poets, including the French symbolists. She was familiar with the work of the symbolists, and other so-called hermetic poets and writers, some of whom she was directly influenced by—including Proust, Ibsen, Baudelaire, H. D., Rimbaud, and Valery. Hermetic writing was often referred to as "intellectual music"—a term that describes Richardson's approach to and invention of the film as a shadow on the wall of Plato's cave, which, with the right combination of musical accompaniment, words, and light, could miraculously suggest something else—an idea, an ideal form—elsewhere. In a letter to her friend Henry Savage, Richardson elaborated on the superior relation that mystics have, as compared to artists, to that which cannot be said.

> Your citations from Freud and Nietzsche: certainly, most "idealism" is enlightened self-interest. Has sprouted mostly amongst Protestants. The R.C. church knows all about that. Yet the word "ideal" keeps its meaning in suitable contexts and within rigid limitations. Language is a very partial medium of expression. Poetry indirectly more direct. Music still more so. Yet all art, as every artist, though not his camp-followers, well knows, can never express, fully, what he wants to express. In the hierarchy of being, the mystics (not the many aberrations of mysticism) the best of them, stand on a "higher" or "deeper" or further rung. Oh the helplessness surrounding the helpfulness and manifold uses of speech, the dangers within the delights of metaphor. By their

> metaphors ye shall know them. Metaphorocrasy, that is what really all thought lives under, all the philosophies.[84]

Richardson's involvement with the Quakers ran parallel to and validated the modernist hermetic aesthetic she developed. In addition, it provided an arena in which she witnessed a different relation of women to public speech than she had seen before. In 1907 she spent almost a year at a Quaker fruit farm on Windmill Hill on the coast of Sussex. This was the beginning of her life-long interest in the Quakers. She wrote two books about the Quakers, both published in 1914: *The Quakers Past and Present* and *Gleanings From the Work of George Fox.* In *The Quakers Past and Present,* she reveals some of the ways in which Quaker philosophy intersected with her concerns about women's relation to God within organized religion and with her concerns about the relation between revelation and aesthetics. As she says in *The Quakers Past and Present,* they [the Quakers] believed in "the possibility here and now of complete freedom from sin," and they recognized the "spiritual identity" of a woman. The "inner light," they felt, was universal; women were not "an appendage to be controlled, guided, and managed by man" . . . they seemed to be searching always for the 'center of being' where one might remain, remote and impersonal, and yet "see freshly all the time." The "center of being," like the "lamplit circle" to which she would "everlastingly return" to write, are very different from that place offered to women by the Anglican church in which Richardson was raised.

Staley describes the connections between the development of Richardson's aesthetic and her link to the Quakers:

> She had moved in her thinking from anarchism to communism and socialism, denying communism for its lack of attention to the individual. The Quaker philosophy introduced her to mysticism and to the quest for a reality that bypassed ordinary perception in order to establish a unity with the Absolute through supersensuous, non-rational processes. For the Quakers, the experience of mysticism "is not a gift of grace to a few, but possible to every man by virtue of his partaking of the spirit of God in himself."[85]

These ideas evolving from her immersion with the Quakers and the formal literary results of her aesthetic hermeticism are manifest most clearly in *Dimple Hill,* the second-to-last novel-chapter of *Pilgrimage.*

Richardson's writing was a hermetic activity accompanied by all of the overtones that the word "hermetic" brings. For example, in the "Continuous

Performance" columns, film is at times referred to with a capital "F" indicating that it is other, or ideal. Capitalized or lower case, film served as the source of dense possibilities and demands for interpretation. In an almost blatantly platonic vein, she frames film as the location of seemingly direct visual revelation and at the same time the scene of concealment of meaning. It is not surprising that her particular hermeticism regarding film includes a platonic twist. The climate of the turn-of-the-century philosophy and mysticism in which she was immersed was infused with a brand of Neoplatonism primarily influenced, in Richardson's case, by McTaggart, Bergson, and the Quakers.

The aesthetic spirituality Richardson spins out in her writing is closely related to the figure of Hermes as both a "literary" conveyor of messages and the embodiment of the alchemical belief in language as a mode of transfer and transformation. This belief was echoed in the discourse of psychoanalysis. Hermes helped the Fates compose the alphabet, was located at boundaries as a boundary marker or herm, and as a hermaphrodite was also a figure of boundary crossing—the perfect figure for Richardson's focus on gender and its relation to language.

The Neoplatonic philosophers called Hermes the "Logos," or "word of God made flesh." Richardson's cinema was the new flesh of the word of God given physicality through the continuous performance of representation—the spectacle. By extension, the "Continuous Performance" columns were a continuous speculation about spectacle, occurring at the juncture of two scenes of spectacle's performance, the novel and film. In the last of the "Continuous Performance" columns, she gives an ecstatic account of the difference between a play and a film. It is the "continuous[ly] sparking representation" that interests her most and is unique to the film. What happens in a film that cannot in a play is "the dim, blurred continuously sparking representation of a locomotive advancing full steam on the audience, majestic and terrible." Fascinated with the "majestic and terrible" (words of awe that might be used to describe the appearance of a god, adjectives referring to the transformative powers and potentials of representation) she implies that mechanical reproduction suggested a hermetics and hermeneutics of representation in which the capacity for reproduction had redemptive and transformative potential.

NOTES: Part II

1. Henry James, as quoted by Leon Edel in *The Modern Psychological Novel* (New York: Grove Press, 1955), 23.

2. Benjamin, *Illuminations*, 220.

3. Virginia Woolf, "The Cinema," *The Captain's Death Bed and Other Essays*, (New York and London: Harcourt, Brace and Jovanovich, 1978), 180-186. Quotes from pages 183 & 184. Originally published in 1926.

4. William James, as quoted by Edel in *The Modern Psychological Novel*, 20.

5. Henry James, Edel, 23.

6. As quoted by Stephen Kern, *The Culture of Time and Space 1880-1918* (Cambridge, MA: Harvard University Press, 1983), 39.

7. Kern, *The Culture of Time and Space*, 68.

8. Kern, 72; and Henri-Martin Barzun, as quoted by Kern, 72.

9. Kern, 72-74.

10. Kern, chap. 3.

11. Benjamin, 237-38.

12. Benjamin, 232.

13. Kern, 70.

14. Kern, 71-72.

15. Stephen Heath, *Questions of Cinema* (London: Macmillan, 1981), 228.

16. Rachel Low, *History of the British Film 1918-1929* (London: G. Allen & Unwin, 1971), 231.

17. Heath, *Questions of Cinema*, 228.

18. Benjamin, 237.

19. M. H. Abrams provides a highly useful historical account of the metaphoic use of the lamp and the mirror in critical discussions of aesthetics.

> The title of the book identifies two common and antithetic metaphors of mind, one comparing the mind to a reflector of external objects, the other to a radiant projector which makes a contribution to the objects it perceives. The first of these was characteristic of much of the thinking from Plato to the eighteenth century; the second typifies the prevailing romantic conception of the poetic mind (*The Mirror and the Lamp: Romantic Theory and the Critical Tradition*, New York: Oxford University Press, 1953).

In Abrams' terms, Richardson did not entirely abandon the mirroring function of the novel. Consistent with the turn-of-the-century late romantic and early modernist moment in which she writes, Richardson uses both the neo-classic mirror and romantic lamp as metaphors that describe her work and the techniques operative in it. The film lends itself perfectly to this hybrid as it embodies both the mirror and lamp functions. As a mirror it is mimetic and at the same time reflects the mind of the viewer; and as a lamp it projects and invokes the mind of the viewer to contribute, to be like a lamp and cast light, to project, as well. Thus indirectly invoking James' "centre of experience," Miriam refers to the original scene of writing to which she imagines repeatedly returning as "a lamplit circle."

As Abrams states, "The recourse to a mirror in order to illuminate the nature of one or another art continued to be a favorite with aesthetic theorists long after Plato" (32). In this vein Abrams sites an especially striking parallel between Plato's, Locke's and Richardson's use of the mirror and lamp metaphors: "Or (suggesting the *ut pictura poesis* of the aesthetic of that period) [the mind] is a *tabula rasa* on which sensations write or paint themselves. Or (employing the analogy of the camera obscura, in which the light, entering through a small aperture, throws an image of an external scene on the wall) external and internal senses are said to be 'the windows by which light is let into this *dark room*'" (57). For further discussion of Richardson's relation to platonic thinking see the "Magic Fingers Writing" section of Part II.

Although Richardson does use the film in a way strikingly parallel to Locke's use here of the camera obscura, she also departs from this metaphoric use radically. The most significant element of her departure from this and other neo-classic metaphoric uses of the mirror figure is that for Richardson the mind is not solely a tabula rasa, but, as in the use of the figure of the lamp, the mind contributes.

Again, the issue of Miriam's name is raised by these figures. Naming the main subject of the novels "Miriam" is perhaps more a modernist than a romantic or neoclassic gesture. As Richardson states, she views all writing to be in some sense autobiographical, but if the name of the main subject suggests that the subject is a mirror then it also begs the question, Whose life are these novels about? The presentation of a subject as a reflective surface raises further questions such as, Who is or is not the author? What and who is an author? A subject? An autobiography?

20. Stephen Heath, *The Nouveau Roman: A Study in the Practice of Writing* (London: Elek, 1972), 21.

21. Heath, *The Nouveau Roman*, 21.

22. Heath, 22.

23. Unless otherwise stated, all information regarding *Close Up* is derived from Anne Friedberg, *Writing About Cinema: Close Up 1927-33*, (Ph.D. 1983, N.Y.U. 44/12A, 3522). This is an especially rich and wonderful work which has been essential to this book.

24. Roland Cosandey, "On Borderline," *Afterimage* 12 (Autumn, 1985), 69.

25. Friedberg, *Writing About Cinema*, 228.

26. Sigmund Freud, as quoted in *In Dora's Case, Freud-Hysteria-Feminism*, ed. Bernheimer and Kahane (New York: Columbia University Press, 1985), 11.

27. Elizabeth K. Helsinger, Robin Lauterbach Sheets, and William Veeder, *The Woman Question* (New York: Garland, 1983), 16.

28. Freud, Bernheimer and Kahane, *In Dora's Case*, 5.

29. Linda Dowling, "The Decadent and the New Woman in the 1890's," *19th Century Fiction*, vol. 33, no. 4 (March, 1970), 32.

30. In this book the word "feminine" is always actually or figuratively in quotes since we don't know what it is.

31. Carolyn Burke, "Supposed Persons: Modernist Poetry and the Female Subject," *Feminist Studies*, vol. 11, no. 1 (Summer, 1985), 147.

32. Sergei Eisenstein, "Through Theatre to Cinema," *Film Form*, ed. and trans. Jay Leyda (New York: Harcourt, Brace & Company, 1949), 17.

33. Friedberg, 57.

34. Friedberg, 235.

35. Friedberg, 11.

36. As previously stated, in both content and technique, Richardson's *Close Up* columns circle around many of the same themes with which *Pilgrimage* is concerned. The concerns common to *Pilgrimage* and the "Continuous Performance" columns include acute attention to the formal implications of the frame of the page and attention to the function of the film frame; a similar concern with the spatiality of reading and viewing, often discussed in the "Continuous Performance" columns in terms of the spatial arrangements of the projector, screen, and audience in the cinema house; the connections between constructions of textual identity through uses of punctuation and a filmic grammar of editing; the linguistic and visual narrative functions of sound, silence, and light; and the notion of the act of reading as a solitary pilgrimage toward a shrine, and the parallel notion of film as "a small ceremonial prepared for a group."

37. During the 1920s the cinema was sometimes discussed in psychoanalytic terms, and much of this discussion was published in *Close Up*. One such article, which particularly resonates with Richardson's ideas, is "The Film in Its Relation to the Unconscious," by L. Saalshutz, vol. V, no. 1 (July, 1929), in which he speaks of the cinema as "an instrument of mass fantasy" and states that "the film is a visual reality . . . light patterns on a screen. But the content of the cinema is fantasy."

38. Benjamin, "The Work of Art in the Age of Mechanical Reproduction," *Illuminations*, 228.

39. Luce Irigaray uses the word "suffer" in this way in *This Sex Which Is Not One*, trans. Catherine Porter (Ithaca, NY: Cornell University Press, 1985), 38.

40. Richardson's engagement with and fantasy about the film manifests her view of writing and thus her view of the readerly and authorial subject. In this way her psychological novel experiment differs from those of her contemporaries, particularly those of Joyce and Woolf who, although interested in the cinema, do not use it as a primary phenomenological model for writing and subjectivity. The other way in which Richardson's engagement with the film distinguishes her experiment from those of her contemporaries is the way in which the silent film enacts her narrative theories regarding feminine writing. Thus, as discussed throughout Part II, the silent cinema becomes a model for and spectacle of the narrative effects Richardson would like to embody in her writing. This is quite distinct from the engagement of Joyce or Woolf with the early cinema. Although they may have been fascinated by the film, it never gained the aesthetic status and power for either of them that it occupied for Richardson.

41. Eisenstein, "Achievement" in *Film Form,* 182.

42. Eisenstein, "Achievement" in *Film Form,* 60.

43. Eisenstein, "The Structure of the Film," in *Film Form,* 154.

44. The platonic echoes here are very loud. They are given closer consideration in the sections of Part II titled "Inner Speech and Uttered Speech" and "Richardson's Aesthetic Mystification of the Cinema." Without launching a discussion that would be relevant, but at this point too tangential to the present one, it can be noted that some of Richardson's thinking can be seen as quite platonic. Two of the most striking examples in this regard are what she refers to as "that immortal part of us" which she believes lives on "after our bodies perish" and her notion of an "eternal feminine"— something essential yet invisible whose existence and operation she explains in a way that is resonant with Plato's theory of the Forms. I am not aware of any direct reference to Plato in *Pilgrimage* or of any statement Richardson may have made in regard to Plato, but this sharp resonance between their cosmological views certainly was highly influential in her attraction to the cinema as a spectacle of her aesthetic practice. It is perhaps more likely that she encountered Plato through the neo-Platonists whom she did read, such as McTaggart, Bergson, and to some extent the Quakers.

45. This inability to identify whose will or what will is causing all of the transformations conveyed by the projector also signals the cosmopolitan ability of the film to be nowhere and everywhere at once. Light itself—that which fuels the film—is cosmopolitan; it has the ability to be nowhere and everywhere, and a spectator who identifies with the will of the projecting apparatus identifies with the light and also travels everywhere, while staying in one place, while going nowhere.

46. Jane Gallop and Carolyn Burke, "Psychoanalysis and Feminism," *The Future of Difference,* ed. Eisenstein and Jardine (New Brunswick, NJ: Rutgers University Press, 1985), 111.

47. Gallop and Burke, 111.

48. Gallop and Burke, 111.

49. Gallop and Burke, 111.

50. Julia Kristeva, "Linguistics, Semiotics, Textuality," in *The Kristeva Reader,* ed. Toril Moi (New York: Columbia University Press, 1986), 93-105, 196, 232-34.

51. Eisenstein, "Achievement," in *Film Form,* 182.

52. Heath, *Questions of Cinema*, 36.

53. Heath, 36.

54. Heath, 38.

55. Examples of the power of words to evoke rather than merely accompany are discussed in detail in the last section of Part III, "Linguistic Shrine Sites and Corporate Silence." One of the elements necessary to the potence of the shrine-site passages is exactly this musical power of words to evoke a mental synesthetic state, a memory or epiphany beyond or through linguistic sense.

Shirley Rose also discusses the way in which the evocative and powerful sound of words acts as a trigger to what she calls a "form of spiritual ecstasy" which Miriam repeatedly experiences in *Pilgrimage.* Rose quotes the following passage from *Clear Horizon* and then goes on to discuss the nature of this "spiritual ecstasy:"

> It was as if some inexorable force were holding her here on this chill promontory of consciousness, while with the progressive mesh of interwoven sounds dark chasms opened (*Clear Horizon*, 298).

> While the appearance of the musical phrase recalls Proust, we see that Richardson does not use it as a trigger to memory. Miriam's reflection upon the phrase results in a form of spiritual ecstasy, and as such the event is more closely analogous to Joyce's aesthetic of epiphany. However, in *Dawn's Left Hand* (IV, 229-230), the sudden intrusion of a musical phrase does encourage memory; but more importantly, it arouses in Miriam both a sense of the future and an intense appreciation of the sound for its own sake in the present. The difference between Dorothy Richardson and Proust on this point may be clarified by Joseph Frank's analysis of the nature and effect of Proustian revelation. "Each such experience, Proust tells us, is marked by a feeling that 'the permanent essence of things, usually concealed, is set free and our true self, which had long seemed dead in other ways, awakes, takes on fresh life as it receives the celestial nourishment brought to it.' This celestial nourishment consists of some sound or odor, or other sensory stimulus, 'sensed anew, simultaneously in the present and the past.' Proust's words to this point may apply equally to Dorothy Richardson" (Shirley Rose, "The Unmoving Center," *Contemporary Literature*, vol. 10, no. 3, 1969, 366).

Indeed these words may apply equally to Richardson's use of linguistic musical accompaniment in the novels. They also apply to the way in which Richardson frames the silent film as a scene of potential "spiritual ecstasy" and epiphany, as well as a trigger to memory. The parallel Richardson draws here depends largely on an expansion of the meaning of the word "accompaniment" from simply the function of illustrating, or going along with, to the power of sound to evoke something entirely new beyond itself.

56. See the Foreword of *Pilgrimage*, page 10, where Richardson describes her writing process as evoking a "longing for participation."

57. As de Lauretis describes,

> Medusa and the Sphinx, like the other ancient monsters, have survived inscribed in hero narratives, in someone else's story, not their own; so they are figures or markers of positions—places and topoi—through which the hero and his story move to their destination and to accomplish meaning (Teresa de Lauretis, *Alice Doesn't: Feminism, Semiotics, Cinema*, Bloomington: Indiana University Press, 1984, 109).

58. Miriam is describing what de Lauretis and others have described as the gendered apparatus of "the gaze."

59. Heath, *Questions of Cinema*, 33-34. Regarding the relation between the window frame and notions of the screen and film frame, Heath says,

> Notions of screen and frame are fundamental in the elaboration of the perspective system. Leonardo da Vinci writes: "Perspective is nothing else than seeing a place (or objects) behind a pane of glass, quite transparent, on the surface of which the objects behind that glass are drawn. These can be traced in pyramids to the point in the eye, and these pyramids are intersected on the glass pane." The pane is at once a frame, the frame of a window and a screen, the area of projection on which what is seen can be traced and fixed; from the Quattrocento on, the "pane" delimits and holds a view, the painter's canvas as a screen situated between eye and object, point of interception of the light rays. It is worth noting, indeed, in Renaissance (and post-Renaissance) painting the powerful attraction of the window as theme, the fascination with the rectangle of tamed light, the luminously defined space of vision.

60. Robert Herring, "A New Cinema, Magic and the Avant Garde," *Close Up*, vol. IV, no. 4 (April, 1929), 49.

61. Barbara Low, "The New Cinema," *Close Up*, September, 1927, 50.

62. Sigmund Freud, "A Note on the 'Mystic Writing-Pad," XV, 1925, *Collected Papers 1888-1938*, vol. V, ed. James Strachey (New York: Hogarth Press, 1959), 177. Also see, David Farrell Krell, *Of Memory, Reminiscence, and Writing—On the Verge* (Bloomington and Indianapolis: Indiana University Press, 1990). See especially the chapter titled "Wax Magic, Freud and the Typography of Effraction." And, Jacques Derrida, "Freud and the Scene of Writing," in *Writing and Difference*, Alan Bass, (Chicago: University of Chicago Press, 1978).

63. Freud, "A Note on the 'Mystic Writing-Pad,'" 170.

64. Sergei Eisenstein, "Film Form: New Problems," *Film Form*, 130.

65. Eisenstein, 130.

66. Eisenstein, 130.

67. See the following sources for further discussion of the western equation of the eye with the theoretical view and of the dichotomy between the male logocentric gaze and the other senses associated with the "primitive," the "feminine," and the close-up (as opposed to the broad view or theoretical view). It is this economy of the eye that Richardson wishes to disrupt by retaining the importance of sight but making "distributed listening" equally important.

Stephen Tyler, "The Vision Quest in the West, or What the Mind's Eye Sees," *Journal of Anthropological Research* 40, no. 1, 23-40.

Donald Lowe, *The History of Bourgeois Perception* (Chicago: University of Chicago Press, 1982).

Jacqueline Rose, *Sexuality in the Field of Vision* (London: Verso, 1986).

Teresa de Lauretis and Stephen Heath, eds. *The Cinematic Apparatus* (London: Macmillan, 1980).

68. *Vanity Fair* (May, 1925), 6.

69. Mary Ann Doane, *The Desire to Desire—The Woman's Film of the 1940s* (Bloomington: Indiana University Press, 1987), 82.

70. Ferdinand de Saussure, *Course in General Linguistics*, eds. Bally, Sechehaye and Riedlinger, Trans. Wade Baskin (New York, Toronto, London: McGraw-Hill, 1959), 80-82. Richardson's descriptions and analyses of the "feminine" silents and the "masculine" talkies and their relation to language are strikingly resonant with much of de Saussure's analyses, particularly those notions that pivot around the idea that "synchrony and diachrony designate respectively a lan-

guage-state and an evolutionary phase" (81). It is almost as if Richardson added a consideration of gender to de Saussure's analyses and applied them to writing and the film. In this sense she again anticipates much of the work of contemporary feminist theorists, especially the French feminists who align feminine language practices and experience with the synchronic axis and male practices with the diachronic. De Saussure believes that both axes come together in communication, but, as Richardson, the French feminists and feminist psychoanalytic theory suggest that with the entrance of the Father into the Oedipal scene the synchronic always remains present though it is subsumed by the diachronic.

71. Joan Riviere, "Womanliness as a Masquerade," *Formations of Fantasy*, ed. V. Burgin et al. (London: Methuen, 1986). First published in *The International Journal of Psychoanalysis*, vol. 10 (1929). The background information on Riviere comes from Stephen Heath's essay "Joan Riviere and the Masquerade" in the same book.

72. Heath, "Joan Riviere," *Formations of Fantasy*, 46.

73. Riviere, "Womanliness," *Formations of Fantasy*, 35.

74. Riviere, 37.

75. Riviere, 37.

76. Riviere, 43.

77. Doane, *The Desire to Desire*, 106.

78. Doane, 82-83.

79. Doane, 82.

80. See the passage from *The Tunnel* (105) quoted in full in Part II on pages 72-74. Of Mr. Hancock, Miriam says, "even he was one of those men who do not know that an effect like that was just an effect, a deliberate 'charming' feminine effect."

81. Irigaray, *This Sex Which is Not One*, 89.

82. Irigaray, 78.

83. It is important to recall here that, for Richardson, ideal contemplation is not necessarily or strictly a solitary act. The fact that it has occurred, even if it occurs while one is alone reading a book, indicates that a kind of "participation" has happened. Whether it be in the cinema or in a solitary scene of reading, Richardson's contemplation or meditation always imagines and projects the

accompaniment of an audience or presence. Indeed one of the main reasons for her defense of the silent cinema is that it instigates more collaboration from the audience than the talkies, which by being "so speaking" in their "masculine" way, impose rather than invite a collaborative story or experience from the viewers. Thus the ideal "contemplative state" which Richardson aims to invoke is a state of participation or collaboration. Richardson makes it clear that silence and solitude are conditions favorable to this state, but even if a reader or viewer is physically alone, the contemplative state itself involves a dissolution of boundaries and a sense of unity with the visible and invisible things of the world.

84. Horace Gregory, *Dorothy Richardson: An Adventure in Self-Discovery* (New York: Holt, Rinehart and Winston, 1967), 11.

85. Thomas Staley, *Dorothy Richardson* (Boston: Twayne, 1976), 23.

PART III
Recreative Delights and Spiritual Exercise

Jesus said: Become passers-by (*The Gospel According to Thomas*, Log. 42).

If only she could make Eve see what a book was . . . a dance by the author, a song, a prayer, an important sermon, a message. Books were not stories printed on paper, they were people; the real people . . . (*Honeycomb*, 385; Richardson's ellipses and punctuation).

. . . to see God everywhere is pantheism. What is Christianity? What are Christians? Evangelicals are humanitarians; rushing about in Ulsters. Anglicans know all about the beauty of life and like comfort. But they are snobs and afraid of new ideas. Convents and monasteries stop your mind. But there is a God or Christ, there is something always there to answer when you turn away to it from everything. Perhaps one would have to remain silent, for years, for a lifetime, and in the end begin to understand (*Interim*, 358).

Richardson rejected the Anglicanism of her family as well as many other religions and forms of spirituality that she subsequently investigated. The only organized religion for which she ever felt an affinity was that of the Quakers, though she never considered herself one of them. She invented her own pantheistic aesthetic based on the possibility of seeing God everywhere, exactly the project in which Miriam is engaged. Through the character of Miriam in *Pilgrimage*, and in her other writings, Richardson reveals that the nerve of her spirituality is a pantheistic worship of language and objects as animate. This belief served simultaneously as a model of how to live and how to write. In her life, Richardson (and Miriam) aimed at an always-increasing contact with the "god" that is "everywhere." In her writing, she wished to reproduce both the idea and the experience of contact with a divine presence that permeates the world.[1]

As part of her search to articulate and define her own spirituality, Miriam often muses on the ideas embedded in a wide array of religions. There are also many moments (often continuing for a number of pages) in which she does not discuss religion but actually experiences "God" in the things, people, or sounds around her. In these mystical or transformative moments Richardson does not tell the reader Miriam's thoughts, but attempts instead to animate the language so that the reader is also infused with Miriam's experience. Richardson attempts in these passages to endow the words themselves with a sensual vitality that replicates the teeming linguistic waters that both she and Miriam inhabit.

In calling her technique of feminine prose a "form of spiritual exercise," Richardson asserts that all of her aesthetic choices are also spiritual choices. In the foreword to *Pilgrimage*, she indicates a merging of the aesthetic and the spiritual in her discussion of feminine prose, stating that "feminine prose," like James' technique, should demand "upon the first reading a perfection of sustained concentration akin to that which brought it forth, and bestowing, again upon the first reading, the recreative delights peculiar to this form of spiritual exercise." Thus she aims at reproducing, through the techniques of feminine prose, the ecstatic moments of "sustained concentration" that she experienced in the writing of *Pilgrimage*. Her "spiritual exercise," and the "exercise" in which she wishes to engage the reader, is one of a quest for consciousness beyond language. This is achieved through a sensual glut of narrative and through the filmic techniques of feminine prose, at times including disrupted language practices. The "sustained concentration" on and in language, an immersion in language that leads beyond words, is best exemplified in those passages from *Pilgrimage* in which the syntax and space of the page are altered to the extent that the prose is transformed and appears to hover between ideogram, poetry, and music. These passages are like prayers to be uttered in linguistic shrines. In this section I will investigate some of these "shrine sites" in *Pilgrimage*, since it is in their shelter that Richardson's "spiritual exercise" is most fully embodied.

The particular hybrid of genres Richardson employs for *Pilgrimage* indicates, on a broader scale, the kind of spiritual practice in which she was engaged as a writer. With the title *Pilgrimage*, for example, she signals the genre of travel or spiritual quest. In making her work a continuous, unending epic she signals the tradition of what is now often referred to as the "long poem."[2] In using the outline of her own life as the structure of Miriam's, she locates herself in the realm of autobiography. These choices made at the level of genre and style reflect another significant aspect of the merging between her writerly technique and spiritual practice.

Just as the spirituality is manifest as an aesthetics at the more local level of the word and the page, it also reveals itself as a politics through these generic choices. She chose the pilgrimage-epic-autobiographical hybrid as the vehicle appropriate to feminine prose for many of the same reasons that she practiced syntactic disruption in the novels themselves. The underpinnings for some of Richardson's choices are addressed by Derrida in "The Law of Genre," in which he states that genre appears to be a description of literary types, a taxonomy that borrows from the biological system of classifying species. But description, he argues, always implies proscription. "Thus, as soon as genre announces itself," he writes, "one must respect a norm, one must not cross a line of demarcation, one must not risk impurity, anomaly or monstrosity."[3] It is precisely out of a desire to risk impurity, anomaly, and monstrosity as a gesture of disrespect for the norm that Richardson chose to write outside the borders of a single genre, and in the same spirit would not become a member of an organized religious or political group.[4] Although she refused to join, her spiritual practice was devout and her political views reflected much thought and investigation. Similarly, though her writing does not conform to one genre, like her spiritual and political practices it draws on the structures and figures of many.

In her views of the relations between women and writing, Richardson anticipates much contemporary feminist thought. She views genre distinction as a political territory fraught with power relations rather than a neutral realm of naming. Embedded in her desire to produce a "feminine equivalent to the current masculine realism" is Richardson's recognition that it is not only syntax and form which are governed by "overdetermined" and gendered categories, but that the notion of a "transcendental . . . ideal type" also reigns and requires disruption at the level of genre.[5]

Moving from the pan to the close-up in the following section, it is clear that Richardson's generic choices reflect on a broad scale the kind of aesthetics and spirituality operative in the writing of feminine prose. Consistent with these choices, but manifest more locally, the shrine-site passages in *Pilgrimage* can be seen to most fully embody the spiritual exercise of feminine prose.

Monstrosity and Impurity: The Generic Hybrid—Pilgrimage, Epic, and Autobiography

As described in the foreword to *Pilgrimage*, Richardson, in choosing a genre in which to write, was faced with the issue of whether to follow a male tradition or to "attempt to produce" a "feminine equivalent" of that tradition. In giving the novel-chapters the title of *Pilgrimage*, Richardson both situated herself in and departed from a tradition of pilgrimage narratives written by an army of "male regiments." Among these predecessors, the ones to whom Richardson refers in the body of *Pilgrimage*, and thus who most likely had the greatest impact on its writing, include Bunyan, George Fox, Chaucer, Dante, and Goethe, whose *Wilhelm Meister* she pays homage to in the Foreword.

Richardson attempted to produce a feminine equivalent of the pilgrimage genre by altering the usual terms and structure of pilgrimage narratives. Generally and schematically speaking, the traditional pilgrimage and travel narrative written by one of the "male regiments" features a young male hero who must leave home, often in search of a lost father or in order to avenge a dead father. He must travel through perilous territory and pass a series of tests and trials. As de Lauretis suggests, the territory of the young male hero's travel is usually figured, metaphorically or otherwise, as feminine, thus emphasizing the agency of the male hero and the fact that his quest is as much a search for gender identity as for any external goal.[6] Because his physical travel manifests personal and psychic development, if he passes the trials and tests presented to him, he is rewarded with a symbol of newly gained manhood, usually either a woman, a sword, another kind of weapon, or an instrument endowed with magical powers. He then returns home transformed by his journey and no longer in search of his father because he has now become the symbolic father or male authority. The evidence of his transformation is both in the object (or woman) with which he returns and, even more so, in the story of the journey which he brings home. Because the story counts in the community as evidence of his transformation and therefore evidence of his wisdom, the story itself and the telling of it become the most important prize brought back from his travels. The ability to use language to explain the unseen, to tell the story of overcoming perils and of the customs of people in foreign places, is to possess knowledge, to gain status in the community, and to become a hero.[7] Richardson inverts the pilgrimage genre by putting Miriam, a traveling female hero, at the center of the male quest, by giving her the male wilds of London as the territory of her travel and the exploration of the untraversed jungles of existence outside of traditionally defined gender roles as one of the goals of her journey.

The double register present in travel or quest, in which actual physical travel and landscape can also always be read as signifying psychic transformation, is featured and highlighted in pilgrimage narratives. The pilgrimage genre itself always signals a realm in which physical travel should be read as an allegory for spiritual travel. Describing the history of the structure of European pilgrimage narratives and the various ways in which allegory has operated in them, Howard says,

> The image of the pilgrimage kept a place in European thought into the nineteenth century. The pilgrimage itself, dead as an institution in England by the end of the sixteenth century, lived on as an idea preserved in books. There was never a time when the words pilgrim and pilgrimage didn't have force, and . . . they connoted a one-way journey to a destination, made for a purpose worthy of reverence. Purchas's use of the word in his titles already shows [*Purchas His Pilgrimage* or *Relations of the World and the Religions Observed in All Ages and Places Discovered, From the Creation unto this Present* (1613)] secularization: his pilgrims' purpose was to return home with knowledge. And of course Bunyan's *The Pilgrim's Progress* comes at once to mind. In such allegories, as in spiritual guides and autobiographies of the period, the individual Christian's internal struggle in the world was reckoned a pilgrimage. . . . For, as was always true, pilgrimage was a metaphor for human life: life is a one-way passage to the Heavenly Jerusalem and we are pilgrims on it. In the eighteenth century, the metaphor of the pilgrimage never disappeared, but it was in various texts supplanted or augmented by other images, especially that of life as theatre: this image allowed the author to be not a returned traveller and omniscient narrator but a privileged spectator, exploring personages in relation to one another and to the world, uncovering their masks and roles—an important step in the history of fiction.

It is no accident that in the eighteenth century, a time when the novel was first stirring, the image of pilgrimage was altered in such a way that the position of the author was no longer that of a "returned traveller and omniscient narrator" but instead a "privileged spectator, exploring personages in relation to one another and to the world." In the eighteenth century, the author was a kind of pilgrim-novelist-ethnographer engaged in a writing that was realistic in its description as well as fictional and analytic. This combination aptly describes Richardson's position as an author, a position which was also modeled by the writers of the nineteenth-century bildungsromanen.[9]

The bildungsroman has much in common with the pilgrimage narrative in its altered eighteenth-century form. It is significant that Goethe's *Wilhelm Meister's Apprenticeship*, generally considered the prototype of the bildungsroman and influential to Richardson, contains an intratext called "Confessions of a Beautiful Soul." The development of the woman in this text ultimately serves Wilhelm's development, but even the presence of a female counterpart may have been suggestive to Richardson.[10]

In *Pilgrimage*, Richardson acknowledges the influence of some of the nineteenth-century bildungsromanen that were written by women. Miriam especially identifies with the pilgrim-heroines of Charlotte Bronte, whose lives are a long journey of learning. At fifteen, for example, Miriam acquires a copy of Villette and, in keeping with her sense of life as a series of circlings—a kind of travel that includes a return journey but does not end at the pilgrim's return—she says of *Villette*, "When I've finished it, I begin again" (*The Tunnel*, 259). As discussed in previous chapters, Miriam's various ways of reading throughout *Pilgrimage* are often meant to serve as models for the reader's reading, for writing and spiritual practices. Thus to begin *Villette* again after finishing is to suggest a view of quest as repeated processual return rather than as a goal to complete. Again merging a spiritual model with the literary in *The Tunnel*, Miriam says, "Your reading is a habit, like most men's, not a quest. You don't want it disturbed" (279). Miriam wants to disturb male reading habits so that, as in a quest, a reader does not know what will come next, though one may know what she or he seeks.[11]

With the rise of the novel in the nineteenth century, the many different types of quest and travel narrative became less and less distinct:

> By the nineteenth century, kinds of journeys which to the medieval mind would have little to do with pilgrimage—the voyage of exploration, the chivalric quest, the sojourn, even the prodigal's return—had become conflated. The romantic quest, even when as with Byron it is called a pilgrimage, was a new and different image: it had become internalized. It was a journey into the self, and the antagonist was no longer exterior temptation (as in the Middle Ages) or external nature (as in Defoe) but identity, selfhood: the romantics had to shake off selfhood to attain their interior Edens of love and knowledge, of triumphant imagination.[12]

For Miriam, the internal journey into the romantic self is the route by which she gains access to the "triumphant imagination" beyond the self. "Triumphant imagination," or the goal beyond the self, is signified for her by the desire to write and her eventual ability to actually write. As with the traditional male hero, one of the most compelling aspects of her journey was the telling and writing that it would yield. But, unlike the traditional male hero, for Miriam there can be no final return home, just as in the writing, or telling, of *Pilgrimage*, there can be no formal closure. Rather than returning to one final home with the prize of the story, Miriam circles back continuously in order to return to moments of prayer, which are the moments of being "at home" in the universe.[13]

In framing this internal journey as a pilgrimage, Richardson reveals her more romantic nineteenth-century leanings. It is evident that Richardson was aware of many pilgrimage and travel narratives, and it is likely that her awareness could partly be attributed to the fact that in the

> nineteenth century, though the pilgrimage per se no longer found its way into the substance of literature, the medieval accounts of pilgrimage passed to a different and no less avid readership. They became the objects of an international scholarly craze. . . . The vogue passed at the turn of the century, and they were forgotten.[14]

Richardson began writing *Pilgrimage* at the turn of the century and may have been one of those who was affected by the pilgrimage "craze."[15] Whether she was or not, it is clear that in titling her epic *Pilgrimage* she made use of an amalgam of many early and modern pilgrimage models in order to serve her idea that "the journey is always to where one already is, that the quest is for what is already possessed if not firmly grasped, that the discovery is always a rediscovery and the illumination a repetition."[16]

Since each type of pilgrimage also presents a storytelling structure, Richardson used different elements of different pilgrimages to convey her notion of quest as rediscovery and repetition. Like Chaucer, for example, her pilgrimage is an allegory of allegory, or a writing about writing. In its ironic mode it is also like Chaucer in that it is an allegory and catalogue of character types and their lives. The theme of mystical journey to fulfillment and understanding of self is reinforced throughout the novels with allusions to Dante. As Staley points out,

> In *The Tunnel* . . . there are thirty-three sections just as there are thirty-three cantos in each of the three books of Dante's *Divine Comedy* along with allusions to the "inner circle," "outer circle," and "rim of the world." The Dante parallel reaches its climax in the middle of *Interim* when Miriam attends a Dante lecture and feels the absence of love in her being, in her inability to feel for humanity in universal terms.[17]

In its sensual relation to language, *Pilgrimage* is also closer to Dante than any of the other pilgrimage authors that Richardson mentions. In its spirituality, *Pilgrimage* is closer to that embodied by George Fox's pilgrimage narratives that express the faith that Christ can enter and speak through anyone who is properly receptive—that "God is everywhere." The Quaker practice of testimony and belief in the power of voice and the equality of women in spiritual quest and transmission also resonates with Richardson's other concerns. Echoing a Quaker spirituality, Miriam amplifies the belief, in many moments throughout *Pilgrimage*, that "there is a God or a Christ, there is something always there to answer when you turn away to it from everything" (*Interim*, 358). It makes sense in terms of the strong link between Richardson's aesthetic and spiritual development that the 1914 publication of *The Quakers Past and Present* (London: Constable), one of her two books on the Quakers, coincided so closely with the beginning of her writing of *Pilgrimage* in 1913. Her description of George Fox's method and that of mystics in general in *The Quakers* is also a description of a method and effect she attempted to manifest in her writing.

> The religious genius, as represented preeminently by the great mystics—those in whom the sense of an ultimate and essential goodness, beauty, and truth is the dominant characteristic—have [sic] consciously bent all their energies to breaking through the veil of sense, to making a journey to the heart of reality, to winning the freedom of the very citadel of Life itself. Their method has invariably included what—again borrowing from psychology—we must call the deliberate control of all external stimuli . . . as we have seen with Fox, a setting forth to seek something already found—something whose presence is in some way independent of the normal thinking and acting creature, something which has already proclaimed itself in moments of heightened consciousness—in the case of the religious temperament at "conversion" (35).

Richardson emphasizes here the conscious direction of energy or "deliberate control" necessary to "breaking through the veil of sense" in order to make a journey to "the heart of reality." Using Fox and the methods of the mystics as a guide, she attempts through the "deliberate control" of language and the departure from "the veil of sense" and "normal thinking and acting" to make *Pilgrimage* a conduit for moments of "heightened consciousness." It is her hope that by practicing this method in writing, the presence of "something which has already proclaimed itself" will pervade *Pilgrimage* and the experience of that presence will hold the vital power of "conversion" for readers.

Besides Fox, the other pilgrimage writer who had major impact on Richardson's conception of her work was Bunyan. The ways in which Bunyan served as a model for Richardson's writing is described by Miriam speaking in *Honeycomb* about authors in general.

> You don't have to sympathize with authors; you just get at them, neither happy nor sad; like talking, more than talking. Then that was why the people who wrote moral stories were so awful. They were standing behind the pages preaching at you with smarmy voices. . . . Bunyan? . . . He preached to himself too . . . crying out his sins. . . . He did not get between you and himself and point at a moral. An author must show himself. A moral writer only sees the mote in his brother's eye. And you see him seeing it (*Honeycomb*, 385; Richardson's ellipses).

Thus, although *Pilgrimage* is riddled with social critique and allegory, Richardson does not intend it to be a moral story. If there is any preaching in *Pilgrimage* it is, as Miriam makes clear, like Bunyan's preaching, directed as much at the author as at the reader. As a story about one's own travels, the pilgrimage genre necessarily features, through the autobiography inherent to its form, the relation between the author and his or her soul—or the parallel relation between the author's life "outside" of the writing and the author's life as writing. Thus if, as Miriam says, "An author must show himself," then the pilgrimage genre presents the perfect set of mirrors for such viewing. If the author shows through the choice of metaphors he (sic) uses to describe his travels that the travels have provided a means by which he can see himself seeing himself, then the reader also sees him seeing himself. If not, the author (unlike Bunyan or unlike Richardson's intentions) sees only that which is wrong with others—"only the mote in his brother's eye"—and as readers, "You see him seeing it." Using Bunyan's model and Miriam's voice, Richardson reveals in the above passage that she wishes for the reader to see her seeing herself. She wishes to use the pilgrimage genre as the theater in which to "show" herself as an author in the mirror that is Miriam. In so doing, she wishes the reader to be provided with a model of a mode of travel, a model of writing or of self-reflection which could, in turn, be used as a vehicle for his or her own pilgrimage. As Miriam says in *Honeycomb*,

> Then you read books to find the author! . . . I have just discovered that I don't read books for the story, but as a psychological study of the author . . . . It was rather awful and strange. It meant never being able to agree with people about books, never liking them for the same reasons as other people. . . . It meant things coming to you out of books, people, not the people in the books, but knowing, absolutely everything about the author (384).

In addition to the presence, or imagined presence of the author, the many modes of travel and metaphors of motion in *Pilgrimage* are also always figures of different kinds of spiritual quest. Fleishman notes that in *Pilgrimage*

> particularly in chapter openings [there] are images of journeying. The working girl making her way through the world is represented time and again in biblical figures of exile, Bunyanesque allusions to pilgrimage, and the Dantesque language of a journey through stratified layers of reality. *Honeycomb* had opened with repeated references to Miriam's reaching the end of her journey, on arriving at the Corries' mansion, though this turned out to be little more than a way station. *The Tunnel* covers no spacious ground as Miriam's movements are restricted to the short distance from her Bloomsbury room to her nearby office. In place of outdoor movement, this part begins with Miriam's arrival at her rooming house and adds small gestures of locomotion as it proceeds. Indeed, Miriam takes up cycling to further her progress (for 1896 this is a bold stride) and she is almost killed in an accident. She begins making walks through London that will become progressively larger, both in territory covered and prose devoted to them, in later volumes. And she is able self-consciously to proclaim the style and significance of her movements as "wanderyahre" (*The Tunnel*, 92). It is her equivalent of the male romantic's assertion of freedom: "I am going to lead a man's life, always getting away."[18]

Each mode of travel—the bicycle, the walking, the trains—indicates another turn in the spiritual journey, another vehicle, like those of the "feminine equivalent" in reading or writing, in which to "lead a man's life, always getting away." Since Miriam was a woman leading a man's life and "always getting away," it was necessary for Richardson to alter many elements of the traditional quest or pilgrimage structure and capitalize on others. In addition, pilgrimage narratives were usually by and about men and were usually structured according to a particular religious ideology, and since, as Miriam says, "Religion in the world had nothing but insults for women," it was necessary to parallel the invention of a writing technique that departed from that of her male regiment with a technique of spirituality that in its practice also departed from that presented by "religion in the world" (*The Tunnel*, 222). Thus, in terms of the "recreating" that was Richardson's project, the appropriation of spiritual pilgrimage—that is, of the position of its hero and the territory of its travel—was a particularly powerful move, especially given the heavy weight of Christian patriarchal tradition embedded in the genre.

In her disruption of the traditional male pilgrimage, Richardson's "feminine" quest, like her "feminine sentence," moved inside the consciousness of its hero and inside her room. Often the scene of Miriam's travel is the outlandish solitude of Miriam's room while she is in communion with a book (outlandish for a turn-of-the-century woman to have her own room and to spend many hours alone in it reading). Rather than physically going to exotic, wild, or faraway lands, Miriam engages in an exotic and forbidden activity in the land in which she was born. It is no accident that in *The Tunnel* when Miriam first moves into her own room in a boardinghouse in London, she is reading *The Voyage of the Beagle*. The undisturbed reading of this book in her own room points up Miriam's elation with her own voyage.

> She left her things half unpacked about the floor and settled herself on the bed under the gas jet with *The Voyage of the Beagle.* Unpacking had been a distraction from the glory, very nice, getting things straight. But there was no need to do anything or think about anything . . . ever, here. No interruption, no one watching or speculating or treating one in some particular way that had to be met. . . . Reading would be more of a distraction than unpacking. She read a few lines. They had a fresh attractive meaning. Reading would be real. The dull adventures of the Beagle looked real coming along through reality. She put the book on her knee and once more met the clear brown shock of her room (*The Tunnel*, 17).

Miriam's adventure is to read while alone in her room and to choose to live in a situation in which she was not required to respond to the needs of others or to be interrupted by them, as women at home are usually required to do.[19] This adventure was far more exciting than the "dull adventures of the Beagle." Miriam here occupies the position of the pilgrim on pilgrimage, in the sense that, like the turn-of-the-century middle-class British woman, she is at the same time a member of society and an outsider. This double position not only applied to Miriam but would have particularly applied to women who, like Miriam, were adults but not married, were childless and not desirous of becoming mothers and wives, had left their family homes in order to work and live alone, and were thus not explainable or "good" as women—were perhaps not women. Because they had altered the terms of their physical and social existence, these pilgrim women, or "new women," found reading as well as many other acts to have "a fresh attractive meaning."

Victor Turner uses the term "limnar" to describe the condition of a pilgrim on pilgrimage. "Limnar" also describes the condition of Miriam and other turn-of-the-century women in her position.

> What I call liminality, the state of being in between successive participations in social milieux dominated by social structural considerations, whether formal or unformalized . . . is a sphere or domain of action or thought rather than a social modality. Indeed, liminality may imply solitude rather than society, the voluntary or involuntary withdrawal of an individual from a social-structural matrix. It may imply alienation from rather than more authentic participation in social existence. . . . liminality [can] refer to any condition outside, or on the peripheries of, everyday life . . . [since] there [is] an affinity between the middle in sacred time [the "middle" is the time of pilgrimage or rites of passage] and the outside in sacred space.[20]

As a "limnar," Miriam is neither completely home nor completely away from home, neither completely female nor completely male. As *Pilgrimage* spans the years 1891-1915, Miriam, like other British women contemporary to herself, is a citizen but cannot vote. If she married she would have minimal property rights, would only recently have been granted a separate legal existence from her husband and would not have equal access to divorce. If divorced, she would have no custody rights over her children.[21] Thus, employed and unmarried, Miriam does not fully take part in the current "social-structural matrix." She is indeed "alienated" from the "everyday life" that goes on about her, but at the same time she is vitally occupied by the details of her own daily life. Miriam's position of temporal alienation and her sense of being constantly involved in a pilgrimage to "break through the veil of sense," or a rite of passage that leads beyond sense, allows her to transform and spatialize the mundane into moments of "heightened consciousness." In this vein there is a direct parallel for her between the "middle" sacred time of pilgrimage and the outside or external manifestation of the sacred in space.

Just as the later internalized Protestant pilgrimage provided a vehicle for mental or spiritual travel outside the home, the medieval pilgrimage also provided women with one of the few means of travel outside of the confinement of domestic space. The "wanderyahre" with which Miriam's movements are endowed, her daring to ride a bicycle and to walk through sections of London traditionally forbidden to women, combines the privileges inherent for women in Protestant and medieval pilgrimages and presents the possibility of an altogether different notion of travel and space for a woman. The psychic/spiritual geography which Miriam maps is, like the genre of pilgrimage and the "technique of the feminine equivalent," both traditional and innovative, transformative of both the internal and external, and both romantic and modernist. Like the state of Turner's "limnar" pilgrim, the narrative in *Pilgrimage* often hovers between realism and oneiric utterance, which is also often the case in the language of traditional pilgrimage narratives. This language signals the edge or the borders that the pilgrim occupies.

The second genre that Richardson uses in the generic amalgam that makes up *Pilgrimage* is that of the epic or the "long poem." Situating the epic in its cultural tradition, Friedman states that

> as poems on the greatest historical-metaphysical-religious-aesthetic questions, big-long-important poems have assumed the authority of the dominant cultural discourses—even when they speak from a position of alienation, like Pound in *The Cantos* or Williams in *Paterson*. The generic grid within which these and other big long poems are read has been established pre-eminently by the epic, which has a very big long history of importance in western culture. The epic has been the preeminent poetic genre of the public sphere from which women have been excluded. As a narrative of brave men's deeds, the epic often centers on the "destiny" or "formation of a race or nation." It reflects a comprehensive sweep of history, a cosmic universality of theme, and an elevated discourse of public ceremony . . . . These genre codes for the epic intersect with societal gender codes to identify the epic as a pre-eminently masculine discourse. The "law of genre" prescribed in the practice of the epic is fundamentally phallic. Within the dominant discourses of western culture, women have never been allowed the authority to pronounce on history, philosophy, religion and aesthetics. The epic has consequently been the quintessential male territory whose boundaries enforce women's status as outsiders on the landscape of poetry.[22]

In trespassing the boundaries of the "quintessential male territory" in *Pilgrimage*, Richardson speaks from a "limnal" position of alienation. Her position is similar in some senses to that occupied by Pound and Williams, but she refuses the status that the epic prescribes for her as an "outsider on the landscape of poetry." Instead she uses a poetic prose that at moments dissolves entirely into poetry. *Pilgrimage* is epical because of the enormity of its scope and the breadth of time and issues it encompasses. Realizing that the epic is the genre from which women have been "preeminently excluded," Richardson uses it, just as she uses the pilgrimage genre as a potentially powerful point of intervention into the practices of the ranks of the "male regiment" that preceded her, some of whom (such as Pound and Williams) were her contemporaries. Taking the authority from within a dominant western cultural discourse that has not traditionally allowed women to speak from positions of authority, Richardson pronounces on history, philosophy, religion, and aesthetics, among many other broad subjects. As an epic, *Pilgrimage* is comprehensive, but instead of covering a "sweep" of public history, it refers to many different historical moments and surveys the myriad details of panoramic but private consciousness. Rather than presenting itself in the discourse of "public ceremony," it is an associative collection of the most idiosyncratic "inner speech," snatches of internal conversation, dialogue, and the music of prayer or poetry.

As an intervention, Richardson's use of both the pilgrimage and the epic genres has the effect of dismantling the boundaries of inside/outside that Derrida identifies with the phallogocentrism of "the law of genre." As Friedman states,

> Aware of their absence within the tradition, women poets of the "long poem" often defensively and defiantly assert their presence. They engage in a feminization of the form—refusing the victim status of woman's objectification in men's texts and making themselves agents in the form's evolution, subjects in its creation.[23]

The inside/outside boundaries are dismantled when women position themselves as women writing inside a tradition from which women have been excluded. The doubleness of this position provides a distance that is often manifest as irony, satire, or the exaggeration of an element characteristic to the genre. In Friedman's words, "This means . . . a comedic mockery of what she cannot possess, a carnivalesque disruption of the authority that the form of the poem evokes."[24]

In her 1939 piece on Joyce's *Finnegan's Wake* called "Adventure for Readers," Richardson discusses the "shift," marked in her mind by the writing of Henry James, from romanticism to modernism and the parallel shift manifest by the "last ditch effort of the epic" in the development of the modern novel.

> How, or just why, or exactly when the shift occurred from concentration upon various aspects of the sublime and beautiful to what may be called the immediate investigation of reality, it is not easy to say, though a poet-novelist, Richard Church, in his recent address to the Royal Society of Literature, made, one feels, some excellent guesses as to the practical reasons for the changeover. Whereunto may be added the widespread application, for some time past, of Pope's injunction as to the proper study of mankind.
>
> Whatever the combination of incitements, certain of our poets have now, for decades past, produced short stories rather than lyrics and, in place of the epic and foreshadowed by *The Ring and the Book*, so very nearly a prose epic, have given us, if we exclude *The Testament of Beauty*, rearing a nobly defiant head in the last ditch of the epic form, the modern novel.

Explaining the way in which the poetry of epic has woven itself into the modern novel, Richardson goes on to state that the reader of the modern novel

> finds himself within a medium whose close texture, like that of poetry, is everywhere significant and although, when the tapestry hangs complete before his eyes, each portion is seen to enhance the rest and the shape and the intention of the whole grows clear, any single strip may be divorced from its fellows without losing everything of its power and of its meaning. ("Adventure for Readers," *Life and Letters To-Day*, no. 22, July, 1939, 2)

This description is consistent with the traditional structures of the pilgrimage and epic genres, which focus on the spiritual development of the self allegorized through the symbolic significance of daily mundane details and events in the author's life, any one of which, if "divorced from its fellows," would not lose "its power and its meaning." In emphasizing and exaggerating these elements of the pilgrimage and the epic, and in using the outline of her own life to structure Miriam's, Richardson also writes in the genre of autobiography, specifically that of spiritual autobiography. It is not surprising in this respect that Bunyan and Fox provided the primary models for the

English autobiographical tradition.[25] As Fleishman says of *Pilgrimage*'s relation to those autobiographies that preceded it,

> as exceptional as *Pilgrimage* is among novels, it is firmly in place in the autobiographical tradition and forges stronger ties with its predecessors than any other modern self-writing. Indeed, from its title to its frequent references to spiritual autobiographers like Bunyan and Fox, the work declares its preoccupation with the religious searchings and moments of vision that have animated Western autobiography and that continue to do so even when the writer is unorthodox in her creed, staunchly combative in her version of feminism, and iconoclastically individualist, if not bohemian, as an artist.[26]

Richardson structures *Pilgrimage* with the repeated appearance of the traditional figures of autobiography. These figures include Edenic childhood and its loss, aimless wandering and hellish torment, vision and conversion, and return to origins.[27] In addition to her deep affinity for these figures of autobiography, the genre of autobiography itself served to raise questions that she wished to feature. Through these tensions inherent to autobiographical writing, which are the desire to both chronicle "actual" events and to make those events into "art," the autobiographical genre raises questions regarding what is appropriate to expect from any form of writing.

> Since the concept of genre designates an aesthetic as well as a historical function, what is at stake is not only the distance that shelters the author of autobiography from his experience but the possible convergence of aesthetics and history. . . . Empirically as well as theoretically, autobiography lends itself poorly to generic definition; each specific instance seems to be an exception to the norm; the works themselves always seem to shade off into neighboring or even incompatible genres and, perhaps most revealing of all, generic discussions, which can have such powerful heuristic value in the case of tragedy or the novel, remain distressingly sterile when autobiography is at stake.[28]

It is precisely because "autobiography lends itself poorly to generic definition" that Richardson chose to use it. As part of her project of inventing, on the genre level, a "feminine equivalent to the current masculine realism," Richardson uses a genre in which to write that intervenes in the male tradition by throwing into confusion the whole question of what counts as a genre. Thus, in relation to *Pilgrimage*, a "heuristic" discussion about genre is frustrated, and this is exactly the kind of discussion that Richardson would wish to frustrate. It is exactly the kind of discussion among "literary" men that she documents in order to mock and satirize repeatedly in *Pilgrimage*.

The blur between the impulse to document and the impulse to create "art" that is inherent to autobiography also points to another hazy area that autobiography, and especially *Pilgrimage*, features. This is the area in which representation itself becomes the subject of an autobiographical work in the sense that it may appear that a life is producing an autobiography, but it may be equally true that the writing of an autobiography is producing a life. Fleishman states that one of the functions of self-writing is to keep oneself alive. Other functions of self-writing are to remain alive, at many different times at once, to remind oneself that one is alive and to continue to remain alive after death. Autobiography, then, raises the same questions about the relation between the original and the copy, the author and the fiction, that film and other forms of mechanical reproduction raise. In this vein, de Man states,

> Are we so certain that autobiography depends on reference, as a photograph depends on its subject or a (realistic) picture on its model? We assume that life produces the autobiography as an act produces its consequences, but can we not suggest, with equal justice, that the autobiographical project may itself produce and determine the life and that whatever the writer does is in fact governed by the technical demands of self-portraiture and thus determined in all its aspects, by the resources of his medium? . . . does the referent determine the figure, or is it the other way round: is the illusion of reference not a correlation of the structure of the figure, that is to say no longer clearly and simply a referent at all but something more akin to a fiction which then, however, in its own turn, acquires a degree of referential productivity?[29]

In the realm of *Pilgrimage* we cannot be "so certain" that the autobiography depends on reference to the life of a realistic subject. True to its circular structure and its belief in eternal circular process, the autobiographical project of *Pilgrimage* itself produces and determines the life of the writer. The subject of Richardson's writing is Miriam's development into a writer, and as Richardson writes she invents and becomes Miriam, a writing writer. In this sense the autobiographical form serves Richardson well as it reveals her identity as mirror-I-am: Miriam, both revealed and concealed in writing. These writing and written lives are referred to simultaneously as an illusion or a fiction and as actual "real" lives. In this sense, *Pilgrimage* produces a reading of myriad and ambiguous reference. This is an effect of Richardson's "feminine equivalent," and it is consistent with the effects of autobiography in the sense that autobiography is not a genre or a mode, but a figure of reading or understanding that occurs, to some degree in all texts—a figure in this case that signals multiple referentiality.[30] To a very high degree, then, Richardson wishes to emphasize autobiography as a figure of reading and to use it as a means of mocking the legitimacy of the other genres she employs. Pilgrimages and epics, for example, contain closure, but, as de Man says, "The interest of autobiography . . . is not that it reveals reliable self knowledge," as the pilgrimage and the epic are meant to do—it does not—"but that it demonstrates in a striking way the impossibility of closure and of totalization of all textual systems made up of tropological substitution."[31] As a vast fabric of turns and substitutions that do not resolve into an ending or into a closed system, *Pilgrimage* as autobiography, as a journey without end, mocks the pilgrimage and parodies the epic in its revelation of many selves rather than self-knowledge.

Bruss provides a list of "common tendencies" characteristic of autobiography which is striking in that it can also be read as a catalogue of the ways in which Richardson's aesthetics formally embody her spirituality. This list is not only a meticulous catalogue of Richardson's spiritual practices but also a precise description of an aesthetics operative in many other modernist texts. These "common tendencies" of autobiography include:

> a leaning toward discontinuous structures . . . with disrupted narrative sequences and competing foci of attention. The "story" the autobiography tells is never seamless, and is often not a story at all but a string of meditations and vignettes—fractional events that may be painful or joyous in their partial disinterment, irrepressible or simply casual in their transient spontaneity. Never, except in cases of deliberate iconoclasm . . . can one speak of an autonomous and self-sustaining textual pattern. The order, the meaning or rhythm of the composition, becomes clear only when we look for the person and the personality which holds it all together, whether by means of publicly ascertainable religious convictions or by a private, implicit set of values and associations. This is not a failed coherence but a different kind of coherence. . . . there must always be something which is just outside the autobiographer's immediate field of vision, something he can reach only by turning his text back upon itself to examine the vantage point rather than the view. Thus an autobiography typically calls attention to its own devices,

> to the progress it is making in unfolding its tale, to its successes and even more often its failures to capture and communicate its subject.[32]

This list could be read as a set of poetics as well as an allegory of how to view one's life. Though there is nothing mentioned on the list that Richardson does not do in *Pilgrimage*, one of the "tendencies" that she most vehemently practices is that of "calling attention to [the writing's] own devices, especially its failure to capture and communicate its subject." In a characteristic statement that illustrates the kind of "calling attention" that recurs throughout *Pilgrimage*, in *Interim* Miriam laments the impossibility of words to communicate. In doing so she points to the failure of Richardson's writing and her own speaking, a failure made bearable by the process of traveling to something that is present in language but, like Eisenstein's inner speech, does not serve the function of communicating information. Miriam states that "the pain of the failure of words so set out, was made bearable by the wonder of the journey from speech to speech" (*Interim*, 344).

It would be possible to cite many examples from *Pilgrimage* for each "common tendency" on Bruss' list, but from the entire list the tendency that perhaps most sums up Richardson's project is the notion of the autobiography as embodying "not a failed coherence but a different coherence." This notion echoes Heath's "readability and unreadability" discussed in Part I. As Heath states, that which is unreadable no longer duplicates or reproduces the dominant cultural ideology in its use of the culture's conventions of genre, coherence, grammar, and syntax. Many modernist texts, including *Pilgrimage*, are in this sense "unreadable" and waver at what Heath calls "the horizon of sense." Rather than making no sense at all, they make a different kind of sense or possess a "different coherence" which cannot be detected through traditional habits of reading. Wavering on "the horizon of sense," the "unreadable" text comes potentially close to crossing the horizon and falling instead into the land of incoherence or "failed coherence." Wavering on this horizon Richardson signals traditional generic expectations while she disrupts those expectations through her particular use of, or exaggeration of, all the "tendencies" common to the autobiography, the pilgrimage, and the epic. As Miriam is on a journey toward writing, *Pilgrimage* also gestures at the tradition of the kunstlerroman. This tradition is often characterized by an internal split in an artist-hero manifest as a choice that must be made between life and art. The aim of the classic journey of this artist-hero (rarely female) is to reconcile this split. Describing the traditional narrative poles of this split, Beebe states,

> If we grant the divided nature of the artist, we can readily see why he is pulled in contrary directions. The man seeks personal fulfillment in experience, while the artist-self desires freedom from the demands of life. One result is that conflicting traditions of art have existed side by side for more than a century. What I call the Sacred Fount tradition tends to equate art with experience and assumes that the true artist is one who lives not less, but more fully and intensely than others. Within this tradition art is essentially the re-creation of experience. The Ivory Tower tradition, on the other hand, exalts art above life and insists that the artist can make use of life only if he stands aloof. "The artist, like the God of the creation, remains within or behind or beyond or above his handiwork, invisible, refined out of existence, indifferent, paring his fingernails." Crucial in this statement by Joyce is the comparison of the artist with God, for the Ivory Tower tradition equates art with religion rather than experience. The frequency with which the authors of artist novels describe the creation of art as "divine," the sanctuary of the artist as "holy," or the nature of the artist as "godlike" or "priestly" is a heritage from the classic analogy of creator with Creator.[33]

Indeed Miriam does exhibit some of the above traits. She seeks personal fulfillment through experience—particularly her exploration of London—while she is also compelled by the idea of being free from practical demands and remaining at the Quaker fruit farm of Windmill Hill. Richardson and Miriam remain, if not invisible, as Joyce would have it, illusive in their seeming presence. Perhaps the most striking element of this tradition that Miriam displays is that of viewing her art as a religious act and the scene of its performance as divine and separate from others. However, Richardson and Joyce part ways at his view of the God function of the author. As an authorial position more easily accessible to a male than a female writer, this is a stance Richardson deliberately wished to forgo. Although Miriam's character partakes of elements from both sides of this useful but perhaps overly schematic tower/fount divide, the position and the conditions and options for the female artist-hero are highly complex. Her choice is not between what Beebe calls "the man" and the "artist-self" but between the woman and an "artist-self" for which there is little or no traditional model or acceptable social position. Women are traditionally heroic in what Richardson calls their "being" rather than their "becoming." Using similar terms Stewart describes the implications of Beebes's schema for women.

> If this tower/fount polarity is repeatedly depicted in terms of doing and being, then Faust's divisiveness between his earthy and his spir-

itual nature becomes a dual dilemma for the female artist as heroine. For the female novelist, Beebe's label of Ivory Tower and Sacred Fount have a different meaning. Women placed on ivory pedestals traditionally are consciences of society, decorative ornaments, or angelic agents to a heavenly realm. Women playing the role of fountains traditionally become Dianas of Ephesus, sources of an erotic, earthy, or hellish life. . . . Sometimes women play both roles.

> She must choose: She may consciously or unconsciously reject this tradition of polarity or of the female form as synthesizing agent. She may write didactic fiction which critics will debase as art. She may create a hero or adopt a masculine identity and remain within the tradition. She may create fictions which transmute the old or construct new myths . . . which prove unacceptable to readers dependent on the traditional. She may seek to erase all sexuality and establish an androgynous or asexual protagonist. When as a female she creates an artist as heroine, she is denied these convenient escapes. Her heroine may therefore remain disintegrated, estranged, or unsuccessful—a failure as a woman or as an artist.[34]

In looking specifically at the case of Richardson and Miriam and their modes of working out these polarities, Stewart states,

> Ruling out the possibilities of role-playing as pianist, certified teacher, governess, painter, dental secretary, Lycurgan, Jew's wife, doctor's wife, feminist, hostess, international socialite, free-liver, ex-seminarian's wife, Quaker, and Quaker's wife, Miriam eventually settles into her role as a writer. She must express the revolving polarity of such abstract concepts as masculine and feminine, solitude and companionship, Toryism and socialism, language and silence, subjectivity and objectivity, marriage and freedom, ecstasy and peace, free will and determinism, as well as the metaphoric entities of walled gardens and open spaces, or light and darkness. Rather than resolve these polarities, Richardson revolves them, keeping them in suspension to emphasize life's fullness rather than its directness.[35]

In this useful summary of Miriam and Richardson's dealings with the traditions of the kunstlerroman Stewart invokes the title of the seventh *Pilgrimage* novel-chapter, *Revolving Lights*. Whether or not this is a deliberate echo on Stewart's part, it serves to link her analysis to Richardson's project of disrupting rather than reinscribing any generic tradition from which she might of choice or necessity partake.

The uniqueness of this generic amalgam keeps a reader of *Pilgrimage* from sinking comfortably back into any set of expectations. It forces the reader to be actively on a "quest" rather than to rely on "habit," since without "sustained concentration" and interaction, *Pilgrimage* is unreadable—which indeed it has been for many readers. On the level of genre, then, this pilgrimage-epic-autobiographical amalgam alters the experience of reading and thereby performs one of the same functions as the "feminine equivalent."

Consistent with Richardson's desire to both signal and disrupt generic reading expectations and habits, and to make the text of *Pilgrimage* constantly turn back on itself in order to examine itself from another vantage point, Miriam makes ironic statements throughout the novel-chapters such as the following about the genre of *Pilgrimage* itself, or the value of literary discussions in general.

> What are books? What is the novel? I don't care for novels. . . . I can't see what they are about. They seem to be an endless fuss about nothing (*Deadlock*, 45).

And:

> It seemed always useless and dangerous to talk about books. They were always about something else. . . .Why must a book be a masterly study of some one single thing? (*Deadlock*, 61).

Instead of "useless and dangerous" talk about books, Miriam inhabits the realm of myriad forms and figures. As Rose describes, Miriam

> . . . becomes a complex unity of observer, mediator, interpreter, creator, contemplator of her own creation, new interpreter and so forth, in the perpetual condition of reexperience. . . . The link is established between the inner reality of self and the outer reality of the actual world, for in affirming the reality of subjective experience, the phenomenal world which initiates the subjective response also becomes real. . . . The important quest for the link between the subjective and objective reality made apprehensible through a literary work introduces the pilgrimage metaphor.[36]

Consistent with the nature of Miriam's journey as subjective and objective metaphoric pilgrimage toward the powerful silence on the other side of words, "books were always about something else," something else for which words and their subjects were a conduit, since words themselves were "an endless fuss about nothing." Indeed, within her method of operating, books could only always be "about something else" because they could only be viewed as vehicles to unknown destinations, pilgrimages to the state of "wanderyahre." As Miriam says in reference to tangents and proper subjects,

> their adventure took them away from their subject into what "clever" people would call "side issues." "Nothing is a side issue," she told herself passionately with her eyes on the green glare beyond the window (*Backwater*, 249).

Miriam in her daily life, and Richardson in her writing practice, looked through the windows or framing devices used by "clever people," to the view beyond the requirements of framing devices. Passionately committed to wandering in the territory of the tangential with her staunch belief that "nothing is a side issue" and her eyes always on the "green glare beyond the window," Richardson refused to stick to a single genre, subject or mode of behavior. Instead she remained, as she reveals in the following paradigmatic passage, "watchful and silent," inhabiting the "shifting . . . moving . . . strolling" of the "little drama," the "pilgrimage" of forms and movements that embodied the "ceremony of the game."

> All the other forms were standing or moving in the gloom; standing watchful and silent, the gleaming ends of their cues held in rest, shifting and moving and strolling with uncolliding ordered movements and little murmurs of commentary after the little drama—the sudden snap of the stroke breaking the stillness, the faint thundering roll of the single ball, the click of the concussion, the gentle angular explosion of pieces into a new relation and the breaking of the varying triangle as a ball rolled to its hidden destination, held by all the eyes in the room until its rumbling pilgrimage ended out of sight in a soft thud. It was pure joy to Miriam to wander around the table after her ball, sheltered in the gloom, through an endless "grand chain" of undifferentiated figures that passed and repassed without awkwardness or the need for forced exchange; held together and separated by the ceremony of the game (*Honeycomb*, 435).

She refers in this passage to the game of life or the life of the book. In framing the game of pool, a man's game, as a "wandering around the table after her ball" on a "rumbling pilgrimage," Richardson again takes a man's form, a male game, and plays it in a "feminine" way. In using the allegory of a pool game she signals all of the figures in *Pilgrimage* that have come to hold an allegorical and symbolically laden value. The "passing and repassing" of "figures and forms" immediately transforms the game of pool into a repeating spectacle of writing. The "rumbling pilgrimage" of the pool ball makes the act of observing the spectacle of writing into an internal and spiritual travel—a "wandering around the table after her ball" or a "wanderyahre" after tangential "side issues." This "passing and repassing," wandering as writing, gave Miriam and Richardson "pure joy." These implied relations between the "ordered movements" of the game and the "ceremony" of writing capture the aesthetic/spiritual collapse that is one of the primary "subjects" of *Pilgrimage*.

Finally, Richardson quite deliberately and ironically calls the thirteen volumes of *Pilgrimage* "novel-chapters." In naming them novel-chapters, she signals a genre that marks generic collapse. In this sense the novel is the perfect umbrella to shelter the pilgrimage-epic-autobiographical hybrid, since as the most elastic of genres it contains generic and other impurities and monstrosities that are consistent with the intentions of feminine prose. As Miriam says, "What is the novel? I don't care for novels."

Linguistic Shrine Sites and Corporate Silence

> Even the business people who went about intent, going to definite places, were in the secret of London and looked free. The expression of the collar and hair of many of them said they had homes. But they got away from them. No one who had never been alone in London was quite alive. . . . I'm free—I've got free—nothing can ever alter that, she thought, gazing wide-eyed into the fire, between fear and joy. The strange familiar pang gave the place a sort of consecration (*The Tunnel*, 77).

> This year, with dinner in the cool dining-room and the balcony for the evening, the summer would not be so unbearable. She sat still, lifted out into garden freshness. . . . Benediction (*Interim*, 404).

> To go forward now, from this moment, alive, keeping alive, through the London summer. Even to go away for holidays would be to break up the wonder, to snap the secret clue and break the secret life (*Interim*, 405).

As evidenced in the above quotes, Miriam's experiences of merging with the sensual details of a place, time, and state of mind gave an otherwise mundane place "a sort of consecration" and could serve to transform a passing moment into "Benediction" or reveal the "secret clue" and "secret life" lodged in "the London summer." Through the use of signal words such as "consecration," "benediction," or "secret" and other elements of what Miriam calls the language of "praise and prayer," Richardson repeatedly sanctifies and amplifies the secular of daily life in *Pilgrimage*. In using the language of praise and prayer to ignite the mundane, Richardson highlights the links between writing, speech, silence, the miraculous, and the sacred. Through Miriam's perceptions, Richardson shows a spiritual practice that pivots around a constant careful observance and fierce awe of the daily detail surrounding her, from a slant of light to a chipped teacup.[37]

In the "Continuous Performance" columns Richardson speaks of the "miracle" of "confrontation" between an audience and an art form, a reader and a book, an audience and a film or play. She refers to the film's "miracle of compelling the creative consciousness of the audience." It is the same "creative consciousness" of the reader and the same kind of miracle that she wishes to compel through the benediction in those of Miriam's experiences quoted above. These "miracles" capture secret or inarticulable truths and what Miriam calls a daily "sense of astonishment." The miracles are characterized by the heightened experiences of merging, "collaboration" or confrontation during which Miriam's physical, linguistic, and sensual boundaries either dissolve or are intensely and distinctly defined. In all "astonishing" or miraculous, and therefore sacred, moments, Miriam is carried to the edge of language where it is possible to glimpse what she calls "nothing" or the silence beyond words. In another form, the edge of language, or "nothing," is characterized through voice that turns to music or through narrative that turns to oneiric utterance—noises on the border of linguistic meaning. Addressing this miraculous nothing beyond "the meaning of things," Miriam states in *Interim*,

> There was no thought in the silence, no past or future, nothing but the strange thing for which there were no words, something that was always there as if by appointment, waiting for one to get through to it away from everything in life. It was the thing that was nothing. Yet it seemed the only thing that came near and meant anything at all. It was happiness and realization. It was being suspended, in nothing. It came out of oneself because it came only

> when one had been a long time alone. It was not oneself. It could not be God. It did not mind what you were or what you had done. It would be there if you had just murdered someone (*Interim*, 322).

It is "this strange thing for which there were no words," this thing without past or future, outside of time, that Miriam seeks on her quest because it gives meaning to "anything at all." As an internalized Quaker-like peregrination toward an internal shrine, Miriam's pilgrimage in an avalanche of words is a journey toward "the thing for which there were no words," a journey toward "meaning" or what the Quakers call "the beyond that is within."[38] This "beyond" is characterized by the Quakers as "corporate silence out of which a message comes."[39] The striking resonance between Richardson's "spiritual exercise" and Quaker language and imagery can be seen in the following passage in which the ecstatic "miracle" of being alive yields "happiness and realization," while also opening onto "perfectly still," death-like silence or "nothing."

> If one were perfectly still the sense of God was there. Things were astounding enough; enough to make you die of astonishment, if you did nothing at all. Being alive. If one could realize that clearly enough, one would die. Everything one did was just a distraction from astonishment (*Honeycomb*, 458).

In order to commune with the "astounding" "corporate silence," the Quakers believe that it is necessary to empty oneself and become like "a hollow tube."[40] One's body can then become the conduit for the "message." Richardson uses this same technique in the writing of feminine prose. This notion of the body as source of message begins to address how and why the spiritual is so closely allied to the aesthetic, and particularly to writing, for Richardson. Like the medieval Catholic pilgrim, Miriam bestows the status of relic on both the book and the word, revering books and language as charms or amulets in the same way that a pilgrim might have treated the fingernail clippings of a saint. In the context of this belief in language as animate, certain kinds of words become sacred because, like relics, they are remnants of, or "messages" from, an original holy body. These messages of silence therefore invoke the finalities of death and the possibility of birth: "Being alive. If one could realize that clearly enough, one would die." Like the large niches in medieval shrines in which pilgrims curled up in fetal position while praying for cures, the shrine of the "beyond that is within" is both a womb and a tomb. The "corporate silence" that the Quakers seek is precisely what the medieval shrine contained. Like many other shrines throughout the world at various times, the medieval shrine was a tomb in which the corporate but inanimate, usually in the form of the dead body or skeletal remains of a saint, emanated the power to transform or to heal; that is to say, out of the "corporate silence" of the dead body or skeleton a "message" was delivered.

Just as pilgrims travel toward a shrine that contains the silence of death from which emanates a mysterious vitality, so does Miriam travel toward such a shrine. The medieval pilgrim's life is revitalized through proximity to death, and both the Catholic and Protestant pilgrim's travel, or spiritual journey, is shaped by the powerful absence located at its center. This absence is represented by a body in an actual shrine or the "corporate silence" at the center of being. In this vein, written words are like the dead body of a saint in that they are traces or "message" relics of the living that, in their inanimate vitality, occupy a border between life and death.

The relationship between writing and healing, or writing and birth and death, has a long tradition. Charms that were condemned by the church of the Middle Ages as a form of magic (as opposed to a form of religion) were often written down and then placed on a patient's body. Sometimes miracles were written on parchment and bound to an ailing person. In the early twentieth century in parts of France, it was believed that toothache could be relieved by touching the sore gum with a piece of paper on which a prayer was written. The fourth book of the *Iliad* used to be placed under the pillow to cure ague, but in twelfth-century England the Gospel of John or a relic was used. A third-century Roman doctor recommended writing "abracadabra" repeatedly on a piece of parchment, which was then folded up and carried around in the pocket of a good Christian.[41] The interchangeability between the Gospel of John and a relic is striking and speaks to the way in which writing was endowed with the power to perform miracles. Interestingly, the reasons that the book could also serve as a relic is that both the relic and the written word are kinds of representations substituting for an original body and voice.

The power of writing in Christian tradition has been dependent on the notion that there is an original body. The word is potent due to its literal association by displacement to the body of Christ. Within this Christian framework written words always refer to the written revelations of the New Testament. The most holy act in relation to writing viewed in this way is to transcend beyond or through the words to the original body. In the context of

Jewish tradition there is no original body to return to. Thus in the realm of Old Testament exegesis, the text, the letters and words themselves on the pages, invoke endless return for further interpretation. Within this context it is the acute attention brought to the text—the act of interpretation itself—which is the divine act that animates and gives potence to the words. Thus in a Jewish framework the text itself is an original always-changing body rather than a window through which to view another body or presence far more divine.

Given Miriam's deep ambivalence about Christ, her alliance with the Quakers and her (also ambivalent) fascination with Jews throughout *Pilgrimage*, it is not surprising that both aspects of these traditions operate in her relation to language. But Miriam and Richardson's overriding sense of "metaphorocrasy" as the most potent and desirable state to which to aspire, is closer to what can be conceived of as an Old Testament relation to the word. Richardson's metaphorocrasy—"giving up thinking in words"—is a giving up of thinking in univocal reference, in terms of one original. It is a desire to inhabit multi-referentiality so fully that words disappear into their own body—the shape of writing on a page, the music of their sound. Although in the context of *Pilgrimage* reference is made to a corporate body outside the text, unlike the body of Christ this is an unstable body. Inasmuch as it is an original body, it is at times a Christ-like figure, yet more often reference is to the body of Miriam's mother or a symbolic mother (also potentially linked to the early iconography of Christ). As will be evident in the shrine-site passages, sometimes the body of the reader is signalled by being included in the sensation of Miriam's transport; at other times the body of a writer is called up—possibly the autobiographical writer of the text we read, but not necessarily—and sometimes a nameless, absent other is signalled.[42]

To touch a sore gum with a piece of paper on which a prayer was written is not far from Miriam's feeling that a book was "a dance by the author, a song, a prayer, an important sermon, *a message*" (my italics). It is also not far from the belief that "books were not stories printed on paper, they were people; the "real people" to the belief that as a "real" person a book holds life, just as the dead body of a saint emanates transformative powers. A book, like the dead body or skeletal remains of a saint, does not move or speak, though through its author it has spoken before and having spoken, therefore retains the promise or possibility of future speech. Like the "real" corpse of a saint, a "real" book or writing radiates the power to make people retell the stories of their lives in an altered form, thus changing their spiritual condition and their relation to their own mortality.[43]

Believing that women had more access to the silence beyond words and thus to the healing power embedded in written words because of their link to "the being at the heart of all becoming," Richardson proposed the "feminine equivalent" as "spiritual exercise," not simply modernist experiment. Herself a "woman in a book," Miriam displaces the reader by talking about the affinity she has for (other) "women in books" who share an understanding of and access to a "sacred beauty" beyond words.

> She understood what women in books meant by sacred: "It is all too sacred for words." There was no choice in all that; only secret and sacred beauty; unity with all women who had felt in the same way; the freedom of following certainties (*Interim*, 392).

As a follower of the certainty that there was "secret and sacred beauty" beyond words and a sense of "unity" with "all women who had felt in the same way," Miriam may have been named for, among other things, the Marian shrines of the Virgin and her Son, which sprung up throughout Europe in the late fourteenth to mid-fifteenth centuries.[44] As shrines of the Mother, this naming would be consistent with the beauty of the "sacred silence" and the dead body (always so closely linked in Richardson's aesthetics) which is located at the center of *Pilgrimage*. The silent body at the center is the suicidal body of Miriam's mother. This body and this suicide, as well as the actual suicide of Richardson's mother, for which she always felt responsible, structure much of Miriam's travel. It is toward this body that Miriam travels and from it that she flees. Thus to travel toward the shrine of Marian, the universal Virgin Mother, or to travel toward her personal mother, is also for Miriam to travel toward herself.

Richardson always wrote in the vicinity of her mother's death, as if hovering around a shrine. The death itself is never directly mentioned, though through writing Richardson is able to approach it without entirely merging with the death and dying herself. She thereby fills the "corporate silence" with the "miracle" of "messages" from the womb/tomb of the death she only barely missed preventing. Richardson's "spiritual exercise" and Miriam's journey toward writing represent an approach and avoidance of the dead mother. Because, as Miriam says, "Coming events cast light," writing is always simultaneously a seeing into the future and "a walking backwards to something you know is there," though that "something" may have previously been missed. As Miriam suggests, to be awake in dream time is to be, as the audience is in cinematic time, in the past, present, and the future simultaneously. Travel toward the mother also occurs in this kind of collapsed time in which one writes in a "real dream" while one is simultaneously awake in "the real part of [one's] life." The "feminine equivalent" is, in this sense, a vehicle not only for writing outside of the constraints of linear time but also a vehicle for unconscious travel.

> that idea of visiting places in dreams. It was something more than that . . . all the real part of your life has a real dream in it; some of the real dream part of you coming true. You know in advance when you are really following your life. These things are familiar because reality is here. Coming events cast light. It is like dropping everything and walking backwards to something you know is there (*The Tunnel*, 13).

The places in *Pilgrimage* where the written message becomes dream, music, or prayer epitomize that wavering border between sense and nonsense, speech and silence, the corporate silence of death, and the incorporate speech of life. These moments are, as previously stated, most exemplified on the page by narrative disruptions achieved through a deep engagement with the "contemplative state" of feminine prose. The words break up and break down or dissolve into music: the blank spaces on the page in between type give way to that which is "all too sacred for words," the "nothing" that provides "meaning" even if "you have just murdered someone" or, even if someone has just murdered themselves and you feel responsible. Thus, the nerves of Richardson's spiritual practice can be seen where the writing wavers between words and hieroglyphic marks on the page, embodying her "habit of ignoring, while writing, the lesser of the stereotyped system of signs" and her "Small unconscious departure from current usage." In the following shrine-site passages these "spiritual exercises" of "feminine prose" will be illustrated.[45]

The Spiritual Metronome that Operates on Sentences

> Some kind of calculation is at work, a sort of spiritual metronome, imperceptible save when something goes wrong. It operates, too, upon sentences (*Clear Horizon*, 352).

As a self-proclaimed "wandering of meaning," or, as Miriam calls it, "wanderyahre," Richardson's feminine prose presents a theory of reading similar to that which Susan Handelman describes in the Methodological Preface to her book *The Slayers of Moses*.

> In the broadest sense. . . [it] is a kind of midrash, a search for hidden elements and correspondences, a tropism or "wandering of meaning," which proceeds as much by analogy and association as by linear logic.[46]

Thus to overlay a single theoretical framework or method on the reading of *Pilgrimage*, or any of Richardson's other writing, would be to ignore the theories of reading that are developed and proposed in the work itself. As Handelman goes on to say,

> Freud himself recognized that what distinguished his method of dream interpretation from all others was that he treated the dream as "holy writ," and assumed meaning to lie hidden in the most trivial and inconsequential details. Freud . . . showed us that in a sense, every text is holy writ—has multiple meanings, none of which are arbitrary.[47]

Emanating multiple meanings and written from locations or states of consciousness to which Richardson refers as "sacred," *Pilgrimage* is also a kind of "holy writ" filled with what might easily be (and actually has been) mistaken for "trivial and inconsequential details." Its writing involves and its reading invokes a dreamlike state of consciousness in which, as in Freud's method, "the most trivial and inconsequential details" are the most important. As Richardson states in a set of unpublished notes from January 1908 that eventually served as a basis for the Foreword, she had a

> growing conviction that the extraneous matter was more essential than the interesting deliberately composed narrative, incidents and figures

and she was

> perpetually haunted by the mutability of ideas. Giving no satisfaction to a growing desire to express the immutable. ("Literary Essays," title handwritten at the top of the first page, unpublished papers, Yale University: The Bienecke Rare Book and Manuscript Library, 1908, 1-2).

Haunted by the "mutability of ideas" and attempting "to express the immutable," Richardson's writing practice increasingly became submerged in a dreamlike state that allowed her to be a conduit for the "holy writ" that arrived from the unconscious or from the closely allied silence of death. In a description of this contrapuntal dialogue between her own consciousness and the material that arrived from the other side and became writing, she says,

> Assume life. Describe humanity in terms of humanity, therefore not at all. The essential is the dialogue or conflict between the individual &— ("Literary Essays," 2).

This "essential dialogue" between the individual and a dash that stands in for something unnameable required a relinquishing of thought. In the spirit of "wanderyahre" and of Handelman's "wandering of meaning," Richardson's method of writing allowed her to do what Miriam does: " '*Pass into nothingness, but always keep*'—evade thought" (*March Moonlight*, 619).

Richardson believed, as did Freud, that thought was a manifestation of a deeper structure of individual beliefs and consciousness. Thinking about thought, as Richardson demonstrates through Miriam, becomes immediately and necessarily thinking about language—which quickly presents the complex predicament that thinking about language is also thinking in language. In an attempt to both investigate and short-circuit the predicament, in an attempt to occupy the source of thought by evading thought itself, Miriam says, "I must remember to tell Jean about thought. About the way its nature depends upon the source of one's metaphors. We all live under a Metaphorocrasy. Tell her I'm giving up thinking in words" (*March Moonlight*, 607).

As is evident in the following first example of a shrine-site passage, to think about the source of one's metaphors, and to practice metaphorocrasy by giving up thinking in words, are means of access into this room of *Pilgrimage*. Elaborating on the workings of metaphorocrasy Miriam says, "...thought is cessation, cutting one off from the central essence, bearing an element of calculation. 'Ye must become as little children.' Meaning, as those who do not calculate" (*March Moonlight*, 607). In the realm of metaphorocrasy the notion of origin disappears and endless comparison and substitution reign. Only motion is left in perpetual deference to more motion, as one thing, one thought, replaces another without a calculated trajectory. As elsewhere in *Pilgrimage*, motion in this passage is figured as an actual journey, as a self-conjugation and as a grammatical aliasing mirrored by the motion of an actual train.

Resembling the profile of the other novel-chapters, all of *Pointed Roofs*, the first novel-chapter of *Pilgrimage*, is punctuated by many ellipses and various-sized blank spaces that appear between paragraphs. One of the paragraphs most densely sprinkled with ellipses in all of *Pilgrimage* is located in Chapter II of *Pointed Roofs*. In this chapter Miriam and her father are in the midst of a journey from London to Hanover, Germany. The chapter begins with the completion of their "crossing" as they are "arriving" on land. Miriam's father has had financial troubles, and in order to alleviate the strain on her family and urged by the desire to become financially independent and to have an adventure, Miriam goes to an "agency" in London. She secures a job as a teacher-governess in Hanover. At the turn of the century this was a dramatically independent move for a girl of seventeen or eighteen years. In addition, the position, as well as the need to secure it, was also dramatically outside of the middle-class expectations of Miriam's background. After hesitantly consenting to Miriam's plan, her father escorts her to Hanover. The following densely elliptical paragraph occurs in the midst of this journey when "late at night, seated next to her sleeping companion, rushing towards the German city, she began to think." Directly after this statement is a blank space on the page the width of approximately four printed lines. In this space both the invisible time "late at night" and the invisible space of "rushing" merge. Following the blank space the thoughts that Miriam "began to think" arrive.

> It was a fool's errand. . . . To undertake to go to the German school and teach . . . to be going there . . . with nothing to give. The moment would come when there would be a class sitting round a table waiting for her to speak. She imagined one of the rooms at the old school, full of scornful girls. . . . How was English taught? How did you begin? English grammar . . . in German? Her heart beat in her throat. She had never thought of that . . . the rules of English grammar? Parsing and analysis. . . . Anglo-Saxon prefixes and suffixes . . . gerundial infinitive. . . . It was too late to look anything up. Perhaps there would be a class to-morrow. . . . The German lessons at school had been dreadfully good. . . . Fraulein's grave face . . . her perfect knowledge of every rule . . . her clear explanations in English . . . her examples. . . . All these things were there, in English grammar. . . . And she had undertaken to teach them and could not even speak German. Monsieur . . . had talked French all the time . . . dictées . . . lectures . . . Le Conscrit . . . Waterloo . . . La Maison Déserte . . . his careful voice reading on and on . . . until the room disappeared. . . . She must do that for

> her German girls. Read English to them and make them happy. . . . But first there must be verbs . . . there had been cahiers of them . . . first, second, third conjugation. . . . It was impudence, an impudent invasion . . . the dreadful, clever, foreign school. . . . They would laugh at her. . . . She began to repeat the English alphabet. . . . She doubted whether, faced with a class, she could reach the end without a mistake. . . . She reached Z and went on to the parts of speech (*Pointed Roofs*, 29).

It is no accident that this significant passage occurs while Miriam is on a train traveling through country that, in daylight, she called the "Dutch landscape" in which "one level stretch succeeded another." During the day she had wanted to get off the train and "go out alone under the gray sky and walk over the flat fields." As "she looked at the dikes and the windmills with indifferent eyes her desire for the flat meadows grew." Now, when it is "late at night," Miriam goes out into the flat meadows of her thoughts, walking where "one level stretch" succeeds another. As a visual map of Miriam's "walking" and "going out," the complete and incomplete phrases on the page, separated by varied lengths of space and ellipses, resemble the flat horizontal meadows that Miriam "desired" in the daytime. When it is "late at night" her desire to go out and walk is met, not through a dream or wish, the usual night visitors, but through something similar—Miriam's going out into the "flat fields" of her thoughts. Like the landscape seen in the daylight and like the phrases on the page, "one level stretch" of Miriam's thought "succeeds another," and one thought replaces a previous thought in the same way that one scene out the window of a train is quickly replaced by another. Here, as in other passages in which the figure of the train is present, the train and its motion serve as a physical manifestation or model of the associative action of displacement and replacement by which Miriam's consciousness travels. Thus the quick succession of flat fields of prose, some fragments and some complete sentences, embodies Richardson's feminine prose as it mimes the shape of traveling consciousness on the page. By "ignoring . . . the lesser of the stereotyped system of signs" and "depart[ing] from current usage," Richardson is able to meet and manifest on the page Miriam's growing desire for the "flat meadows."

Embodying another important element of feminine prose, Miriam occupies many different temporal locations at once in the passage. It is as if she conjugates herself, practicing the grammar of which she speaks, to imagine herself into various times. Some of her phrases sound like a sequence of grammar exercises for the non-English speakers who will be her students in

Hanover: "to go to the German school and teach . . . to be going there." Through these statements she places herself simultaneously in the present and the future imperfect. Again she is in the present when she states, "It was too late," and she locates herself again in the future imperfect when she thinks, "The moment would come" and "She must do that for her German girls." The indefinite past is marked by "The German lessons at school [which] had been dreadfully good and are symbolized in Fraulein's grave face" and by "Monsieur . . . [who] had talked French all the time." Thus as she "rushes" through the specific time "late at night" toward "the German city," Miriam occupies at once many different times and places.

The "careful voice" of Monsieur "reading on and on . . . until the room disappeared" signals the way in which this conjugation of time through Miriam's thoughts, or by means of the memory of Monsieur's voice reciting conjugations out loud, also conjugates or alters space. This alteration is visually demonstrated on the page, where the text appears in a spatial arrangement dramatically altered in comparison to those that preceded it or those that follow. Just as Monsieur's voice was able to make the room disappear, the recitation and disjunct nature of Miriam's thoughts are able to effect the arrangement of words in the room of the book. Like Monsieur's thoughts, Miriam's thoughts also create a disappearance. In Miriam's case it is a disappearance into ellipse. It is through the act of "reading on and on" that this disappearance is made to occur. Since the "reading on and on" of Monsieur and the resultant disappearance is, according to Miriam, a desirable effect which she hopes to reproduce for "her German girls," it can also be taken as a clue to the reader of *Pilgrimage* of a desirable method with which to read *Pilgrimage*. If a *Pilgrimage* reader uses this method of reading "on and on" in a recitative fashion, then he or she will also experience the "happy" pleasure of disappearance.

The pleasure of disappearance rendered by this passage is displayed in the elliptical disappearances on the page. The passage is also bordered on top and bottom by the disappearance of two blank rectangles of space. These typographical blanks—the disappearance due to the darkness of the carriage in which Miriam sits, the dark rectangle of window giving only a view of night, as well as the memory of the disappearance of the room caused by Monsieur—are all manifestations of one of the aims of Miriam's journey and Richardson's "spiritual exercise"—to arrive at "the strange thing for which there were no words." These blanks are the pools out of which words issue and to which they return in Richardson's phenomenology.

After the "happy" memory of the extraordinary way in which Monsieur's voice "made the room disappear," Miriam states that "she must do that for her German girls," but in the elliptical space that soon follows this thought, the question or problem of how Miriam will "do that" is implied and is then answered in the statement, "But first there must be verbs." This statement reads like a proclamation regarding more than simply the teaching of English to her German students. Its emphatic expression implies its reflexivity in the context of this passage and in the larger context of *Pilgrimage*. That is, in order for Monsieur's voice, or any voice to make space disappear, or for there to be "flat meadows" of thought continually replacing one another as the phrases in the landscape of this passage replace one another, there must first be verbs or motion. In the context of *Pilgrimage*, the word of God that begins creation is a verb. The verb as grammatical location of motion in the passage and elsewhere has divine status—creation depends on verbs.

The statement "But first there must be verbs" is also self-reflexive in that this passage itself is powered by verbs or motion, particularly by the "rushing towards" momentum of the train. The passage also serves to instruct the reader in how to read this or any other dense example of feminine prose. The statement "first there must be verbs" is an instruction to readers as well as to German girls. It refers to the instruction of all who are foreign to the English language usage present in the passage—an English that is the foreign language of feminine prose. Because instruction in how to participate in the "spiritual exercise" of feminine prose involves an understanding that one is "setting forth to seek something already found," metaphors that signal travel and motion, as well as verbs that signal motion, have a special symbolic and heuristic value in reminding the readers of the repeated "setting forth" required in a reading that is quest rather than habit.

After the proclamation regarding verbs, Miriam descends backwards in language as, earlier in the passage, she descended back in time to memories of her own school days. As if learning to speak all over again, she recites the alphabet with great doubt as to whether she will be able to reach the end. When the beacon of the capitalized letter Z stands out in the last line of the passage, the reader, like Miriam, is assured to have faith and continue on "to the parts of speech." Miriam is modeling the process of learning to read all over again, a process that may be necessary for readers who set forth on the "fool's errand" of reading *Pilgrimage*. The "fool's errand" of writing

Pilgrimage also requires of Richardson an entire relearning of English, since part of the project of feminine prose is a dismantling of the elements of English grammar and a reinvention of its uses. In this vein Richardson both shares Miriam's doubts regarding the success of her "fool's errand" to Hanover and is in the position of a teacher not sure that she will be able to convey the different "rules" of her English grammar to her reader/students.

Many different spatial locations are simultaneously present in the passage. As with the temporal locations, the reader is told in the last line that, spatially, Miriam is in a state of "to be going there." She is not literally able to see her destination and occupies the past as much as the present. She is in a state of both going and about to be going, as the train takes her through the dark. She is no place as she rushes along inside the train compartment "opposite her sleeping companion" in the late night. At the same time, being no place allows her to be in the space of imagination. This space is introduced by the statement, "She imagined one of the rooms at the old school." All of Miriam's memories about "the old school" were, as she says, present in "English grammar." English grammar is a locus of memory which Miriam occupies in imagination. The words "English grammar" are triggers for memories and a place to which association and memories adhere. Established as a space in the imagination and in memory, Miriam continues to occupy various elements, spatial and temporal locations of English grammar throughout the remainder of the passage. She is in the English alphabet as she repeats it and as she simultaneously faces an imagined class. When she reaches Z she goes on, by means of repetition, to occupy "the parts of speech."

For the first time in *Pilgrimage* this passage presents the idea that will become a thematic problem. This problem, one that requires of Miriam continual examination, is presented as the paradigm that, in order to take on the authority of the "male regiments" it seems to be necessary to follow the proper rules of grammar. Miriam's independent choice to leave her family and work in Germany, like Richardson's project to alter the proper use of grammar, is a challenge to the male regiments or to a tradition of male authority. At this early point in Miriam's development, with her father asleep beside her in the railway carriage, the confidence with which she challenges that tradition wavers, as her father and other male authorities still serve as a yardstick by which she measures her competence. Her doubts as to whether she will be able to take on the position of authority as a teacher rest on her doubts as to whether she knows and can convey "the rules" of English grammar. Not to know the rules is "shameful." But since this passage, riddled with Miriam's concern about proper usage, is a flamboyant demonstration of improper usage, Richardson presents Miriam's doubt in an ironic light.

The passage is itself an argument for the necessity of improper usage. In it Richardson illustrates that thinking, even thinking about grammar, is not grammatical—thus in order to map the motion of thoughts or consciousness in writing, particularly those of a feminine subject, the proper rules of grammar will not be useful. Instead it is necessary, as Richardson argued in the Foreword, to depart from the authority of the "male regiments" who represent the rules of "proper usage" and attempt to "produce a feminine equivalent to the current masculine realism." While the embodiment of male authority, her father, is asleep beside Miriam, her thoughts can rush ungrammatically out of sequence toward the "German city."

Since deviation from proper punctuation is one of the signs of Richardson's spiritual practice as it comes to bear on the page, a short detour into her 1924 essay "About Punctuation" will be worthwhile before going on to look at the next shrine-site passage ("About Puncuation," *Adelphi* 1.11, April, 1924, 990-996). In "About Punctuation," Richardson discusses in detail the ways in which the implied but submerged notions regarding punctuation, as suggested in the above passage, are part of her aesthetic and spiritual practice. She opens the essay by lauding the "patient reading" that is the only method that will render "the charm concealed in ancient manuscripts." She uses the example of an ancient manuscript to introduce the idea of "patient reading" because an ancient manuscript is a text that, in contrast to modern texts, "moves along unbroken, save by an occasional full stop." The reader who persists, she states, will win familiarity with the writer's style and begin "to punctuate unconsciously as he goes." At this point the "patient reader" will also begin "to be aware of the charm sacrificed by the systematic separation of phrases." Finally this reader will "[find] himself listening. Reading through the ear as well as through the eye." It is to this kind of reading that Richardson refers when she states in the Foreword that she wishes, like James, to engage the reader in a "perfection of sustained concentration akin to that which brought it [the writing] forth."

Again citing James' prose as a model for her own, she later states in emphatic italics that "It [his writing] is a spiritual Swedish Drill." Richardson also aspires to the "Swedish Drill" effect, intending through the kinds of ellipses and fragments evidenced in the above passage from *Pointed Roofs* to, as she puts it, "fuse the mind and heart" through a writing that, like James', also serves as a system of therapeutic spiritual exercises.

As she goes on to state in "About Punctuation," this spiritual exercise of "patient reading" has transformative powers: "Quite modest matter, read thus, can arouse and fuse the faculties of mind and heart." But most modern reading, she says, is "a superficial swift gathering, as we loll on the borderland between inertia and attention." This is largely because punctuation has become so highly standardized that there is no need to attend to it: "the machinery of punctuation and type" have "devitalized the act of reading." However, since Richardson believes that punctuation is the "pace-maker for the reader's creative consciousness" and the rules of grammar have become, as she puns, "the letter of the law," it is necessary to transgress these rules. The proper rules of grammar must be transgressed because "the sole aim of law is liberty; in this case, liberty to express."

Beyond expression, Richardson continues in this brilliant essay to analyze the necessary connections between uses of punctuation and the kinds of reading that various types of punctuation will cause. Again, illustrating the ways in which the technicalities of punctuation and the spiritual exercise of reading are united, she states that the main aim of any revitalized reading, and presumably any writing, is "to yield all we are and suffer change." This segue into "About Punctuation" should illuminate some of the ways in which the passage from *Pointed Roofs* is a shrine site. Through its punctuation and the rhythm that the punctuation affects, the passage requires of the reader the acute listening that an imagined "patient reader" might bring to a medieval manuscript. In its emphasis on the relation between voice and the transformation of space through Monsieur's recitations, or through Miriam's recitation of her thoughts and the alphabet, the passage points to the relation between the spatial arrangement of the words on the page and the consciousness that they map. With this heightened awareness of the relation between the arrangements of words and of consciousness, the "patient reader" can listen closely and hear the rhythm and tempo of Miriam's thoughts as well as the blank pauses which, as temporal commas, serve to punctuate her thoughts. In the passage from *Pointed Roofs* the reader is submerged in this alternation of noise and silence that mimics the noise of the train in which Miriam travels, ostensibly on a journey to a German city but equally on a journey that could be described—as Richardson describes the travels of a mystic—as a "journey to where one already is, a quest for what is already possessed, a discovery that is always a rediscovery." Miriam is both submerged in English language and grammar and traveling toward it. She both already possesses it and doesn't yet understand in what form she has it at all. The "strange thing for which there were no words," one of the primary elements of Miriam's transfigurative experiences, is present in the silence outside the dark train window and in the ellipses of Miriam's thoughts. Whether or not this has been a "mystic" moment for Miriam, it has without doubt been a moment of heightened awareness of transition, a literal being in motion while watching the motion of her own consciousness. If the passage has successfully propelled the reader across "the borderland between inertia and attention" into the territory of "sustained concentration," then, with transformative powers similar to that of a prayer or relic, it has engaged the "creative consciousness" of the reader, and the ceremony of reading, a communion with the unseen and the newly seen, can continue renewed.

Into Ellipse

The next shrine-site passage occurs in the first two pages of the four-page long Chapter VI of *Honeycomb*. As in the passage from *Pointed Roofs*, these pages are also heavily sprinkled with ellipses. Thus, before looking at the text itself, a brief discussion of the varieties of ellipses and Richardson's use of them will be helpful.

According to the *Princeton Encyclopedia of Poetry and Poetics*, the word "ellipse," from the Greek, is a "leaving out" or a "defect." It is

> a figure wherein a word, or several words, usually of little importance to the logical expression of thought but ordinarily called for by the construction, are omitted. . . . The device may be used for a number of psychological reasons, including, according to Qunitilian, considerations of modesty. . . . Qunitilian distinguishes ellipse from aposiopesis (q.v.) on the ground that in the latter it is uncertain what is suppressed.[48]

The ellipse is the perfect figure for Richardson, who wishes to disrupt the "logical expression of thought" and call attention instead to the asequential workings of consciousness. That which is left out in Richardson's ellipses is indeed often left out "for a number of psychological reasons." "Modesty," however, could only be considered to be one of those reasons if modesty were thought of as a kind of personal secret. Miriam does keep personal secrets, sometimes unarticulated even to herself. In addition, Richardson's ellipses often conceal a secret about reading or the secret silence beyond words. In more "psychological" terms, the ellipses may also contain repressed material that is secret by the nature of its inaccessibility to Miriam or to Richardson.

Richardson also makes use of the figure of aposiopesis. True to the character of the aposiopesis, in many of these instances it is clear exactly what words or fragments of thought are being excluded from a sentence or phrase. As "a becoming silent," aposiopesis is particularly appropriate to Richardson's aesthetic and spiritual practice. According to the *Princeton Encyclopedia*, it is

> a conscious anacoluthon (q.v.) that is, a speaker's abrupt halt midway in a sentence, accountable to his being either too excited to give further articulation to his thought, or thinking to impress his addressee the more with this kind of vague hint of an idea too awesome to be put into words. . . . A. is always followed by the speaker's explanation that he is passing over in silence matters either already known to the addressee or too sordid to be mentioned. . . . Qunitilian remarks that it is sometimes used as a merely transitional device, where the speaker wishes to introduce a digression or announce an impromptu change in the planned conduct of his argument, such as the circumstances of the moment might suggest.[49]

The "midway halts" in Miriam's discourse occur for all the reasons listed in the above definition. Particularly in the shrine-site passages, Miriam is often too "excited" or too caught up in the "astonishment" of a transfigurative moment to give words to what she perceives. In such a moment, Miriam's statement "It is all too sacred for words" often comes to bear on the writing down of a word, and consequently no words appear on the page (*Interim*, 392). Certainly the absence of words is also intended to impress upon the reader that the idea or experience is too awesome to articulate. Sometimes, as in the case of Miriam's mother's death, the ellipses and blank spaces do indicate, as the above definition suggests, a matter too sordid to mention, or perhaps too taboo or repressed. In other cases the ellipses occupy the silent knowledge of that which is already understood, or they serve as "a merely transitional device" linking one digression to another in a narrative where "everything is a side issue."

In addition to the ellipse, Richardson deploys with care and invention all other marks of punctuation though she pays special attention to the comma. This is clear throughout *Pilgrimage* but most evident in the shrine-site passages. As she states in "About Punctuation,"

> for those who stand between purists and rebels, the rules of punctuation are neither sacred, nor execrable, nor quite absolute. No waving of the tablets of the law has been able to arrest organic adaptation. The test of irregularities is their effectiveness. Verbless phrases flanked by full-stops, the use of and at the beginning of a sentence, and kindred effective irregularities, are safe servants, for good, in the cause of the written word. And always there has been a certain variability in the use of the comma. As the shortest breath of punctuation it is allowed, without controversy, to wander a little. Yet the importance of the comma cannot be exaggerated. It is the angel, or the devil, amongst stops. In prose, everything turns upon its use ("About Punctuation," *Adelphi*, April, 1929, 6).

As the visual and aural imprints of the spiritual exercise of feminine prose, these uses of and observations about punctuation amount to an aesthetic manifesto for the writing of feminine prose. Richardson characteristically practices, in the above passage, the idea and techniques that she also presents. Illustrating the "good" of using the word "and" at the beginning of a sentence, she begins the sentence following that statement with And. She demonstrates her notions about the wandering use of the comma by sprinkling the sentence preceding the one beginning with "And" with five commas. Beyond the above-quoted passage, she goes on in "About Punctuation" to catalogue the various important uses and personality types of the comma. In this essay Richardson also reveals that punctuation itself is as vital and animate for her as language. This is evident in her use of ellipses and in her personification of "spontaneous" commas: "Spontaneous commas are as delightful in their way as spontaneous spelling; as delightful as the sharp breath drawn by a singing child in the middle of a word" ("About Punctuation," *Adelphi*, April, 1929, 6).

Heavily riddled with ellipses and lightly sprinkled with commas, the following passage from *Honeycomb* is both a site of epiphany manifest in punctuation and the site of a merging between the "beyond" that is "within" and without.[50]

> The West End street . . . grey buildings rising on either side, angles sharp against the sky . . . softened angles of buildings against other buildings . . . high moulded angles soft as crumb, with deep under-

shadows . . . creepers fraying from balconies . . . strips of window blossoms across the buildings, pouching out along the dipping sill . . . a wash of green creeper up a white painted house front . . . patches of shadow and bright light. . . . Sounds of visible near things streaked and scored with broken light as they moved, led off into untraced distant sounds . . . chiming together.

Wide golden streaming Regent Street was quite near. Some narrow street would lead into it.

Flags of pavement flowing—smooth clean grey squares and oblongs, faintly polished, shaping and drawing away—sliding into each other. . . . I am part of the dense smooth clean paving stone . . . sunlit; gleaming under dark winter rain; shining under warm sunlit rain, sending up a fresh stony smell . . . always there . . . dark and light . . . dawn, stealing . . .

Life streamed up from the close dense stone. With every footstep she felt she could fly.

The little dignified high-built cut-through street, with its sudden walled-in church, swept round and opened into brightness and a clamour of central sounds ringing harshly up into the sky.

The pavement of heaven.

To walk along the radiant pavement of sunlit Regent Street for ever.

She sped along looking at nothing. Shops passed by, bright endless caverns screened with glass . . . the bright teeth of a grand piano running along the edge of a darkness, a cataract of light pouring down its raised lid; forests of hats; dresses, shining against darkness, bright headless crumpling stalks; sly, silky, ominous furs; metals, cold and clanging, brandishing the light; close prickling fire of jewels . . . strange people who bought these things, touched and bought them.

She pulled up sharply in front of a window. The pavement round it was clear, allowing her to stand rooted where she had been walking, in the middle of the pavement, in the midst of the pavement, in the midst of the tide flowing from the clear window, a soft fresh tide of sunlit colours . . . clear green glass shelves laden with shapes of fluted glass, glinting transparencies of mauve and amber and green, rose - pearl and milky blue, welded to a flowing tide, freshening and flowing through her blood, a sea rising and falling with her breathing.

> The edge had gone from the keenness of the light. The street was a happy, sunny, simple street—small. She was vast. She could gather up the buildings in her arms and push them away, clearing the sky . . . a strange darkling, and she would sleep. She felt drowsy, a drowsiness in her brain and limbs and great strength, and hunger.
>
> A clock told her she had been away from Brook Street ten minutes. Twenty minutes to spare. What would she do with her strength? Talk to someone or write . . . Bob; where was Bob? Somewhere in the West End. She would write from the West End a note to him in the West End (*Honeycomb*, 416-17).

The proper name "West End street" opens the first paragraph and immediately situates the reader on a street heading toward an unknown destination. The "West End street" leads into an external architecture that is simultaneously an internal landscape imbued with the ultra-lush quality of imagination. The quality of light is important because it is the external element that infuses the landscape with a heightened, palpably sensual character, so close to the light and landscape of dream: "angles . . . soft as crumb, with deep undershadows." The soft "West End street" about to crumble, promises to lead somewhere and to be something to follow, not exactly like a sentence leads, more like one glance leads to another or like a series of phrases. Each time a comma appears, the sight that has been glanced before the comma is now seen in more vivid detail in the phrase that follows. For example, "grey buildings rising on either side, angles sharp against the sky" becomes even more specific in the following clause: "high molded angles soft as crumb, with deep undershadows." As the narrator walks down the West End street, her attention to one area and observation shifts and leads to another area and more detailed glance. These glances are indicated by the terraced ellipses descending down the paragraph. As though the typeface on the page were three-dimensional, these ellipses cast "patches of shadow and bright light" on the page. Rather than the "full stops" of periods, the use of ellipses and commas lend the sense of constant movement and the accumulation of many details into a fused atmosphere of internal consciousness and external place.

Near the end of the first paragraph, the "bright light" that has illuminated everything seen up to this point, gives way to "sounds of visible near things." The merging that begins here between light and sound presents the first of many mergings of disparate elements presented in this chapter. The "bright" quality of the light is that of dream light, though it is a light that can also be seen in a heightened dreamlike state while awake. We know the quality of the light more from the luminosity it casts on the buildings and plants than from any direct description of the light itself. We know it, for example, by the "deep undershadows" and "patches of shadow" that it casts. It has both the seductive and the transcendent quality of the light in Renaissance religious paintings and, as in allegorical religious light, it emanates from an unnamed and therefore mysterious source. It signals both an unusual time of day and an unusual state of mind. The places in the narrative where the light dims to shadow, pull the reader and the narrator's glance toward investigation of the mystery that is beyond "the deep undershadows." We are then told that just beyond the "deep undershadows" are "creepers fraying from balconies . . . strips of window blossoms . . . scarlet, yellow, high up." A profusion of color emerges from shadow matched by a lush density of language as foliage.

When the light merges with the sound of unspecific "visible near things," the words on the page, which are also "near things," are "scored." As in the arrangement of notes in a musical score, or like the words that, as arranged structures are like buildings or architecture, this scoring sets the linguistic and imaginative arrangements in motion. It is with "broken light" that both the sounds and the "visible near things" are "scored," significantly "as they moved." As a result of being "scored" with light, the objects in the environment are set in motion, as the words are set in motion, "chiming together," if they are read like music.

When the light merges with sound, the passage becomes voluble. "Sounds of visible near things streaked and scored with broken light . . . led off into untraced distant sounds . . . chiming together." These lines emphasize the importance of the ear to the reading of the passage; they describe what would occur if one were to read this passage out loud. Reading aloud this paragraph leads "off into untraced distant sounds" and becomes a walk through written and aural image.

In the second paragraph, the more general "West End street" is more specifically located with the name "Regent Street." It is a place "golden and streaming," both with light and with the noise of activity. Its name and golden character lead to an even more specific and richly textured place: the opening out of the chapter, and the scene of action. Not accidentally named, the "regent" in "Regent Street" signals the ruler, or the ruling principle that is the companion in this walk down Regent Street. It becomes increasingly clear that as Miriam gains momentum toward Regent Street, she also comes into closer proximity with one of the regents, or one of the most highly valued spiritual principles of Richardson's practice: she approaches "the being that is at the heart of all becoming." This "being" is present in the increasing sense of sensual merging that she experiences.

At the apex of this momentum, fueled by ellipses, light and sound, the motion from one name, the "West End," to another more specifically located name, "Regent Street," gathers to become a "sliding into each other" of the "flags of pavement." The merging of the paving stone with the sudden entry of the first person narrator—"I am part of the dense smooth clean paving stone"—lends the sense of a subject that is both autonomous and part of the environment.

Continuing with the sense of one element merging into another, the narrator describes Regent Street as "streaming" and the "flags of the pavement" as "flowing." The hard has become soft and now flows like lava, just as in the first paragraph the light melts into sounds and enters our ears as words. Light and sound, soft and hard, subject and object have lost their boundaries. There is a "shaping and drawing away—sliding into each other" of which the narrator partakes. It is this acute sense of merging that allows the narrator to speak. This is a speaking "I" whose joyously crumbling loss of subjectivity causes a heightened awareness of itself as a precariously constructed subject. As "part of the dense smooth clean paving stone," the words spoken by the "I" from the center of this first page personify the convergence of all the inanimate architecture, names, light, and sound that are present. The words "I am part of" also anticipate those moments of merging that will follow.

Next, in the same paragraph, the eternal cyclic alternation of light and darkness is stated to be "always there." This eternal alternating presence of light and darkness, darkness and light, signals another of the principles of Richardson's spiritual writing practice that locates the scene appropriately again in Regent Street, street of ruling principles. In the eternal presence of the alternation of light and dark, in its nature of being constant, "always there," yet always alternating, appearing and disappearing, the light and darkness manifest the eternal stillness in motion, or "being at the heart of all becoming," that is basic to Richardson's spiritual/aesthetic practice. The experience of stillness in motion, particularly portrayed here through the alternating figures of light and dark, is constantly returned to throughout *Pilgrimage*. These figures always serve as invitations to merge with the atmosphere created by day and night, light and darkness, and their rhythmic alternation is often mirrored musically in the language. The presence of these figures almost always signals a shrine site or the opening of a transfigurative moment.

In the end of the second paragraph the precise time and light of this particular transfigurative moment are located as "dawn"—a beginning underlit with promise. Out of this promise, in the third one-line paragraph, issues "Life" which "streams up from the close dense stone." The narrator continues to remain merged with the paving stone, from which "Life streamed up." Since the narrator's life is part of the paving stone, the "Life" that "streams up" at the narrator is also her own life. Yet, through the act of merging with the paving stone, her own life has also become depersonalized and is now the same as the life of the street. Thus it is both her personal life, "Life" as a universal principal, and the lives of myriad other flaneurs not currently present, that "stream up" at her from the pavement.

The intense subjectivity of the narrator, manifest in the previous paragraphs through her acute observations, breaks into this merged universality where there is no distinction between all subjects and objects, by means of the fiercely intense concentration on a self's perceptions of itself. Gendered as "She," but still nameless and only a walking observing feminine subjectivity, the narrator illustrates here a technique of thought or contemplation that serves as a means of transport out of the self and back into a self transfigured by the journey out. This "Life" streaming up at the narrator makes her feel that she could fly. Altered by her intense concentration on her surroundings and not limited by the usual corporeality of her own body, she is elated and uplifted by the merging of her body with the body of the light, sounds, and buildings around her.

Next in this walking lesson—or phenomenological allegory of consciousness as act, as a walk at dawn—a spiritually proper emptied-full, light-dark state of mind is approached as the narrator comes upon a "sudden walled-in church." This church contains and concentrates the "brightness" and "clamour of central sounds ringing harshly up into the sky." The presence of the church also indicates that a sacred realm has been entered in the text. Merged with the brightness and the sounds and already feeling that she could fly, the narrator is transported, with the "central sounds," "up into the sky." With the gesture of this upward transport, the flagstones of the previous paragraph and the narrator as part of them are transformed, in a single line isolated from any other lines, into "The pavement of heaven."

This increasing transport of the narrator upwards, first to the feeling of being able to fly, and next to the sounds "ringing harshly up into the sky," and finally up to heaven, is simultaneously a drop down closer to the page for the reader. The "*pavement* [my emphasis] of heaven" signals that which is closest to the narrator as it is directly beneath her feet. Through its divine status as the pavement of heaven, it is also, in the register of spiritual allegory, the road farthest away and most difficult to reach. In the limnal time of pilgrimage or ritual, the sequence of perceptions of secular time is typically reversed so that, as is the case here, the close becomes the allegorical distant, or the right-side-up becomes upside-down.[51] Since the "pavement" is the material on which one must travel in order to reach "heaven," the reader also must traverse the pavement or the paving stones of words, the street made of linguistic marks, on which she or he must walk in order to be transported upwards. This pavement is shown to be a state of mind produced by the spatial practice of walking, that is, by this journey down terraces of ellipses, through these comma-less, breathless streamings of language rivers, these big space-lapses between paragraphs on the page, these names.

Next, a large blank space on the page punctuated by one line marks the location of the narrator's desire. She wishes to remain inside of this shrine in words "for ever." To remain in this shrine-like state of consciousness "for ever" she states that it would be necessary to walk forever "along the radiant pavement of sunlit Regent Street." Since it has been established that the pavement is the symbolic material on which this walk in words takes place, and since we know from *Pointed Roofs* that verbs must be first in propelling motion through language, the desire to walk along "the radiant pavement of sunlit Regent Street for ever" is also the desire to remain forever merged with the "close dense" streaming of language. This desire to remain merged harkens back to Richardson's notion of a feminine film which satisfied the pre-Oedipal desire to remain merged in the realm of the synchronic.

Following the heavenly transcendence of the previous passages, the first line of the following paragraph, the seventh in the chapter, "She sped along looking at nothing," reveals what is inside of this actual church as well as this shrine site in written image. Inside is the convergence of light and sounds, and a glut of images that obliterates all ability to "look at" anything. A rich list of vitally animated objects pass by, but there is now a distance between them and the narrator: though they pass they do not enter and become part of her. As she speeds along looking into windows, familiar inanimate objects take on a strange disturbed animation, as in the "bright teeth of a grand piano," or "dresses shining against darkness, bright headless crumpling stalks." The vitality with which these objects are infused, in comparison with that of the preceding paragraphs, has become menacing in its vision of bared teeth and beheaded women. In this paragraph the heightened quality of Miriam's perceptions continues without the merging that earlier accompanied it. Her detachment is evident not only in the now-menacing quality of what she perceives, but particularly in the intrusion of a thought that removes her for the first time in the chapter from the immediacy of the moment. The thought is about the "strange people who bought these things, touched and bought them." Not only has the familiar become strange, but the people who buy these familiar objects are infected with that strangeness through their ability to touch what she cannot. Looking at their things through the invisible and powerful glass of class the strangers are conjured but not present. Unlike other objects, their untouchable objects do not invite contact. The strange ability to buy and touch these objects, visible signs of class access, coupled with their acutely conjured menacing presence, makes the strangers doubly strange as even in their absence they remind her of her own estrangement from their world.[52]

Following the sudden intrusion of this thought, the eighth paragraph opens, "She pulled up sharply in front of a window." Next she stands "rooted where she had been walking." The condition of her standing and its relation to the pavement is mentioned three times, again pointing up the importance of the pavement as the material of her transport. First the pavement "round [the window] was clear." Next, her rootedness is positioned "in the middle of the pavement." Finally, she has stopped speeding along the pavement "looking at nothing," as she was doing in the previous paragraph. Now her full descent from "the pavement of heaven" to her rootedness "in the midst of the pavement, in the midst of the tide flowing from the clear window" allows her to look at the "soft fresh tide of sunlit colours" as something separate from herself.

The "flags of pavement flowing" in the second paragraph have become stationary. This lack of motion in the material of the narrator's walk is manifest in the dense profile and absence of blank spaces in this paragraph. The paragraph begins with a complete sentence and is followed by a sentence of layered phrases separated by a series of commas that allow the phrases to spill gently from one another for nine lines, all the way down to the end of the paragraph. The only ellipse in the paragraph follows the phrase "a soft fresh tide of sunlit colours," which comes in the middle of the second and last sentence of the paragraph. In this sentence, the series of carefully placed commas, the solitary ellipse and the dash that arrives a few lines later, serve to link thoughts connected by associations that move too quickly to catch whole. The punctuation also indicates the inhaling and exhaling sea in which Miriam is now submerged and which is "rising and falling with her breathing."

The solidity of the pavement beneath her and the density of the paragraph are emblematic of her return to her own personal body and the cessation of her merging with the sound, light, and buildings about her. This return allows her to look at the objects in the window and see the "soft fresh tide of sunlit colours" flowing from them. Since the danger and pleasure of merging with all about her has abated, she does not perceive the objects behind this window to be menacing as were the "bright teeth" and beheaded dresses of the previous paragraph. Though she is returning from the experience of ecstatic merging to the more mundane separation of subject and object, she remains "welded to a flowing tide." Both her return and her continued connection are apparent in her acute consciousness of her body. It is as a physical synesthetic sensation that she feels the beautiful tide of light emanating from the objects in the window as the tide enters her, "freshening and flowing through her blood, a sea rising and falling with her breathing."

In paragraph nine the change in the quality of light marks Miriam's return from the "keenness" of her experience to a "simple street" and a simpler frame of mind: "The edge had gone from the keenness of the light." Though the street returns to its former self, "a happy, sunny, simple street—small," and Miriam is on her way to returning to her former self, she remains "welded to a flowing tide." As the tide expands with the "rising and falling" of her breath, and as the street becomes smaller, she rises and becomes "vast." It is not that, as previously, she is now merged with all about her, but instead this paragraph maps the effect that remains after having been merged. Instead of becoming the buildings that were "soft as crumb," as in the opening of the chapter, the vast sea inside of her has made her feel powerful enough to "gather up the buildings in her arms and push them away, clearing the sky." Following this statement comes the only ellipse in the paragraph, a gap like the "clearing" Miriam has made in the sky, out of which issues the change in the "keenness of light." The change arrives in the guise of "a strange darkling." This change on the other side of the experience of heightened consciousness is sleep—a "darkling" and "drowsiness in her brain." Having traveled far away from mundane space and time, she now returns fully to corporeality, to "brain and limbs." The residue of her experience is manifest in her body as "great strength" and as desire in the form of physical "hunger."

With the return to her body in paragraph ten, time intrudes and a clock tells her how long she has "been away." It has been "ten minutes. Twenty minutes to spare." Infused with a strength gleaned from experiencing the collapse of space and time, subject and object, she manifests strength as a desire to do something in the time left before her appointment. She wishes to address this strength to someone, to transform an element of her extraordinary experience into a message: to either "talk to someone or write." Following this statement the only ellipsis in paragraph ten appears. Its silence marks the desire beyond words, the "hunger" of her spirit to transform by talking and writing, and to address this transformation to another. The paragraph closes with the line, "She would write from the West End a note to him in the West End." This line captures perfectly the sense that the journey is always to where one already is, as Miriam will write from where she is in the West End and address her note to someone else who is also where she is in the West End. As in the preceding paragraphs, the name "West End" is shown to be a marker for a shared state of consciousness, both a way of reading a place and a spatial/psychological location in a city.

This chapter continues for three more paragraphs that are mainly concerned with the procuring of materials for writing and the actual writing of the note. After she has written and mailed the note, the chapter ends with the statement, "She, too, now had a mysterious secret face—a West End life of her own." Something has happened to change Miriam, and the change is signified by the fact that she now has "a mysterious secret face—a West End life" that she did not have before the event of this chapter. As illustrated in the chapter and true to Richardson's spiritual practice, it is out of a secret face and life, the secret of walking on the "pavement of heaven," that writing issues. The words that Richardson uses to describe Fox and his spiritual practice, as well as the practices of those she calls "the mystics," also apply to the epiphanic walk in a sea of light depicted in this chapter of *Honeycomb*. To recall Richardson's statement in *The Quakers Past and Present*, Fox and the mystics seek

> something whose presence is in some way independent of the normal thinking and acting creature, something which has already proclaimed itself in moments of heightened consciousness—in the case of the religious temperament at conversion (35).

The thing "whose presence is in some way independent of the normal thinking and acting creature" fully proclaims itself in the "wide golden streaming" of the passages from *Honeycomb*. It "proclaims itself" in these "moments of heightened consciousness" and causes a religious "conversion" in Miriam, or a new faith in or "face" with which to view the "beyond that is within." In traveling afresh to where she already is in the West End, Miriam's discovery of "the strange thing for which there were no words" is also a rediscovery and renewal of the desire to write. As with Fox's journey, the aim of Miriam's pilgrimage down the West End street is "to break through the veil of sense, to journey to the heart of reality" (*The Quakers*, 35). Through the veil of sense, on the other side, lies unpunctuated or unconventionally punctuated landscape and language. It is here where typography and content, Miriam and her environment, merge—here also that the "spiritual exercise" of feminine prose performs its transfigurative music. In this shrine where the writer and reader participate, playing with prose and following the motions of its poses, the "ceremony of the game" is shown to lead inexorably back to the hunger for more writing.

Metaphorocrasy— Giving Up Thinking in Words

The death of Miriam's mother is closely linked to the hunger for more writing, a hunger that returns throughout *Pilgrimage*. The last two paragraphs of *Honeycomb* and the space between them stage the death. As can be seen in the following quote, for Richardson writing and death are intimately connected. It is no surprise then that this death, which parallels exactly the actual death of Richardson's mother and her close involvement with it, plays an important role throughout *Pilgrimage* in generating the desire that always leads back to a hunger for more writing. As Miriam states in the last novel-chapter, *March Moonlight*,

> To write is to forsake life. Every time I know this, in advance. Yet whenever something comes that sets the tips of my fingers tingling to record it, I forget the price; eagerly face the strange journey down and down to the centre of being. And the scene of labour, when again I am back in it, alone, has become a sacred place (*March Moonlight*, 609).

For Miriam, to write is to commit a kind of self-immolation. This loss of subjectivity is different from, though related to, the kind experienced in the intense merging depicted in the previously discussed passage from *Honeycomb*. Each time Miriam feels the desire to write she knows this loss will occur. In this sense writing brings Miriam closer to her mother, who cuts her throat with a kitchen knife in the end of *Honeycomb*.[53]

Although the price of writing is the forsaking of life, "something comes" out of writing and that "something" makes Miriam "eagerly face the strange journey down and down." At the bottom of the journey down is "the centre of being" out of which writing issues. Though life has been forsaken in order to journey "down," Miriam remains alive and alone when she is in "the scene of labour," this "sacred place." Writing, then, is a medium by which Miriam can experience the limnal state of being both alive and dead. It is to this state that she is drawn back and back when "something comes" setting her "fingers tingling to record it." One manifestation of this something, that appears in the passage from *Honeycomb*, is the intense sensual merging of subject and object as well as the intense pleasure that Miriam finds in the loss of a discrete sense of self and the simultaneous ability to be her own mirror: to watch herself lose herself. As will be seen in the following passages, it is not necessary that the sense of merging and loss be pleasurable in order to perform the transformative work that is characteristic of a shrine site.

When Miriam writes she forsakes life, just as her mother has forsaken life, but, unlike her mother, her act of forsaking life allows her to occupy a "centre of being" that is "sacred" due to the intensity of its detachment from any other "being" or life. Because of the intensity of detachment there is also death at this "centre of being." Like their mothers, Richardson and Miriam desire this death and choose repeatedly to inflict it upon themselves. Indeed, it is the exalted destination of their pilgrimage travels.

Miriam strikes the chord here of the traditional sex-and-death analogue. She "eagerly faces the strange journey down" to writing. The nature of this journey, possibly her eagerness for it, and the language she uses to describe it, imply that erotic and/or sexual desire fuel this pursuit. The pleasure that arrives from following out this desire may, like the circumstances that arouse it, be both violent and gentle. The pleasure of death framed as a loss of self accompanied by an intense merging of subject and object suggests the presence of an erotic other. But it also may not imply an explicitly physical, sexual encounter. To echo Fox, much of *Pilgrimage* is redolent with the desire "for something whose presence is in some way independent of the thinking and acting creature." *Pilgrimage* is also full of the desire to merge, to be "part of the dense smooth clean paving stone," and full of the hunger for more writing. These desires are clearly related, as earlier discussed, to desires described in the language of mystical and psychological discourse. However, there is a way in which they are also related to the sexual and erotic. The sexual and erotic in *Pilgrimage* is more repressed, or at least less directly signalled in the narrative than mystic and psychological desire. However, many of the same elements of Miriam's experience in the shrine sites that speak of the desire for a mystical other, a desire for merging or writing, can also be seen to signal the erotic. One example of this is the characteristic regression into a pre-symbolic undifferentiated realm in relation to objects and language always present in the shrine-site passages. This element of Miriam's desire suggests a polymorphously perverse sexuality: for her, contact with language, sound, light—almost anything can be erotic.[54] The close alliance between hunger, the desire for sex, death and writing, with the death of the mother in the following passage, further raises the question of the nature of desire in *Pilgrimage* and particularly in the realm of these peak shrine-site moments.

There is also a difficulty in thinking of Miriam as sexual or embodied that is present in the content of the text as Miriam's difficulty. As Stewart describes,

> Just as she [Miriam] begins to identify with some women, Shatov, who wants to marry her, confesses to illicit heterosexual activities in his student days. Appalled, she sees leering European men and compares them ill-favorably with prostitutes. But to identify with woman is to identify with "the whole masculine sense of womanhood. One image; perceived only with the body, separated and apart from everything else in life" (III, 208). The only other image offered is that of an idol "within a spiral of unconsuming radiance," but "the cost and demand" (III, 212) of being dependent on Shatov's worship are too much. She pulls back, independent, feeling masculine in her need for freedom and self-direction. She cannot find a way out of the maze. She says, "I'm as much a man as a woman. That's why I can't help seeing things" (III, 221).[55]

Miriam's enormous ambivalence about embodiment arises out of her understanding that woman is body, and the complex, perhaps insurmountable problems this implies. Her sense that she is as much a man as a woman suggests not only ambivalence but an ability to occupy various points of view in relation to gender. Since she sees no solution to the woman-equals-body problem, Miriam chooses to constantly reinvent herself. She becomes a fluid being who can occupy many different male and female points of view in relation to body and desire. Since no one position is in itself acceptable to her, this is the only acceptable solution.

For Richardson, there is also no way out of this complex cultural-gender dilemma Miriam experiences, just as there is no way out of the body. However, it is possible to sustain symbolic escape through the subterfuge of writing. In a way similar to the substitution that operates symbolically in ritual transubstantiation, it may be Richardson and Miriam's wish to substitute the problematics of an actual woman's body for the body of writing. It would then be possible to point at another object and say, "This is my body . . ." And in the case of *Pilgrimage*, Richardson can point to a hefty thirteen-volume corpus.

As does the act of writing for Richardson, Miriam also serves as Richardson's vehicle of escape from the problems of the body. As a narrative sleight of hand, Miriam's escape is performed through image. She is the image lodged in *Pilgrimage*. Thus the problem of woman as spectacle which confronts and concerns Miriam, the problem of being only that which is body, is seen, is framed, is taken and played with, played out, is pastiched by Richardson. We are supplied with a constant litany of Miriam's thoughts, her things, her actions, a veritable catalogue of detail to use in constructing a picture of her, yet she remains largely invisible—un-visualizable—in her hyperpresence. She is an image that dislodges the structure of the male gaze—an image that is not primarily visual. Instead she is an image of that which is many-bodied. She is the site of Richardson's desire, the reader's, a writer's; the site, as Miriam states, of being "as much a man as a woman"—the site of a shift of point of view.

In this sense Miriam is erotic because she is the character of transformation rather than a character. As the figure of a transitive state she is available to, indeed invites readers to desire her, desire to be in her state. Her longing to be alone with the "sacred place" of herself serves as a model of a possible longing for which a reader can also yearn. She is the body of another, one who is, like the mother before separation, outside the problems of embodiment—one through which deliverance can be fantasized.

Miriam can be seen as the locus of a triangulated projection of desire. Jane Gallop describes this in another context as "something we might call the erotics of engagement, a sexuality that is not in the object, however deeply hidden, but in the encounter." It is in the encounter with Miriam, or our fantasy of it, that sex and the erotic is located in *Pilgrimage*. And it is encounter with the convergence of things and people in the world that is erotic and sexual for Miriam. Gallop's description resonates with Richardson's descriptions of that which is compelling about the silent cinema: it is a mediated world of desirable mysterious objects in need of interpretation. In the arena of Richardson's silent film there is also a pre-Oedipal state of merging with the image of desired objects. From that state issues the desire for a continuous performance of writing. This is enacted in the shrine sites with almost the same result. Like the film, Miriam projects a desired image in need of interpretation. At the same time she is also an interpreter. Her interpretation is manifest as writing. As a writer, Miriam, like Richardson, also needs a mediated object or image that is in need of interpretation. Her mother, among others, provides this function.

In the shrine sites Miriam as image sharply dissolves or coheres, as does the projected image of the film. Via her image "otherness enters you in some way that is ecstatic." Gallop elaborates:

> Ecstasy etymologically derives from the Greek ekstasis, from ex-, "out," plus histanai, "to place." Thus it means something like "placed out." Ecstasy is when you are no longer in your own frame: some sort of going outside takes place.[56]

Thus the erotics of engagement in *Pilgrimage* pivot on a triangulated structure of desire by which I, as reader or writer, or reading and writing subject of the novels, wish to encounter a mediated image of something or someone that seduces me to want someone or something else. In Miriam's case something or someone else is always writing. That something I want seems to be hidden there in the object, or image of the object, but is actually hidden in my encounter with the object. This is the being "placed out" inherent to this kind of desire: you arrive at what you want by moving through the desired object. The moving through that the object requires is what eroticizes the object itself. Thus the site of being "placed out" is always a location of excess beyond the parameters of the object. It is always more than this something or someone, always beyond them. In terms of Miriam as image and character and in terms of the participating reader Richardson imagines (itself an image of excess), excess in *Pilgrimage* occurs through the object of the book and outside the frame of the book. What is erotic about *Pilgrimage* is not often stated in *Pilgrimage*. The erotic and ecstatic occur where words are revealed to be unable to do their work anymore: Richardson writes an exorbitant thirteen volumes to invoke a silent body of the book beyond the book. Miriam passionately lives and writes, believing that the more passionately she does so, the more she will eradicate—get beyond—living and writing. Richardson is busy with the way in which Miriam projects and is seduced by this passionate eradication, this death into the fantasy of something else. Thus sex in *Pilgrimage* is not in bodies but in encounter and engagement. Since the vehicle of engagement is linguistic, sex in *Pilgrimage* is in language.

Yet sexuality in *Pilgrimage* is never explicit because it is everywhere overtly implicit—present in and repressed in the eroticized language. Just as there is a space left on the page to mark Mrs. Henderson's suicide, there are spaces or extravagant subtleties used to indicate sexual encounters between Miriam and Hypo Wilson, Michael Shatov, or other male characters with whom she is intimate. It is evident that in her relation to Hypo and other men, Miriam most often takes a motherly role in sexually romantic scenarios. This is not the case in her encounters with women. Sexual innuendo occurs more often between Miriam and other female characters than it does between Miriam and men, yet as sexual interaction these relations still remain subtle and largely unarticulated. Thinking about the other suicide in *Pilgrimage*, that of her young Russian friend who kills herself in a fit of romantic drama, Miriam says, "But sex-love dies unless it grows, for both partners, towards universal love" (*March Moonlight*, 644). Miriam flirts with and documents the details of her fascination with one woman after another throughout the novels. When she meets Amabel she falls in love with an abandon and intensity she never experiences with a man. However, while there is no suggestion or mention of their actually touching, there is also nothing subtle or unspoken about the descriptions of erotic intensity of connection. It is significant that the erotic objects most desired by Miriam, those with whom she has the most passionate, complex and intimate relationships, are also the most socially taboo and thus unobtainable—her mother, Amabel, and other important women. These are also the characters throughout the novels for whom Miriam also has the most divided and ambivalent responses. The absence of overt sexuality in *Pilgrimage*, and the presence instead of an erotics of engagement, can also be partially attributed to Richardson's late Victorian historical moment. Closely interlocked with this moment are all the complexities and ambivalences about gender and having the body of a woman that both Miriam and Richardson express.

In addition to the example of Miriam's triangulated desire enacted in relation to her mother, is the example of the arrangement she engineers for her most intimate friends, Amabel and Michael. She cannot marry Amabel, and she does not want to marry her ex-lover Michael. In a grand gesture (that resembles more closely an author choosing a plot line than a gesture of friendship) Miriam instead arranges for them to marry each other. Throughout the remainder of the novels, Amabel and Michael's romance and marriage act like an ulterior plot, a life that Miriam happily doesn't have to live, but one that she can observe and experience by subterfuge. Much later, in the last paragraph of *March Moonlight*, the last of the novel-chapters which revolves largely around Miriam's coming to terms with being a writer and the ways in which that choice marginalizes her as a socially understandable woman, Miriam takes Amabel and Michael's baby in her arms. In this moment alone picking up the baby Paul, Richardson frames Miriam as an almost Madonna-like woman artist who has chosen writing over an actual child but retains a reverence for both kinds of birth. This is a metaphor bluntly suggested by the associations to her writing work that come to Miriam's mind as she picks up Paul and considers the choices she has made and their consequences for herself as well as the future of Amabel and Michael's unhappy marriage. In *March Moonlight* Miriam has arrived at writing. Writing is "the scene of [her] labour" but rather than the traditional view of artistic creation as birth, Miriam labours in order to forsake life and go out alone to the sacred place of that which is hidden in repeated erotic encounter.[57] Displacing the usual assumption that the mother-child bond is the closest possible, interrupted while writing by "Jean's tired voice...murmuring good night" Miriam tells that she is left "...alone with the realization of a bond, closer than any other, between myself and what I had written" (*March Moonlight*, 611).

In the following passages that bring *Honeycomb* to an end, some of the many reasons why Miriam is repeatedly motivated to choose the "sacred" death of writing are demonstrated. One reason is that she is beckoned by a person or thing that is absent. The absent other in the previously discussed *Honeycomb* shrine-site passage is Bob; it is her mother in the following passage. These absent others beckon and seduce Miriam to address them and to address the invisible that represents all of those who are not present, all of those hidden that exceed the frame. Using the "contemplative" process of writing as transformative act, Miriam is able to contact the absent and to engage with some aspects of its presence.

Richardson's method and motivation in writing for and to the absent other represents what Jakobson calls

> the magic, incantatory function [that] is chiefly some kind of conversion of an absent or inanimate "third person" into an address of a conative message.[58]

Though most acutely revealed in the shrine-site passages, all of Miriam's and Richardson's writing is ruled by the "magic" or "incantatory function." This is most evident in the emphasis on sound, rhythm, and repetition in the narrative. In this sense the spirituality of Richardson's aesthetics is derived from the act of converting the absent (and "inanimate," because deceased) mother, into a desire to write, that is, the desire to deliver and receive a message.

The moments of Miriam's and Richardson's most acute reception and delivery of messages are characterized by the shrine-site passages. In their gesturing toward something beyond themselves these passages contain profound absence. The form and substance of their writing demonstrate the ways in which this absence propels the desire to receive and deliver messages from the source of language and absence—"the centre of being." Thus it is in the shrine sites that the height of the incantatory function can be seen at work in the forms of idiosyncratic and missing punctuation, an alternating rhythm of life and death mirrored by thematic alternations of light and darkness and mirrored in the alternations of elliptical phrases and complete sentences. In the shrine sites a heightened consciousness and sensual embodiment that dissolves into loss of bodily boundaries and recurrent reembodiment also displays the incantatory function in action. The profound absence that motivates writing is also present in the text of *Pilgrimage* in the form of "the strange thing for which there were no words" and in the Foreword as "the stranger in the form of contemplated reality" who has "for the first time," through the writing of feminine prose, "its own say." This "stranger" speaks in the dialect of feminine prose, speaks out of centuries of women's silence and of women's being silenced. The Quaker silence that is necessary in order to contact the "God" that is "everywhere" is another face of the stranger or absent other that propels Miriam's and Richardson's writing. In turn, this "stranger" or "strange thing" is summoned by the fierce concentration that Richardson brings to the writing of "feminine prose." And, when present, the stranger draws the promise of writing from Miriam. Manifesting the contemplative state, the stranger is both a present and absent figure, through which, as stated in the Foreword, "revelation comes" and who throughout *Pilgrimage* appears embodied at surprise moments as a nameless, threatening, or inviting other.[59]

According to psychoanalytic and other theories of the subject, the original loss of the mother, often experienced as an actual death, shapes and motivates the desires and patterns of an individual's life. But in Miriam and Richardson's case, the extent of this influence is quadrupled by the intensity of both intimacy and estrangement between mother and daughter, by the daughter's close proximity to and implication in the scene of the death and by the separation that was confirmed and dramatized by the mother's taking her own life. Indeed, mirroring Mrs. Henderson, Mary Richardson occupied a social position of dependency and exemplified a moral state that Dorothy abhorred and from which she wished to distance herself. Yet, in both cases, the mother also had a sensitivity, a lack of rigidity and a capacity for understanding that allowed for the possibility of some profound moments of intimacy between them. As with Richardson, the terms of Miriam's parental identification are complex, but her allegiance is clearly with her mother as opposed to her father. As Richardson's father was fond of calling her his only son, Miriam in turn says, "...I am my mother's son for ever. If there's a future life, all I care for is to meet her. If I could have her back for ten minutes I would gladly give up the rest of my life..." (*Deadlock*, 220). This was far more passion than Miriam or Richardson ever expressed for the fictional or actual father. In addition, in this register of the narrative where the autobiographical is such a heavily informing strand, issues related to class position and Richardson's father's bankruptcy may have become tied up with her reactions, and her presentation of Miriam's reactions to the suicide. The poet Barbara Guest, who interviewed Richardson's friend Bryher in 1948 in Switzerland for her biography of the poet H.D., writes,

> When Bryher said to me that the most traumatic factor in D.R.'s life was her father's bankruptcy, we must recognize that Bryher spoke from an accurate grasp of the mores of British society. British society in the Victorian era—which is where D.R. began—was prejudicial toward the bankrupt and his family. British society then and probably today revolved on the pivot of social position. Most British novels are concerned with this position in a secondary theme and in E. M. Forster it is a primary theme. Society was indeed feudal. But I don't want to go into the further reaches of

> snobbery in England, beyond pointing out that it was of a major concern to D.R. Remember how furious she was in that delicious book *Honeycomb*, at her social superiors who were her moral inferiors. That is her persistent theme.
>
> D.R. indeed must have suffered a lifelong trauma [due to her mother's suicide]—which it would be necessary . . . to examine—. But her mother's death did not change anything. The sisters were married off, Dorothy in her rags was working among richer people and her status had radically changed. Her mother's death was perhaps viewed not only as a result of her mental illness, but a death flavored by a social descent, lack of servants, etc. Although we are reminded how her mother didn't seem to "mind" what happened to them after the bankruptcy. But her daughter did. The mother had accepted it all and then gone mad, or having managed to get through the weddings, just gave up. You don't go mad all at once, so D.R. may have lived for many years under what is known as "this cloud."
>
> Dorothy never introduces Miriam as an adoring, sacrificing for the mother daughter. Harriet appears closer to her mother in their middle-class manners and attitudes. Dorothy distances herself from them all, particularly the vaguely drawn figure of a father whom the novelist can't be bothered to color in.
>
> D.R. is angry about her father's supercilious mistake. Her mother may be considered another victim.[60]

As described in *Honeycomb*, the circumstances surrounding the death of "Mrs. Henderson," Miriam's mother, consist of an account of her desperate mental deterioration.[61] Richardson probably wrote the *Honeycomb* version of the suicide at the same time that she was working on the whole *Honeycomb* manuscript, between 1915 and 1917. *Honeycomb* was published in October of 1917. The writing took place approximately twenty years after the original event occured in 1895. In *Honeycomb*, the extent of Mrs. Henderson's deterioration begins to be revealed a few chapters before the death scene. Miriam realizes the full extent of her mother's desperation in a pivotal moment that occurs during a visit to her mother's home. Mrs. Henderson suddenly says to her daughter, "My life has been so useless." This statement sends "a jolt" through Miriam.

> Here it was . . . a jolt . . . an awful physical shock, jarring her body. . . . She braced herself and spoke quickly blindly . . . a network of feeling vibrated all over to and fro, painfully.

> "It only seems so to you," she said, in a voice muffled by the beating of her heart. Anything might happen—she had no control, having done her duty all her life . . . doing thing after thing had not satisfied her. There was something she had always wanted, for herself . . . even mother. . . .

The conversation continues and "a rain of tears comes down" her mother's cheeks as she says to Miriam,

> "You understand me?"
> "Of course."
> "You are the only one."
> The relieved voice . . . steady, as she had known it correcting her in her babyhood.
> "I should be better if I could be more with you . . . oh Lord . . . impossible.
> "You must be with me as much as you like."
> That was the thing. That was what must be done somehow (*Honeycomb*, 472-3).

Directly following this episode Miriam lights a cigarette in front of her mother whose face "crimsoned unresistingly" at the shocking sight. Miriam then gazes at her mother "boldly, admiring and adoring." We next learn that in this moment Miriam "felt she had embarked on her first real flirtation." Motivated by a desire to be close to and rescue from destruction the object of her "first real flirtation" and burdened by the responsibility of being "the only one" who can understand her mother, Miriam uses money given by brothers-in-law to take her insomniac mother, who "can't see the spring," to the seaside (*Honeycomb*, 475).

Before the journey Miriam anticipates a happy intimacy between them.

> The little bonneted figure . . . happy, shocked, smiling. To go about with her, telling her everything, dreadful things. The two of them going about and talking and not talking, and going about (476).

The rescue does not proceed as Miriam wishes. She and her mother share a room in a boardinghouse where Miriam makes nightly attempts to soothe and lull her mother to sleep by reading the Bible aloud. One night they finally fall asleep at two in the morning, but when Miriam awakes at five she finds that

> in the room yellow with daylight a voice was muttering rapidly, rapid words and chuckling laughter and stillness. Miriam grasped the bedclothes and lay rigid. Something in her led out and away

> refusing. But from end to end of the world there was no help against this. It was a truth; triumphing over everything. "I know," said a high clear voice. "I know . . . I don't deceive myself" . . . rapid low muttering and laughter. . . . It was a conversation. Somewhere within it was the answer. Nowhere else in the world. Forcing herself to be still, she accepted the sounds, pitting herself against the sense of destruction. The sound of violent lurching brought her panic. There was something there that would strike.

After deciding that someone else must know about the "truth" and extent of her mother's illness, Miriam falls asleep again and later awakes to

> the sound of violent language, furniture being roughly moved, a swift angry splashing of water . . . something breaking out, breaking through the confinements of this little furniture-filled room . . . the best, gentlest thing she knew in the world, openly despairing at last (*Honeycomb*, 487-88).

After this performance of her mother's "open despair," they visit an "old homeopathist" who tells Miriam "gravely," after seeing Mrs. Henderson, that "it is very wrong for you to be with her alone." He makes her promise to write for help and refuses a fee. In the following three paragraphs the chapter and *Honeycomb* come to a close.

> On the way home they talked of the old man. "He is right; but it is too late," said Mrs. Henderson with clear quiet bitterness, "God had deserted me." They walked on, tiny figures in a world of huge grey-stone houses. "He will not let me sleep. He does not want me to sleep.... He does not care."
>
> A thought touched Miriam, touched and flashed. She grasped at it to hold and speak it, but it passed off into the world of grey houses. Her cheeks felt hollow, her feet heavy. She summoned her strenghth, but her body seemed outside her, empty, pacing forward in a world full of perfect unanswering silence.
>
> The bony old woman held Miriam clasped closely in her arms. "You must never, as long as you live, blame yourself, my gurl." She went away. Miriam had not heard her come in. The pressure of her arms and huge body came from far away. Miriam clasped her hands together. She could not feel them. Perhaps she had dreamed that the old woman had come in and said that. Everything was dream; the world.. I shall not have any life. I can never have any life; all my days. There were cold tears running into her mouth. They had no salt. Cold water. They stopped.

> Moving her body with slow difficulty against the unsupporting air, she looked slowly about. It was so difficult to move. Everything was airy and transparent. Her heavy hot light impalpable body was the only solid thing in the world, weighing tons; and like a lifeless feather. There was a tray of plates of fish and fruit on the table. She looked at it, heaving with sickness and looking at it. I am hungry. Sitting down near it she tried to pull the tray. It would not move. I must eat the food. Go on eating food, till the end of my life. Plates of food like these plates of food.... I am in eternity... where their worm dieth not and their fire is not quenched (*Honeycomb*, 489-90).

Clearly something cataclysmic has happened in the blank space that separates the second paragraph from the last, but it is nearly impossible for the reader to glean exactly what. It is likely, based on "the sound of violent lurching," the sense that "there was something that would strike," the sounds of "violent language," and the feeling of "something breaking out," that the blank space contains the fruition of this rage. Because the narrator never directly states what has happened, the blank space between the paragraphs where the event resides gains the status of a secret or inarticulable loss. At the same time deliberately, and perhaps to some extent not consciously constructed, the blank as well as the ellipses in the text mark Richardson's lack of resolution or her inability, even from a twenty-year distance, to find words for the event. Capturing all of the above possibilities, Richardson also deploys the blank to mark the "world full of perfect unanswering silence" toward which Miriam's body paces in the line that precedes the blank.

The fluctuations in body size and boundary that are characteristic of the shrine-site passages are also present in the paragraphs quoted above. In the first of the three paragraphs Mrs. Henderson's statement, "God has deserted me," made while she and Miriam walk home from the homeopathist, leads to Miriam's vision of their physical tininess indicating their insignificance in the eyes of a "huge" God: "They walked on, tiny figures in a world of huge greystone houses." Their insignificance is confirmed in the last words that Mrs. Henderson speaks: "He does not care."

In the second paragraph the "touch" and flash of Miriam's thought signify a moment of hope, a possible escape in the form of the positive action to which a thought can lead, and a sense of volition in the face of feeling "tiny" and helpless. But the thought passes "off into the world of grey houses." With the passing of the thought the possibility of action passes and Miriam becomes dissociated from her body, which now seems "outside her, empty." Her body paces forward but something of the rest of her does not go forward with it.

Following the blank space on the page the language takes off from a more diachronic mode of description and enters an aurally mimetic and synchronic realm characteristic of other shrine-site passages. The descriptive complete statements at the beginning of the last paragraph arrive in a straightforward manner, one short line following another. By the sixth line of the paragraph, "Everything was dream; the world," the statements become less complete and often sound like dream utterances. The strange "far away" presence of "the bony old woman['s]" body, indicates the strange and extreme dissociation of Miriam's state of mind, which continues to be manifest in Miriam's experience of her own body as well: she clasps her hands together but "could not feel them."

After one of the last of the linear straightforward statements of the paragraph, in which Miriam wonders whether the old woman had actually come in and spoken to her or whether her presence had been a dream, the language increasingly mirrors Miriam's dreamlike, dissociated state of mind. The line, "Everything was dream; the world," marks Miriam's descent "down and down to the centre of being" where dream and the world outside of dream are undifferentiated. At this point the dramatic shift from third-person to first-person narrative points up sharply the opposites that are united in this world that is dream, or this dream that is the world. With this shift in the terms of identification, the reader, the author, and the subject converge in "I." In the statements, "I shall not have any life. I can never have any life; all my days," Miriam as a subject with volition asserts the vitality of her life and the urgency she experiences in feeling the threat of deprivation of life that arrives with her mother's death.

The presence of the "I" introduces a specific and immediate subjectivity. It is this subject who, in the following lines, perceives the sensations of her own tears and her own body, "moving with slow difficulty against the unsupporting air." These perceptions reproduce on the page, in short jolting fragments, the way in which Miriam's consciousness now moves like a film that has been slowed to a rate at which each individual frame is visible. This sense of hyper-dissociation and the difficult jolting motion that accompanies it is produced by the presence of opposites that unite to immobilize Miriam. For example, the air is "airy and transparent" while her body is "heavy" and "hot," and "light" and "impalpable." Though her body is "impalpable" like a "lifeless feather," it is also "the only solid thing in the world, weighing tons." The "tray of plates of fish and fruit on the table" present life through the sustenance they offer, while they also serve to contrast with their opposite—the vision of violent death that occupies Miriam. These oxymorons embody the extreme pair of opposites that inhabit her: the fact that the ultimate violence has sprung from the "best, gentlest thing she knew in the world." This "thing" is her mother, the original source of food, the one who offered life through the sustenance of her own body.

Gazing at the union of the most gentle and most violent things manifest by the plate of food in front of her, Miriam "looked at it heaving with sickness and looking at it." The emphatic repetition of "looked at" and "looking at" calls attention to the sight of the food and suggests that the "looking" has an extended duration in time. The repeated "looking" also suggests that it is more than simply food as sustenance that Miriam sees on the plates. She also sees the necessity of continuing to live for an extended duration—a necessity that makes her sick.

Even in the face of revulsion for the food Miriam recognizes that, as she states, "I am hungry." The passage previously discussed, from *Honeycomb*, also came to an end with Miriam's hunger, which was then converted into a desire to write. In this case the visceral act of wanting to eat, of knowing the necessity of eating, converts the immobility of her "lifeless," "impalpable," "heavy" body into motion. It makes her into an entity with desire, if not the desire to write, the desire at least to move. This is the small beginning of a desire to transform the death that surrounds her into something else.

The notion that eating could be a transformative act echoes the transubstantiation implied by the particular kinds of food present. The lines from the Gospels that closely follow also suggest transubstantiation since the Gospels are often read during communion. The presence of these Gospel lines strongly suggests that the fish on Miriam's plate is also symbolically the fish that Christ turned into loaves and the fruit is the fruit of the vine. In the Book of Mark, the same book from which the last lines of this chapter come, Christ twice performs the miracle of turning fish into loaves. He anticipates the more astonishing miracle involving bread and fruit a few verses later at the Last Supper, when he compares bread to his body and the fruit of the vine, wine, to his blood, implying that he will soon die and these symbols of his body will become the means of access to God.[62]

Although there was no belief in literal transubstantiation in either the Anglican church of Richardson's childhood or the teachings of the Quakers to which she had such a strong affinity as an adult, symbolic communion was a ritual practice in Anglicanism and had its counterpart in Quakerism.[63] For Anglicans, communion was a means of uniting with Christ, whom they conceived of as a symbolic corporate personality of which all were a part. Anglican communion included a meditation on the passions and wounds of Christ. The prayer "Wounds of Christ Hide Me," a twelfth- or thirteenth-century hymn, was often recited during communion as a concluding devotion in the Eucharist.[64] This hymn was reintroduced by the Oxford movement in Britain in the 1840s and was popular among almost all schools of British Anglicanism by the 1890s—when Richardson was in her late teens.

Without doubt there are strong links between Mrs. Henderson's wound, the lines from the Gospel anticipating Christ's crucifixion, and the references to transubstantiation. Possibly all of these echoed in the back of Richardson's mind with the words of "The Wounds of Christ" hymn from her past, or others containing similar sentiments. Although the Anglicans reacted against the literalness of communion, they maintained the sense that the wounds of Christ were known through communion and that to partake in the wounds was to participate in the passions of Christ. In the strong, mystical tradition of Anglicanism (which was widely influential by the turn of the century), suffering was not sought or welcomed but rather assimilated as having a purpose.

The connections between all of the conscious and unconscious Anglican, Quaker, and other associations that coalesce in the passage and are evoked by the suicide are impossible to pin down. Richardson herself probably did not know how they were linked. Nonetheless, it is clear that, among other things, the feeling presented in and leading up to the passage resonates with the emotions lodged in the hymn "Wounds of Christ Hide Me." The passage itself can be read as a meditation on the wounds of Christ, invoked by the open wound in Mrs. Henderson's throat. Some of the lines from the hymn sound like a small child petitioning a parent, and these speak particularly to the feeling portrayed in the passage: "Body of Christ, save me . . . In thy wounds hide me/Do not let me be separated from you," and—again invoking the potential transformation inherent in the notion of eating—"Blood of Christ inebriate me."[65] Miriam's statement "To write is to forsake life" also implies that, like the redemptive wounds of Christ, all deaths, and, by implication, especially this death of the mother, are for her closely allied with the transfer of word into flesh, flesh into word, or wound into writing. The following statement from Said sheds some light on these connections between writing, death, and transubstantiation.

> If Jesus is the father of the Christian community, every instance of writing signifies his death, or at least the transfer of spoken words to a written document and the community's ambivalent reaction to it. In either case, his presence is transmuted into or sacrificed for word, just as, conversely, he was the Word made flesh.[66]

A few pages before the lines from the Gospel are quoted at the end of this *Honeycomb* passage, Miriam complicates these connections between writing and death by making her attitude toward the Gospels quite clear. She sees the "something" that she believes her mother is "battling to get at" in the room around them. As she attempts to read her mother to sleep, she sees it "clear in the eye of the moon-ray; a real thing." Directly following these recognitions of a mysterious, holy, and yet not-Christian presence in the room, Richardson explains that

> some instinct led away from the New Testament. It seemed impossible to-night. Without consulting her listener, Miriam read a psalm. Mrs Henderson put down her cup and asked her to read it again. She read and fluttered pages quietly to tell the listener that in a moment there would be some more. Mrs Henderson waited, saying nothing. She always sighed regretfully over the Gospels and St. Paul, though she asked for them and seemed to think she ought to read them. They were so dreadful; the gospels full of social incidents and reproachfulness. They seemed to reproach everyone and to hint at a secret that no one possessed . . . the epistles did nothing but nag and threaten and probe. St Paul rhapsodized sometimes . . . but in a superior way . . . patronizing; as if no one but himself knew anything . . . (*Honeycomb*, 486).

But when Miriam begins instead to read Isaiah, something in the room "shifts" and a presence enters that lends a sense of peace and well-being to the atmosphere. Contrasting with this sense of peace evoked by the Old Testament pre-Christian lines from Isaiah, the later invocation of the Gospels, in the lines from the Book of Mark, is Richardson's indictment and critique of the attitudes of reproach and condemnation her mother has learned from the Gospels and internalized. Her mother's self-loathing was an attitude with which Richardson herself, perhaps, also wrestled at times.

The lines from the Book of Mark were probably not among the parts of the Gospels generally read during communion at the turn of the century (the Book of Matthew being an Anglican favorite at that time). Nonetheless, Mark would certainly have been read in private. Every devoted Anglican, which would include Mary Richardson and Mrs. Henderson, read the New Testament regularly. Rather than reading the Gospels aloud in church or during communion, Richardson, consistent with the Quaker tradition, would have more likely meditated on them silently and repeatedly.

In this *Honeycomb* passage, Miriam's hunger, which promises the possibility of desire for more than food, also presents the possibility, or necessity, of transforming the death of her mother into something else. Perhaps later it will be converted into writing, but now the death is transformed into an imperative incantation or prayer of sustenance and survival that begins, "I must eat the food." The repetition of these words in various combinations emphasizes the habitual recurrence of an act as basic as eating in order to remain alive. In the statement "Go on eating food, till the end of my life," Miriam acknowledges that she is doomed to live "till the end" of her life, with the necessity of eating and the necessarily internalized scene of this death. The food is also a sign of the hunger of her mother's soul which Miriam is unable to feed, just as she is now, in turn, nauseated at the idea of feeding herself. But as ellipses appear at the end of the passage and Miriam's broken thought-prayer gives way to the lines from Mark 9:42, it is clear that "the end," for Miriam, is now and that it will continue forever, because she is "in eternity . . . where their worm dieth not and their fire is not quenched." The eternity that she occupies is an ultimate reversal, or union of opposites, in which her life, instead of death, has become an eternal damnation. Her mother's death leaves her to face an eternal last supper. In Miriam's case it is the body and blood of her mother spilled on the floor that must be ingested as a communion. Her mother will live on in Miriam's writing while Miriam will continually die in order to write.[67]

Miriam's reference to writing as "the scene of labour" which is "a sacred place," suggests that Anglican notions regarding work may have been influential in the formation of Richardson's spiritual aesthetic, the elision of writing and death, and her notion that writing work is a means of transformation. In Anglican terms, work is not the good works of Catholic charity but rather, coming out of a more Benedictine tradition, to work is to pray. As the "middle way" between Catholicism and Protestantism, the Anglican tradition sees any work dedicated and offered to God as holy and a part of communion.[68] This view is captured in the first stanza of George Herbert's sonnet "The Elixir."

> 1 TEACH me, my God and King,
>
> In all things thee to see;
>
> And what I do in anything
>
> To do it as for thee.[69]

Although this kind of sentiment could be equally used to dignify domestic work and to keep women and servants in their places, it could also have contributed to Richardson's connecting of the work of writing with that of worship. In Richardson's terms, to write is to pray and although she does not dedicate this writing work to a Christian figure of divinity, her writing is certainly dedicated to a divine faith in that transformative stranger or strange thing.

Richardson's is a faith in the mysterious presence that filled the room as Miriam read from Isaiah—a presence to which Miriam tried to draw "the listener"—her mother's attention on Mrs. Henderson's last night. As a scene of writing, then, the death of Miriam's mother presents the urgent necessity of dedicated writing work as a means by which to remain in contact with a divine presence, a contact that, while it heightens the experience of being alive, is for Miriam and Richardson simultaneously a forsaking of life. The wound in Mrs. Henderson's body, like those in Christ's, is a corridor that can be entered through the dedicated holy work of writing. In this sense writing becomes a constant communion. Miriam's failure to bring her mother into contact with this divine presence is not a failure of writing. However, the parallel failure in Richardson's life may have contributed to the "longing for participation" that she describes in the Foreword as being even stronger than the "longing for publication." In addition, the use of the cinema as a scene through which to speak of writing and Richardson's repeated concern with various aspects of audience participation, of "compelling the creative consciousness of the audience," is an index of how much she wishes to make the "private devotion" of writing also a public communion. Although Miriam must journey alone to the sacred place, one destination of the journey is a return to others. The being alone and the return are not necessarily or always exclusive. Like other events in time for Miriam, they may occur simultaneously. The Quaker meeting is the perfect model of the kind of aloneness in accompaniment that Miriam seeks. To pray or read, alone and together, is also the kind of contact with divine presence in the company of books "that are the real people" that she and Richardson wish to evoke for their audience of reader-listeners.

Beyond the actual lines quoted from the Book of Mark in the end of the passage, there are many other ways in which the language and imagery from Mark resonate in the passage. The themes of this Gospel, healing and the forgiveness of sins, speak to that which Mrs. Henderson desperately needs. Her state resembles that of many of the supplicants in the Book of Mark who come to Jesus for help. Legion, for example, lived among the tombs and

> no one could bind him anymore, even with a chain; for he had often been bound with fetters and chains, but the chains he wrenched apart, and the fetters he broke in pieces; and no one had the strength to subdue him. Night and day among the tombs and on the mountains he was always crying out, and bruising himself with stones.[70]

Not only is Mrs. Henderson like Legion because she is bound, fettered, and damned, but Miriam too is like this man with an unclean spirit, whose name is "Legion" because he is "many." Miriam, whose identity is also myriad, or legion, is in danger of wounding herself or being wounded because she also "breaks out" and refuses to be "subdued." Christ is successful in subduing both Legion and Mrs. Henderson, but Miriam may prefer to be left wandering "night and day among the tombs and on the mountains . . . crying out,"—even if this means being bruised with stones.

In keeping with her preference for the Old Testament, Richardson may have identified more closely with the scribes that Christ warns the people to beware of in the Book of Mark.

> And in His teaching He said, "Beware of the scribes, who like to go about in long robes, and to have salutations in the market places and the best seats in the synagogues and the places of honor at feasts, who devour widows' houses and for a pretense make long prayers. They will receive the greater condemnation."[71]

In the midst of writing a long—indeed an epical—prayer, Richardson may have seen herself in this warning. If not committing a sin, she understood that in writing an epic in feminine prose she had at least heavily trespassed the white European male traditional norms that the Christ of the Gospels had come to represent. The sense of having sinned and of attempting to repent, which pervades the Gospels, pervades Mrs. Henderson's consciousness as well. Mrs. Henderson believes in her sin, which is confirmed by Christ's teachings and by years of humiliation and belittlement from her husband. As Jesus states in a parable, Mark (3:24), she is like "a kingdom divided against itself," who therefore cannot cast out Satan. She is the woman, also in Mark (5:24), "who had suffered much under many physicians, and had spent all that she had, and was no better but rather grew worse."

Directly following the phrase "where their worm does not die, and the fire is not quenched" in the Book of Mark, Christ states, "For every one will be salted with fire. Salt is good; but if the salt has lost its saltness, how will you season it? Have salt in yourselves, and be at peace with one another" (9:48).

But at the scene of her mother's death Miriam cries "saltless" tears, and by implication remains in a hell "salted with fire." Her saltless tears indicate that it is not Christ that she or Richardson believes will redeem them. As Miriam says, "Give up the idea of the divinity of Christ and remain religious" (*The Tunnel*, 233). Rather, it is the act of transubstantiation as manifest in "certain states of being that are favourable . . . to the state of composition" that they worship. Access to these "states of being" are manifest in verbs, metaphors, punctuation and other transformative figures of language, but not in the figures or social forms of Christianity (*Interim*, 402). In a tirade against society, and particularly men, including God (and by implication, Christ), Miriam states,

> If, by one thought, all the men in the world could be stopped, shaken, and slapped. There must, somewhere, be some power that could avenge it all . . . but if these men were right, there was not. Nothing but Nature and her decrees. Why was nature there? Who started it? If nature "took good care" this and that . . . there must be somebody. If there was a trick, there must be a trickster. If there is a god who arranged how things should be between men and women, and just let it go and go on I have no respect for him. I should like to give him a piece of my mind (*The Tunnel*, 220).

And a few paragraphs later:

> They despise women and they want to go on living—to reproduce—themselves. None of their achievements, no "civilization,"

> no art, no science can redeem that. There is no pardon possible for man. The only answer to them is suicide; all women ought to agree to commit suicide (*The Tunnel*, 221).

As *The Tunnel* was published in 1919, Richardson wrote these lines approximately twenty-four years after Mrs. Henderson's suicide in 1895. In Miriam's framework, suicide for women has become an answer to men's demand that women reproduce. The loudest "no" to men could be stated through the agreement of all women to commit suicide. Then there would be no more reproduction. Since it is the male desire to reproduce himself by means of women's bodies that Richardson and Miriam imply was responsible not only for Mrs. Henderson's suicide, but also in varying degrees and modes for the slow suicide or self-destruction practiced by many other women, a "no" to reproduction would be a "no" to men's use of women for their own ends. With Miriam's understanding of her mother's suicide as a gesture of volition, revenge, and retaliation committed within a society of "tricks" played on women by male "tricksters," it becomes possible to view the act as in some sense positive. Suicide, at least in its symbolic form of refusal to reproduce male "civilization," has become a potentially affirmative gesture.[72]

In her impulse to turn away from the New Testament and Christ as representative of male civilization, Miriam manifests Richardson's technique of feminine prose, which, as previously discussed, has more affinity with the absence of Christ and the polyvocity of the Old Testament than with the univocity of the New Testament. Since

> ...for Augustine linguistic multiplicity was the condition of the fall. The loss of a stable referent that grounds the literal and proper meaning of words is a manner of exile. . . . What Augustine seeks is the mode of knowing as being-and-having—not the endlessness of interpretation but the absoluteness of presence.[73]

As an exile, a legion and myriad subject, as well as a living metaphor or interpretation in action, Miriam is in search of the play of presence, not the "absoluteness of presence." But,

> Words for the Greek and Christian are at best only imitations of things; and Derrida stresses that all mimetic theories of language postulate an extralinguistic standard of correctness that privileges proper over figurative language, for figurative language is a departure from the (proper) norm whereby each word points univocally to its referent. Hence for Augustine, as for Christian thought in

> general, language is only a detour from the goal, from the atemporal union with God, the immediate vision of the whole.[74]

In the realm of Richardson's feminine prose where there is no univocal reference and no vision of a completed whole, it is not simply that figurative language is privileged over "proper" language, but that all language is figurative and all words are also things—not simply representations of things. Language is not a detour from the goal in the realm of feminine prose: it is both the goal and the means to the goal. That is, language is both the means to itself and the means to the silence beyond itself—the silence it produces is also within it. In this sense, suicide as a metaphorical act that removes a woman from service to Christ and to all of white male civilization is positive. Figurative suicide and multiplicity or fragmentation of the subject may be coextensive with linguistic disruption and may require, as in the case of feminine prose, the use of idiosyncratic punctuation that breaks apart univocal reference as an ideological as well as an aesthetic act. This may be particularly true of a suicide performed with a knife, so that the intact body is actually cut—almost cut into pieces. Along these lines, the non-naming of the suicide and the concealment of its circumstances, manifest in the text as a gap and by blank breaks between paragraphs, is consistent with the desire to use language to gesture towards the silence it makes.

Although for Miriam and Richardson "to write is to forsake life," the life that has been forsaken at the end of *Honeycomb* is also restored in the body of the book, which replaces the original body and voice and becomes itself a source of multiple messages. As in the case of the medieval Christian pilgrims who slept on books or tied written words to their bodies, Richardson's "holy writ" heals, or at least transforms, by written displacement.

As "spiritual exercise," one of the things that writing displaces is the past. Displacing the past, and, as if in response to the words of "the bony old woman" who holds Miriam after her mother dies—"You must never, as long as you live, blame yourself, my gurl"—Miriam says in *March Moonlight*, eight novel-chapters and many years after Mrs. Henderson's suicide is staged in *Honeycomb*,

> Will begin at once to smite if I pursue the pathway so suddenly opened last night. Towards the past. Inexhaustible wealth. Inexhaustible remorse. Why do they say distance lends enchantment? Distance in time or space does not lend. It reveals. Takes one into heaven, or into hell. From hell, heaven is inaccessible until one

> has forgiven oneself. So much more difficult than accepting forgiveness. Not God, but we ourselves, facing the perspective of reality, judge and condemn. Unforgiven we scuttle away into illusions. But, all the time, we know. We are perambulating Judgement Days. That will make Jean, the permanent forgiver, laugh till she weeps. But it is the truth. If one could fully forgive oneself, the energy it takes to screen off the memory of the past would be set free (*Honeycomb*, 607).

Because writing creates distance in time and space, it provides access to and "perspective" on the past. In this access resides the possibility of heaven, of forgiving oneself. In the shrine site in which Miriam walks on the "pavement of heaven," she and Richardson gain access to a heaven that is characterized by a polyglot merging of language, body, and place. This is what Miriam has called "metaphorocrasy," a state that requires "giving up thinking in words"—and perhaps in its giving up, in its giving over of the self, yields a state of self-forgiveness (*March Moonlight*, 607). When Miriam rides the train to Hanover in the *Pointed Roofs* passage, the first shrine site discussed, a play with and disruption of grammar and punctuation form the pavement that transfers Miriam to heaven. In the later scene of her mother's suicide, Miriam is plunged into hell with its potential for "inexhaustible remorse." Throughout the remaining novel-chapters, moments of heaven and hell are regained but none more extremely ecstatic in its merging or more desperate in its dissociation than these two sites in *Honeycomb*. Instead of screening off memory, the "spiritual exercise" of feminine prose "reveals" the events of the past. In these revelations, distance in time and space are mitigated and the possibility of returning to the scene of any past "crime" and forgiving oneself is presented. By providing release of the enormous energy required to screen off memories of the past, traveling through space and time by these methods of reading or writing can at least transform and reveal if not heal.

As a message from the dead as well as a powerful relic that emanates both from the inanimate dead body and the animate voice, Richardson's "spiritual exercise" serves as a conduit between the past and the present, heaven and hell, life and death, the wounds of the dead body and the work of the living. Richardson writes, for example, in between the echo of Mary Richardson's name and Miriam Henderson's name. Drawing from the death of Mary she produces the life of Miriam, providing her dead mother with an ulterior eternal life and death in the book she simultaneously provides herself with a subterfuge for the past that exists as long as she continues to write. Because, as Miriam states, a book is a "real person," it is possible for an ulterior eternal life to be produced in writing that has the enormous "real" power of physical presence.

This transformative writing, which gives the absent other voice and flesh, occurs in eternity where time retains no linearity and the delivery and reception of a message merge, making the listener and teller, the addresser and the addressee, heaven and eternal damnation, equally accessible. Describing the mysterious workings and the limnal status of writing as relic of the between, Miriam says,

> Some kind of calculation is at work, a sort of spiritual metronome, imperceptible save when something goes wrong. It operates, too, upon sentences. A syllable too many or a syllable too few brings discomfort, forcing one to make an alteration; even if the words already written are satisfactory. Perhaps everyone has a definite thought-rhythm and speech-rhythm, which cannot be violated without producing self-consciousness and discomfort?
>
> The whole process is strange. Strange and secret, always the same, always a mystery and an absence from which one returns to find life a little further on. . . . To open the book is to begin life anew, with eternity in hand (*Clear Horizon*, 352).

Writing, as a "mystery and absence . . . from which one returns," always stages for Miriam, in one form or another, the scene of the death of her mother, the loss of ecstatic and synesthetic moments in the sunlight or garden of her childhood, as well as a loss of a discrete sense of self. This last loss is a result of her absence or departure from mundane life when she writes—a loss that she both longs for and dreads. It is appropriate to this "strange" and "secret" writing, which always invokes absence, that the symbolic connection between the womb and tomb, thematically present in most shrines, becomes literalized for Miriam and Richardson through the womb-mother who turns herself into a tomb. As with actual shrines, there is nothing in these written shrines. The absence they signal, like the absence in a three-dimensional shrine, is marked by a dead body. The graphic marks of print on paper, rather than the usual tomb carvings on stone, give these absences spatial location in the text and leave evidence of the body that has fled. As is also true of physical shrines, to travel on pilgrimage to the site marked by this printed absence is highly compelling. The pilgrim's hope and promise that in the presence of the shrine something transformative will occur is also the hope of the reader. This hope and sense of promise emanating from a spatial location in the world or on the page is perhaps most fully illustrated by the medieval pilgrim's gesture of curling up in fetal position in the cave-like niches of a shrine. This desire to get as intimately close as possible to that which is not there, to the loss and the absence that the shrine marks, is pivotal to Richardson's spiritual aesthetics.

Using the kitchen knife that slit her mother's throat as a writing implement, Miriam presents the possibility of contact with an imaginary mother who may have never been, even in life, as well as the possibility of forgiving herself and her corporeal mother for the suicide. These options exist alongside the possibility of remaining eternally in the presence of the crime and eternally guilty. Neither Miriam nor Richardson indicate that the death of the mother and the issues surrounding it are necessarily redemptive, have been resolved or can be resolved. It is only possible to investigate the personal and social circumstances in which these events and issues are enmeshed. Richardson suggests that there is a danger of duplicating the conditions that caused the crime in exploring, in writing about, the conditions of the crime. In order to avoid this the investigation can only be conducted through the techniques of feminine prose, which, as a "search for hidden elements and correspondences, a tropism or 'wandering of meaning,'" is a mode by which to critique the male regiments without duplicating their practices and to simultaneously investigate the conditions of living and writing. It is no accident that a correspondence can be drawn, for example, between the elements that drove Mrs. Henderson to call her life "worthless" and one of Richardson's main obsessions throughout *Pilgrimage* and her other writings—the social devaluation of women by men.[75]

Following Miriam's mode of analysis, the connection between the unmentioned kitchen knife and the often-mentioned social-religious context is repeatedly explained in *Pilgrimage*, *Close Up*, and other critical writings in terms of men's inability to recognize the "atmosphere" that women create in their "being"—so different from the accomplishments that men achieve in their "becoming" (*Honeycomb*, 384; & "CP: The Film Gone Male," *Close Up*, March, 1932, 38). The violence of the suicide reflects a more widespread social violence, an erasure of women by men who are unable to recognize that women do anything. In this vein Richardson's technique of feminine prose also offers a method by which to contact the "being" that women do, a method that is not only a long prayer but also a mode of social analysis whose aim is to create an atmosphere conducive to heightened alertness—an alternative to the "doing" of the usual conventions of storytelling or analytic method. It is in this atmosphere that Miriam's acute pleasure in being able to "begin life anew" by opening a book is paralleled only by the eternity that is also "in hand" when she writes. She says, "When I write everything vanishes but what I contemplate" (*March Moonlight*, 637). In Miriam's view, we contemplate judgement days that won't arrive later but are instead the current days of our lives. It is, she says, "Not God, but we ourselves, facing the perspective of reality [who] judge and condemn" (*March Moonlight*, 607). Facing that which is seen in the "perspective" provided by distance in time and space, not God but we ourselves are revealed vanishing. That vanishing point is Miriam's destination and Richardson's vehicle. Vehicle and destination are fused in Miriam's words: "Travel, while I write, down to that centre where everything is seen in perspective; serenely" (*March Moonlight*, 619).

NOTES: PART III

1. It is evident that Miriam and Richardson were quite familiar with the Old and New Testaments. In her book *In Memory of Her, A Feminist Theological Reconstruction of Christian Origins*, Elizabeth Schussler Fiorenza suggests a reading of the New Testament that is parallel to some of the views of the New Testament expressed by Miriam.

> Call no one father
> for you have one father
> (and you are all siblings)
> (Matthew v. 9).
>
> This short injunction, "Call no one father, for you have one father," thus maintains the same relationships as did the saying in Mark 10:29-30. The new kinship of the discipleship of equals does not admit of "fathers," thereby rejecting the patriarchal power and esteem invested in them (150).
>
> . . . we must also see that the original logion did not merely address the Christian community and its relationships. It also enjoined the disciples of Jesus from recognizing any father authority in their society, because there is only one father. The social-critical potential of this saying with respect to all patriarchal structures has yet to be brought to bear upon societal-political change. The monotheistic fatherhood of God, elaborated in the Jesus traditions as the gracious goodness usually associated with a mother, must engender liberation from all patriarchal structures and domination if it is to be rescued from the male projection of patriarchy into heaven. Thus liberation from patriarchal structures is not only explicitly articulated by Jesus but is in fact at the heart of the proclamation of the basileia of God (Elisabeth Fiorenza, *In Memory of Her, A Feminist Theological Reconstruction of Christian Origins*, New York: Crossroad Press, 1983, 151).

Although Miriam is more interested in a polytheism than a monotheism derivative of either the Old or New Testaments, one of the main complaints she has about the New Testament is its reliance on the figure of Jesus as an ultimate patriarch. This may be one reason why she shows a preference throughout *Pilgrimage* for the Old Testament. Although the society of the Old Testament is patriarchal, the absence of an embodied man acting to represent God contributes perhaps to her sense of the Old Testament as more effective in evoking an abstract divine presence. This preference for the Old Testament is most powerfully demonstrated in the scene when Miriam is desperate to soothe her spiritually broken mother. She first reads to her mother from the New Testament, then Richardson states that "some instinct led away from the New Testament" and Miriam shifts to the Old, reading her mother a psalm (*Honeycomb*, 486).

2. See Susan Stanford Friedman's discussion of the development and use of the term "long poem" in which she "attacks" the name "long poem" because "in its seeming inclusive neutrality the term may obscure the exclusionary politics inherent in genre categories." From "When a 'Long Poem' is a 'Big Poem': Self-Authorizing Strategies in the Twentieth-Century Women's 'Long Poem,'" paper delivered at MLA 1986.

3. Jacques Derrida, "The Law of Genre," *Critical Inquiry*, 7 (Autumn, 1980) 57.

4. As Staley states,

> By 1907 when Richardson had escaped to a Quaker fruit farm on Windmill Hill on the coast of Sussex . . . she had moved in her thinking from anarchism and communism to socialism. She denied communism for its lack of attention to the individual. The Quaker philosophy introduced her to mysticism and to the quest for a reality that bypassed ordinary perception in order to establish a unity with the Absolute through supersensuous, non-rational processes. For the Quakers, the experience of mysticism "is not a gift of grace to a few, but possible to every man by virtue of his partaking of the spirit of God in himself" (Thomas Staley, *Dorothy Richardson*, Boston: Twayne, 1976, 23).

5. In "All of a Piece: Women's Poetry and Autobiography," Celeste Schenck states,

> Genre is more usefully conceived . . . as an overdetermined locus of political contention than a transcendental criterion or ideal type. . . . Moreover, beneath the western will-to-taxonomize lies not only a defensive history of exclusions constituting a political ideology, but also a fetishization of aesthetic purity . . . which has distinctly gendered overtones (*Life/Lines, Theorizing Women's Autobiography*, eds. Brodzki & Schenck, Ithaca and London, Cornell University Press, 1992, 283-84).

For a more detailed account of Richardson's views regarding the heavily gendered relations between women and the forms of art and attitudes they inherit and within which they must find a way to work, see Richardson's essay "Women in the Arts," *Vanity Fair*, no. 24 (May 1925), 100.

6. Teresa de Lauretis, *Alice Doesn't: Feminism, Semiotics, Cinema* (Bloomington: Indiana University Press, 1984), 109.

7. Albert Lord, *The Singer of Tales* (New York: Atheneum, 1960) and James Clifford "On Ethnographic Authority," in *The Predicament of Culture, Twentieth-Century Ethnography, Literature and Art* (Cambridge, MA: Harvard University Press, 1988).

8. Donald Howard, *Writers and Pilgrims, Medieval Pilgrimage Narratives and Their Posterity* (Berkeley, CA: University of California Press, 1980).

9. A tradition of pilgrimage and travel narratives by women existed but there is little evidence that Richardson was familiar with it. Some of the more significant women pilgrims were Egeria, who in the thirteenth century wrote a fascinating itinerary of her journey to Jerusalem; Lady Hester Stanhope; and Margery Kempe. From the late eighteenth century to the mid-nineteenth there was also a vital English tradition of female popular preachers practicing "cottage" religion. Its lynchpin was the female revivalist preachers, such as Ann Carr, Ann Cutler, Mary Barritt, and other traveling female evangelist preachers, who called for "sanctification of the home and embarkation upon a spiritual pilgrimage." *Egeria: Diary of a Pilgrimage*, translated and annotated by George E. Gingras, Ancient Christian Writers, no. 38 (New York: Newman Press, 1970); William Henry Davenport, *Celebrated Women Travellers of the 19th Century* (New York: E. P. Dutton, 1903), 14. Richardson does not refer specifically to these women preachers or this tradition although she does make a number of references to evangelicals for whom she finds little use: "Evangelicals are humanitarians; rushing about in Ulsters," she says in the quote from *Interim* that appears on the first page of Part III.

10. For an excellent discussion of the female spiritual bildung see Marianne Hirsch, "Spiritual Bildung: The Beautiful Soul as Paradigm," in *The Voyage In, Fictions of Female Development*, edited Abel, Hirsch and Langland (Hanover and London, Dartmouth College, University Press of New England, 1983), 23-48.

11. In a related and excellent discussion of the female bildungsroman, the introduction to *The Voyage* In states,

> The female developmental plot may engender other formal revisions of the bildungsroman. Novels that depict female apprenticeship and awakening not only alter the developmental process, but also frequently change its position in the text. The tensions that shape female development may lead to a disjunction between a surface plot, which affirms social conventions, and a submerged plot, which encodes

> rebellion; between a plot governed by age-old female story patterns, such as myths and fairy tales, and a plot that reconceives these limiting possibilities; between a plot that charts development and a plot that unravels it (*The Voyage In*, ed. Abel, Hirsch and Langland, Hanover and London: University Press of New England, 1983, 12).

12. Howard, *Writers and Pilgrims, Medieval Pilgrimages Narratives and Their Posterity*, 8-9.

13. There are of course many other turn-of-the-century instances of the use of this quest-travel-novel structure. Woolf's *The Voyage Out* and *To The Lighthouse*, Forster's *A Passage to India* and Joyce's *Ulysses* are only a few of the more widely known that come to mind.

14. Howard, 9.

15. The use of pilgrimage as an emblematic metaphor also reflects common modernist concerns with homelessness and worldliness. Some examples of travel literature by modernist women that feature these concerns are *Escapade* by Evelyn Scott, 1923; *The Yangtze Valley and Beyond* by Isabella Bird, 1896; *The Gobi Desert* by Mildred Cable, 1926; *The Desert and the Sown* by Gertrude Bell, 1905; and *The Story of an African Farm* by Olive Schreiner, 1927. See the bibliography for a more complete list of travel and pilgrimage narratives by women dealing with the issues of homelessness and worldliness. These issues are poles in the *Pilgrimage* novels operating on the levels of formal generic construction as well as operating to generate meaning metaphorically and thematically at the level of content.

16. Avrom Fleishman on Richardson's spiritual practice in *Figures of Autobiography: The Language of Self-Writing in Victorian and Modern England* (Berkeley, CA: University of California Press, 1983), 433.

17. Staley, *Dorothy Richardson*, 62.

18. Fleishman, *Figures of Autobiography*, 438.

19. This passage and many others throughout *Pilgrimage* resonate with Woolf's ideas and social critique put forth in *A Room of One's Own*, *Three Guineas* and elsewhere. In addition to the emphasis on a room of one's own and financial independence, some of the other most striking resonances between Richardson and Woolf include a shared attention to women as outsiders and to moments of transcendence. In addition to the discussions in the novels, Richardson's more formal critical discussion of these issues occurs in her essay "Women In the

Arts." This essay was published in May 1925 while *A Room Of One's Own* was published in 1929, and *Three Guineas* not until 1938. It is possible that Woolf's ideas are influenced by or derivative of Richardson's, or that Richardson anticipated Woolf in her critique of and concern with these issues. Indeed, perhaps she did. In her essay "Political Aesthetics: Virginia Woolf and Dorothy Richardson" in *Virginia Woolf: A Feminist Slant*, ed. Jane Marcus (Lincoln and London: University of Nebraska Press, 1983), Diane Gillespie articulates what I view as the most useful angle on this discussion.

> The similarities between a number of ideas Miriam expresses in *Pilgrimage* and Woolf's ideas are clear. Whether Woolf took ideas from Richardson or merely found in her work the expression of what she thought and felt herself is, in the final analysis, irrelevant. More important are the similarities of their views on the novel in theory, their divergences in practice, and the metaphysical-differences accounting for the divergence, all of which contribute to an understanding of political aesthetics (142).

20. Victor Turner, *Process, Performance and Pilgrimage: A Study in Comparative Symbology* (New Delhi: Concept, 1979), 53.

21. As Helsinger, Sheets and Veeder state, the vote was only granted to women in 1918. In addition,

> Some improvement [in women's legal position] was made with the Matrimonial Causes Act of 1884—a wife deserted by an adulterous husband could petition for divorce immediately instead of waiting two years, and the court could no longer imprison a wife for noncompliance with an order for restitution of conjugal rights—but the double standard [women treated simultaneously as chattel and as legal subjects] retained the force of law until the 1920s, in America as well as in England (Elizabeth Helsinger, Robin Lauterback Sheets and William Veeder, *The Woman Question, Society and Literature in Britain and America 1837 - 1883*, Chicago and London: University of Chicago Press, 1983, 21, 23, 37 & 55).

22. Friedman, "When a 'Long Poem' Is a 'Big Poem,'" 4-5.

23. Friedman, 8.

24. This notion of disruption, and the disruption that Richardson practices, is closely related to Irigaray's "mimicry." Mimicry is "an interim strategy for dealing with the realm of discourse (where the speaking subject is posited as mas-

culine), in which the woman deliberately assumes the feminine style and posture assigned to her within this discourse in order to uncover the mechanisms by which it exploits her" (Luce Irigaray, *This Sex Which Is Not One*, Ithaca, New York: Cornell University Press, 1985, 220).

In relation to the doubleness of the position of the pilgrim and the way in which it pivots on the polarity between the power of images of home and images of the unknown, Seidel states, "Exile sets in motion the allegory of separation that circles around to a differently disposed, perhaps even differently located, home. The typical exile in literature, although by nature a wanderer, is also by habit a homebody. Home is locus, custom, memory, familiarity, ease, security, sanctuary. And centuries of tradition do not alter the power of home as an image" (Michael Seidel, *Exile and the Narrative Imagination*, New Haven, CT: Yale University Press, 1986, 10). Richardson summons the allegorical power of the image of home by collapsing the acts of the "homebody" and the wanderer into one activity, that of wandering at home—either inside an actual room or as an exile wandering within her home city.

25. Fleishman, 86.

26. Fleishman, 428.

27. Fleishman, 430.

28. Paul de Man, *The Rhetoric of Romanticism* (New York: Columbia University Press, 1984), 67-8.

29. de Man, *The Rhetoric of Romanticism* , 69.

30. de Man, 70.

31. de Man, 73.

32. Elizabeth W. Bruss, *Autobiographical Acts: The Changing Situation of a Literary Genre* (Baltimore, MD: Johns Hopkins University Press, 1976), 164. This is a fascinating catalogue of "tendencies common" to autobiographies in general, not only because it so precisely describes *Pilgrimage*, but because it also describes the work of Proust, Joyce, some of Woolf, and, as stated above, that of many other modernists who were not deliberately writing autobiography. The reason for this similarity is related to the changing turn-of-the-century conceptions of the subject, which made the internal consciousness of the individual into a new and compelling territory for writing, particularly writing in the new genre of the novel.

33. Maurice Beebe, *Ivory Towers and Sacred Founts, the Artist as Hero in Fiction from Goethe to Joyce*, (New York: New York University Press, 1964), 13-14.

34. Grace Stewart, *A New Mythos, The Novel of the Artist as Heroine 1877-1977*, (Montreal, Canada; St. Albans, Vermont: Eden Press, 1981), 14-15.

35. Stewart, *The Novel of the Artist as Heroine 1877-1977*, 28.

36. Rose, Shirley, "Dorothy Richardson's Theory of Literature: The Writer as Pilgrim," *Criticism*, vol. XII, no. 1, (Winter, 1970), 33-35.

37. Regarding what can be called this "spiritual practice" or attitude, which recurs throughout *Pilgrimage*, Fromm states,

> The "conviction of the wonder of mere existence, the amazingness of there being anything anywhere," is at the philosophic root of *Pilgrimage*, for the sheer overwhelming presence of phenomena and their impact on a receptive sensibility (Gloria Fromm, "What Are Men to Dorothy Richardson?" in *Men and Women*, ed. Janet Todd, New York and London: Holmes and Meier Publishers, 1981, 177).

For an elaboration on one aspect of the experience that occurs in the shrine-site passages, see Shirley Rose's description of what she calls "moments privilégiés," in Shirley Rose, "Dorothy Richardson's Focus on Time," *English Literature in Translation*, vol. XVII, no. 3, (1974), 166.

For an excellent description of the way in which Miriam's contact with the miraculous is translated into Richardson's aesthetic practice see Diane Gillespie, who states:

> Feminine realism . . . reflects an all-encompassing, synthetic, fundamentally affirmative world view. It intuits that life is primarily changeless and stable, in the state of being. In this context a person's inner sense of living fully, joyfully in the all-inclusive present moment is most valuable. Life so experienced has a dimension that might be called spiritual. Such insight, which is the primary reality, is achieved not in conversation or in physical contact with other people, but in silent and usually solitary contemplation, enhanced at times by one's surroundings or by a similar awareness in someone else. Far more significant than any group to which he or she belongs is each individual's awareness or lack of awareness of this dimension. To foster it in others and to share it by means of her art is the task of the feminine realist. Such communication is not achieved by a superior person imparting knowledge to an inferior. It is achieved by equals collaborating in the discovery of

> a reality to which everyone has potential access. The feminine realist does not call attention to her skill and provide a barrier between the reader and the reality she perceives. Instead, she makes her awareness fully accessible in every element of her art (Diane Gillespie, "Political Aesthetics: Virginia Woolf and Dorothy Richardson," in *Virginia Woolf: A Feminist Slant*, ed. Jane Marcus, Lincoln and London: University of Nebraska Press, 1983, 142).

38. Douglas V. Steere, ed., *Quaker Spirituality, Selected Writings* (New York, Ramsey, Toronto: Paulist Press, 1984), 16-17.

39. Steere, *Quaker Spirituality*, 14.

40. Steere, 33.

41. Ronald Finucane, *Miracles and Pilgrims, Popular Beliefs in Medieval England* (Totowa, NJ: Rowan and Littlefield, 1977), 63.

42. I am indebted here to Susan Handelman's excellent discussion of these issues. Particularly illuminating is her statement,

> In Jewish tradition, there were references made in the aggadah to the preexistence of the Messiah and to a personified figure of wisdom. Paul then identified the preexistent wisdom with the preexistent Messiah and claimed that the revelation of the law of Moses and the birth of Jesus were two stages in the earthly revelation of the preexistent wisdom. The first stage was the written Torah, the second the body of Jesus: again the displacement of text or word to a literal body, a person. Paul even goes so far as to call Jesus "the image of the invisible God" (Col. 1:15; Heb. 1:3) (Handelman, Susan, *The Slayers of Moses*, Albany: State University of New York Press, 1982, 100).

43. In connection with this it is interesting to note the statements of two of Richardson's contemporaries, Mallarmé and Baudelaire. In "The Book: A Spiritual Instrument," Mallarmé describes physical aspects of a book as "The foldings of a book, in comparison with the large-sized open newspaper, have an almost religious significance. But an even greater significance lies in their thickness when they are piled together; for then they form a tomb in miniature for our souls." And Baudelaire, "A poet today, in the midst of this society which refuses to let him live, is a man who seeks out solitude in order to sculpture his own tomb." As quoted in *Ivory Towers and Sacred Founts*, Maurice Beebe (New York: New York University Press, 1964), 141.

44. Finucane, *Miracles and Pilgrims*, 198.

45. There is a plethora of possible examples to use to illustrate the "spiritual exercise" of feminine prose in *Pilgrimage*. In addition to the ones I have chosen, some other particularly exemplary passages include *The Trap*, page 498, a one-page chapter that is a beautiful poem in prose; the last chapter of *Interim*, which is one-page long and is the "poetry" that follows the statement "journey towards poetry" made close to the end of the preceding chapter; *The Tunnel*, pages 98-99; *Oberland*, page 124, another single-page chapter, which records the miracle of the moon seen out the window, and *March Moonlight*, the first two pages and the last chapter.

46. Susan A. Handelman, *The Slayers of Moses: The Emergence of Rabbinic Interpretation in Modern Literary Theory* (Albany, NY: State University of New York Press, 1982), xv.

47. Handelman, *The Slayers of Moses*, xv.

48. Alex Preminger, ed., *Princeton Encyclopedia of Poetry and Poetics* (Princeton, NJ: Princeton University Press, 1974), 217.

49. Preminger, *Princeton Encyclopedia of Poetry and Poetics*, 41.

50. In all of the following quotes I have tried to duplicate the spacing and typographical arrangement of words as they appear on the printed page as exactly as possible.

51. Victor Turner, *Dramas, Fields and Metaphors; Symbolic Action in Human Society* (Ithaca, NY: Cornell University Press, 1974), 42.

52. One of the main things, among others, that distinguishes Miriam from these "strange people" is their ability to buy these things and hers to only look in at the things through the window. As previously stated and shortly to be discussed in more detail, Miriam was acutely sensitive to issues of class. She and Richardson are linked by this feeling of being exiled or alienated by the social norm and from a kind of access to social privilege represented by class status. All of this becomes complexly layered with both Miriam and Dorothy's relationship to their fictional and actual fathers. In both cases the father went bankrupt and could thus be seen to be responsible for many of the difficult circumstances of their lives. These circumstances are mapped as the itinerary of Miriam's work life throughout *Pilgrimage*—an extremely difficult trail from one typical working-class job available for a woman of her time to another. In Miriam's eyes they were all trivial and demeaning and represented the fateful fall from better social standing. Perhaps the worst element of this for Richardson and Miriam was that the need for constant employment invaded drastically on writing time.

Much work remains to be done regarding the way in which *Pilgrimage* is itself a symptom of a particular turn-of-the-century white, middle to working-class female subjectivity. Investigation in this direction might develop some of the reasons for the lack of almost any mention of race in *Pilgrimage* while such a sharp gender critique is present alongside a critique of class that is less overtly sharp. Most of the discussion of "otherness" in *Pilgrimage* is concerned with Jews. The lack of blatant discussion of anyone else or any other situation probably duplicates the circumstances of Miriam's own race, class and social position. The silence is certainly in itself a symptom of a particular kind of racism. For a highly useful discussion of Modernism and Judaism see Gillian Rose, *Judaism and Modernity: Philosophical Essays*, (Oxford, U.K.; Cambridge, Mass., U.S.A.: B. Blackwell Publishing, 1993).

53. In terms of a literary tradition in which writing is viewed as a figure of and sometimes an actual suicide, there are many examples from which to draw. This is particularly true of Richardson's time, the turn of the century. Some of the following statements of Mallarmé especially echo those of Miriam and Richardson.

> Mallarmé went beyond self-worship in his ideal of the poet, who "having to read from the book of himself" since it is the only one he has, yet strives ultimately to efface himself. . . "All he can do is work in mystery with an eye to the future or to eternity, and occasionally send his visiting card, a few stanzas, or a sonnet to the 'living,' so they won't stone him, should they suspect him of realizing that they do not exist." If "to create is to conceive an object . . . in its absence," then the source of beauty is *le neant*: "After I had found Nothingness, I found Beauty." Mallarmé's equation of music with silence is not unrelated to the belief developed by Villiers and Huysmans that to desire nothing is to possess everything. Joseph Chiari has summed up his aim in poetry: "Each poem is a new philosophical suicide of the poet's self, a kind of phoenix-like operation to rise from nowhere to nowhere." According to Fowlie, his culminating ritual was that of the absent master who consecrates his work by disappearance. In abandoning himself to *le neant*, in becoming indifferent to self as well as to society, Mallarmé goes beyond Baudelaire and all artists who remain trapped in self. If the ultimate form of alienation is suicide, then "Mallarmé's poetry, dependent as it is on the disappearance of the poet and the effacement of objects so that only the idea remains, is a testimony beyond the frontier of life (As discussed and quoted in Maurice Beebe, *Ivory Towers and Sacred Founts, the Artist as Hero in Fiction From Goethe to Joyce*, New York: New York University Press, 1964, 142-43).

There are also some ways in which Mallarmé's attitude dramatically departs from an attitude toward writing that might have interested Miriam or Richardson. Among others, one major reason for the departures is their different gender positions. While these aesthetic practices and proclamations were bold and heroic coming from a turn-of-the-century male poet, similar statements from a turn-of-the-century female poet or novelist would most likely have been labeled hysterical and delusionary.

54. *Pilgrimage* is redolent with what Norman O. Brown calls "polymorphous perversity."

> Symbolism is polymorphous perversity, the translation of all our senses into one another, the interplay between the senses, the metaphor, the free translation. The separation of the senses, their mutual isolation, is sensuality, is sexual organization, is bondage to the tyranny of one partial impulse, leading to the absolute and exclusive concentration of the life of the body in the representative person (Norman O. Brown, *Love's Body*, New York: Vintage Books, 1968, 249).

In Brown's terms Miriam is "the representative person" of *Pilgrimage*. The life of her body is the narrative sexual organization of the text in which polymorphous perversity is constantly re-enacted.

55. Grace Stewart, *A New Mythos, the Novel of the Artist as Heroine 1877-1977*, (Montreal, Canada; St. Albans, VT: Eden Press, 1981), 114.

56. Jane Gallop, "Carnal Knowledge," in *Thinking Through the Body* (New York and Oxford: Columbia University Press, 1988), 138 & 152.

57. For a related but somewhat different discussion of images of birth in *Pilgrimage* see Shirley Rose, "The Unmoving Center: Consciousness in Dorothy Richardson's *Pilgrimage*," *Contemporary Literature* (Madison, WI: University of Wisconsin Press, vol. X, no. 3, 1969), 375-76.

58. Roman Jakobson, "Closing Statement: Linguistics and Poetics," in *Style in Language*, ed. Thomas Sebeok (Cambridge, MA: Massachusetts Institute of Technology Press, 1960), 355.

59. With regard to the way in which the death of the other becomes a motivation for writing, in his book *Hour of Our Death* Aries describes the change at the turn of the nineteenth century in the cultural attitude toward death. Attention shifted away from "the sense of a universal and common destiny and the sense of a personal and specific biography" in favor of the "sense of the other."

> But this was not just any other. Affectivity, formerly diffuse, was henceforth concentrated on a few rare beings whose disappearance could no longer be tolerated and caused a dramatic crisis: the death of the other. It was a revolution in feeling that was just as important to history as the related revolutions in ideas, politics, industry, socioeconomic conditions, or demography.
>
> An original type of sensibility now came to dominate all others, a type that is well expressed by the English word privacy. It found its place in the nuclear family, remodeled by its new function of absolute affectivity. The family replaced both the traditional community and the individual of the late Middle Ages and early modern times. Privacy is distinguished both from individualism and the sense of community, and expresses a mode of relating to others that is quite specific and original.
>
> Under these conditions, the death of the self had lost its meaning. The fear of death, born of the fantasies of the seventeenth and eighteenth centuries, was transferred from the self to the other, the loved one.
>
> The death of the other aroused a pathos that had once been repressed. The ceremonies of the bedroom or of mourning, which had once been used as a barrier to counteract excess emotion—or indifference—were deritualized and presented as the spontaneous expression of the grief of the survivors. But what the survivors mourned was no longer the fact of dying but the physical separation of the deceased. On the contrary, death now ceased to be sad. It was exalted as a moment to be desired (Philippe Aries, *The Hour of Our Death*, trans. Helen Weaver, New York: Vintage Books, Random House, 1982, 609-610).

The influences of the cultural ideology that Aries here describes can be seen in Richardson's attitude toward writing as a kind of death, in that the death that is required in order to write is "exalted as a moment to be desired." By extension, though she did not literally desire her mother's death (in fact, as Aries states, she acutely feared the death of the other, in this case her mother), this death of a "rare being whose disappearance could not be tolerated" caused a "dramatic crisis," which Richardson and Miriam could look forward to converting into writing. Though not wished for in advance, in retrospect the death was productive in the sense that it generated writing. Miriam's and Richardson's writing in response to the crisis of losing the other was a ritualized ceremony of mourning for the physical separation between the originally merged bodies of mother and daughter.

The "stranger" takes on many different and recurring forms in *Pilgrimage*, especially that of the evil man who appears out of nowhere while Miriam bicycles alone down a country lane, or walks the streets of London alone. There is also a strong resonance between Richardson's stranger—the "strange thing for which there were no words," and her sense of death as fertile—and Neville's way of speaking about Percival's death in Woolf's *The Waves*. Neville says, "'Percival, by his death, has made me this present, has revealed this terror, left me to undergo this humiliation'" (Virginia Woolf, *The Waves*, London: Penguin, 1931), 136. And a few pages later he says, "'Like' and 'like' and 'like'—but what is the thing that lies beneath the semblance of the thing? Now that lightning has gashed the tree and the flowering branch has fallen and Percival, by his death, has made me this gift, let me see the thing'" (139). Perhaps Woolf's and Richardson's common Anglican backgrounds together with their shared historical moment contributed to the similarity of these statements about and approaches to the "thing" revealed by, invoked by, death—this terrible "present."

60. From a letter titled, "Notes to Susan" from Barbara Guest, November 1989. Barbara Guest, *Herself Defined: The Poet H.D. and Her World*, (Garden City, New York: Doubleday and Co., 1984).

61. The parallel circumstances of the death of Richardson's mother, Mary Richardson, as recounted by Fromm, are extensively quoted in the Appendix.

62. The story of the Last Supper occurs in the Gospel According to Mark, Chapter 14.

> And as they were eating, he took bread, and blessed, and broke it, and gave it to them, and said, "Take; this is my body." And he took a cup, and when he had given thanks he gave it to them, and they all drank of it.
>
> And he said to them, "This is my blood of the covenant, which is poured out for many. Truly I say to you, I shall not drink again of the fruit of the vine until that day when I drink it new in the kingdom of God (*The New Oxford Annotated Bible with the Apocrypha*, ed. H. May and Bruce Metzger, New York: Oxford University Press, 1973, 1235).

63. Emmanuel de Mendieta, *Anglican Vision* (London: The Talbot Press, S.P.C.K, 1971), 86-88.

64. de Mendieta, *Anglican Vision*, 30-31.

65. The complete text of the hymn in Latin reads:

Aspirationes ad Ss.mum Redemptorem

Anima Christi, sanctifica me.
Corpus Christi, salva me.

Sanguis Christi, inebria me.
Aqua lateris Christi, lava me.
Passio Christi, conforta me.
O bone Iesu, exaudi me.
Intra tua vulnera absconde me.
Ne permittas me separari a te.
Ab hoste maligno defende me.
In hora mortis meae voca me.
Et iube me venire ad te,
ut cum Sanctis tuis laudem te
in saecula saeculorum.
Amen.
(*Hymns Ancient and Modern*, ed. Biggs, Rev. Couciar, for use in the Services of the Church, London: Novelle and Co., 1867, 202).

66. Edward Said, *Beginnings: Intention and Method* (Baltimore, MD: Johns Hopkins University Press, 1975), 201.

67. In a discussion of these "feeding miracles" and an elaboration on their redactional context Fiorenza illuminates some parallels between the original story and that of Miriam and her mother. Particularly striking is that of the mother and daughter presence. If Richardson was aware of this version of the story this may explain part of her reason for choosing this passage in addition to the more evident reasons related to spiritual hunger and the "eucharistic overtones" so present here. As Fiorenza says,

> If Mark 7:24a is Markan redactional introduction, the original story is located in Galilee. The woman is characterized ethically and culturally as a gentile. Her daughter (her future?) is in bondage to evil and she expects liberation from Jesus. The Greek verb *chortasthenai* ("become satisfied") connects the story with the two messianic pre-Markan feeding miracles, insofar as this verb is only found in Mark here and in 6:42, 8:4, 8). The feeding miracles have strong eucharist overtones which are toned down by Mark. The argument, then, that the children (Israel) should be fed and that their food should not be taken from them and given to the dogs (gentiles) is countered by the woman by referring to the messianic abundance of Christian table community. The gracious goodness of the God of Jesus is abundant enough to satisfy not only the Jews but also the gentiles. The power of the basileia liberates not only the "children" of Israel but also the woman-child who, as a female and as a gentile, is doubly polluted and subject to the "bondage" of ritual impurity (Elisabeth Schussler Fiorenza, *In Memory of Her, A Feminist Theological Reconstruction of Christian Origins*, New York: Crossroad, 1983, 137-38).

68. This notion also runs through the writings of Christian mystic Evelyn Underhill. As her popular contemporary, Richardson was familiar with Underhill's work. Some especially resonant passages regarding work and any act from the smallest to the largest as potential prayer, include the following—the first from her pamphlet published by the Y.W.C.A. in 1926, called "Prayer"; and the second, "Possibilities of Prayer," published in 1927 in *Theology*:

> They begin to realize what Brother Lawrence meant when he talked of "the practice of the presence of God"; a practice, he said, which brought God as near to him when he was busy cooking . . . as when he was in church.
>
> This means a life in which even the smallest and simplest actions have about them something of the quality of worship; in which, like the old scholar in the story, whether absorbed in work or absorbed in prayer, we are "still on the same old terms."

and from "Possibilities of Prayer:"

> Christianity has always taught that work of any kind can be a prayer; but it will not be a prayer unless we make it so, by doing it within the atmosphere of Eternity. In those who do this, physical and mental labor, as well as direct spiritual labour, can become the vehicles of spiritual action. All their odd jobs get woven into their life of prayer; and they can imitate without insincerity the holy woman who boiled her potatoes for the intentions of those for whom she had not time to pray.

Both pamphlets republished in *Modern Guide to the Ancient Quest For the Holy*, ed. Dana Greene (Albany, NY: State University Press of New York, 1988), 142 & 157.

69. George Herbert, "The Elixer," in *Hymns Ancient and Modern*, ed. Rev. Couciar Biggs, 293.

70. Mark 5:3, *New Oxford Annotated Bible*.

71. Mark 12:38.

72. Thinking along similar lines to those proposed by Miriam in the above quote, Hirsch discusses the frequent pattern of resolution by death, often suicide, found in the female spiritual bildung.

> How are we to read these deaths . . . ? It is here that feminist criticism faces one of its most difficult and value-laden questions. Seen in the context of the Bildungsroman's valorization of

> progress, heterosexuality, social involvement, healthy disillusionment, "normality," adulthood, these deaths are pointless, violent, self-destructive. Yet if we look at what adulthood and maturity mean for the female protagonists of these texts, at the confinement, discontinuity, and stifling isolation that define marriage and motherhood, they do not present positive options. Traditional criticism sees the Beautiful Soul, Maggie, Effi, and Edna as neurotic women, afraid of adulthood and sexuality. To adopt this view is to ignore the limited possibilities offered by their societies. I submit that the heroines' allegiance to childhood, pre-Oedipal desire, spiritual withdrawal, and ultimately death is not neurotic but a realistic and paradoxically fulfilling reaction to an impossible contradiction. By showing death to be the only viable response to deep inner needs, these texts lead us to question the very values of Bildung itself, as it has traditionally been understood. Positing a different sexuality (one which erases the distinction between self and other, subject and object) and a different notion of self (marked by attachment rather than separation), this withdrawal, I would argue, is a renunciation in a limited sense only: in another, it emerges as a different kind of affirmation (Marian Hirsch,"Spiritual Bildung: The Beautiful Soul as Paradigm," *The Voyage In, Fictions of Female Development*, ed. Abel, Hirsch and Langland, Hanover and London: Dartmouth College, University Press of New England, 1983, 27-28).

Whether or not it is possible or desirable to view suicide as redemptive, the above discussion raises the issue of the relationship between Miriam and Mrs. Henderson and the kinds of emotional violence or pain embedded in this mother and daughter relationship. I have only barely begun here to touch on the complexities of their relationship. In her study of the novel of the artist as heroine, Stewart states,

> As I read these novels, I find one common experience that informs them. All women are daughters. Some are mothers. The mother/daughter relationship is often central to the novel of the artist as heroine (Stewart, *A New Mythos*, 41).

Stewart goes on to discuss this in the psychoanalytic terms of separation, individuation and object loss which are experienced so differently for female than for male children. Elaborating on this complexity specifically in terms of Miriam and her mother, she says,

> When Miriam is intellectually befuddled, her mother cannot relieve her distress: "She had no reasoning power. She could not help because she did not know" (I, 169). The mother who has lived a life of pain, suffering, and self-abnegation offers only this

advice to Miriam as an entry into femininity: "Don't go so deeply into everything, chickie. You must learn to take life as it comes." (I, 169) . . . .If she is to appear feminine, Miriam believes that she must appear brainless. Consequently she begins to identify positionally with her father's worldliness, his interest in ideas (Stewart, 57).

Thus Miriam's relationship to her mother is highly ambivalent and at the same time charged with an intensity of intimacy which Mrs. Henderson does not share with her other three daughters and which Miriam shares with no one else. It is Miriam whom Mrs. Henderson wishes to accompany her in the worst of her breakdown. This may be partly because Miriam represents one who has escaped from the very issues which torment Mrs. Henderson and make her feel like a failure. However, Mrs. Henderson is not critical of social institutions themselves or her husband—both of which have caused her to believe she has failed. Instead she is critical of herself. Miriam sees her mother's illness as a response to circumstances bigger than herself and in this sense her mother's life serves as a negative model, a model to vehemently avoid duplicating.

Just as Miriam often fills the role of mother in relation to men with whom she is intimate, she is also often in the role of mother to her mother. Her ambivalence about this and about the kind of model and options Mrs. Henderson represents, and in turn, Mrs. Henderson's mutual ambivalence about Miriam is exemplified in the previously discussed scene of Miriam's smoking. The mother and daughter are having an intimate conversation when Miriam says, "Mother! Would you mind if I smoke a cigarette?" In response Mrs. Henderson was "shocked and ashamed and half delighted." Her delight may express the pleasure and hope she feels at having an extraordinary daughter like Miriam who has deviated from the predictable strangulations of female social roles, but her shock perhaps cuts both ways. She is shocked in pleasure at Miriam's deviation, and shocked in shame. Her heavy identification with this closest and most unique of her daughters may be based on how exceptional Miriam is, how exceptionally well Mrs. Henderson feels understood by Miriam. But the half of her response manifest in shock and shame may also be triggered by the sense of her own failure as an ideal woman which she sees reproduced in Miriam. She also may fear for Miriam (as she does for herself)—what will become of her in these hostile surroundings?

Although the terms of her identification are complicated, Miriam's allegiance is with her mother as opposed to her father. As Richardson's father was fond of calling Dorothy his only son, Miriam in turn says, "...I am my mother's son for ever. If there's a future life, all I care for is to meet her. If I could have her back for ten minutes I would gladly give up the rest of my life..." (*Deadlock*, 220).

73. Handelman, 120.

74. Handelman, 120.

75. In this vein, the only other suicide mentioned and discussed in any detail besides that of Miriam's mother is the suicide of Miriam's young Russian friend Olga in the end of *March Moonlight*, the last novel-chapter. The suicide is triggered by Olga's romantic disappointment and despair about life within and outside of Russia and by a bad love affair. It is committed in Paris at night.

Olga drags a settee out onto her balcony, drinks a bottle of veronal and lies down in her nightgown, soon to lose consciousness. The similarity between the image of Olga dying in a reclining position on a settee and many of the images of women in pre-Raphaelite paintings, particularly those by Rosetti, is striking. On Richardson's part this similarity may have served the purpose of invoking a currently popular and romantic image of women in a passive pose in order to critique and comment on it. Distinct from the shadowy mode in which the details of Mrs. Henderson's suicide were presented, the circumstances and details of this suicide are overtly chronicled. Miriam receives a postcard from Olga mailed on the day of the suicide that reads:

> This picture by Rodin shall show you where I have been. In a world so beautiful that I can no more return to the world-life as before. To you alone I can say good-by, with the words of your so wonderfoll [sic] Mr. Wells: "Perhaps there are better dreams."
> *The Sea Lady*
> (*March Moonlight*, 644).

Miriam's response to this suicide is dramatically different from her earlier response. She is saddened, but the suicide also becomes an occasion to ruminate about the natures of love.

> Love carried her [Olga] into a temporary eldorado. But sex-love dies unless it grows, for both partners, towards universal love. Meanwhile it is comedy for onlookers, who yet share and rejoice in its beginnings, whether or no they have themselves experienced them. So various in their similarities (*March Moonlight*, 644).

APPENDIX

Richardson was born in Abingdon, an old market town in England, on May 17, 1873. Having had two daughters already, her father, Charles Richardson, wanted a boy. He was disappointed to get Dorothy but, as Fromm states, "after his fourth daughter was born in 1874, . . . [he] took to referring to his third [Dorothy] as his son."[1] Charles and Dorothy's mother, Mary, were brought up Nonconformist. Charles rejected his family's Nonconformism early, and Mary converted to Anglicanism soon before marrying Charles. Charles was interested in Anglicanism for the worldly pleasure it emphasized and the social standing it provided. His parents did not approve of these reasons for religious conversion.

Charles Richardson's father was a successful wine and provisions merchant. In 1874 he died and Charles inherited the business and the house in which he grew up. He sold them, since trade and all association with it disgusted him. Charles interested himself in current scientific discussion and attended meetings and lectures at Oxford as well as becoming a member of the British Association for the Advancement of Science. He was a conservative gentleman and ran his house according to strict rules and proper rituals. Seventeen years after receiving his inheritance, Richardson declared bankruptcy. When later fictionalized by Dorothy, this moment of Charles Richardson's bankruptcy becomes the moment at which *Pointed Roofs*—the first "chapter" of *Pilgrimage*—opens. Paralleling Dorothy's actual decision, in the beginning of *Pointed Roofs*, Miriam makes the decision to become financially independent for the rest of her life and begins, as did Dorothy, by going off to Germany to be a teacher and governess.

Before Charles Richardson lost his money, the four daughters were brought up in a typically turn-of-the-century middle-class manner. They were sent to upper-middle-class girls schools of the time. Dorothy studied mathematics, science, German, French, Shakespeare, English history, and pianoforte which was her favorite subject. It is not surprising, then, that piano playing is a recurring symbolic theme in *Pilgrimage*. Geography was her least favorite subject, since it seemed to her to be "unrelated to anything else on earth." Because of her dislike she was moved to an innovative class in logic and psychology. She enjoyed the logic, but the psychology made her "uneasy."[2]

The Richardson daughters belonged to a club where they played tennis and went to parties and dances. They rowed in the spring, skated on the Thames in the winter, and, as the century turned and it became more acceptable, they learned to bicycle.

The Henderson family in *Pilgrimage* is structured almost exactly like the Richardson family. Miriam, like Dorothy, is the third of four daughters. Dorothy's parents, Charles and Mary, appear in *Pilgrimage* as Mr. Henderson, or Pater, and Mrs. Henderson, or Mother. In *Pilgrimage*, Dorothy's older sister Richie is named Eve, her younger sister Jessie is named Harriett, and her oldest sister Kate is named Sarah. Dorothy was born in Abingdon and Miriam in Babington. Some of these name changes were difficult for Dorothy. In the original manuscript, for example, she alternated between Babingdon and Babington for the name of Miriam's birthplace. She moved the family's first big house, originally in the London suburb of Putney, to Barnes, a suburb along the Thames. The Henderson family, like the Richardson family, was in trade. In *Pilgrimage* the family is Wesleyan Methodist, while the original family was Anglican. All of this information is conveyed in the process of revealing Miriam's character in *Pointed Roofs*.

One of the most important events in Richardson's life, that of her mother's suicide, barely appears in *Pilgrimage*. Richardson maintained an extraordinary silence regarding the suicide, both in her life and in *Pilgrimage*. There are no recorded conversations about the episode and no mention of it in journals or letters. Neither is it clear from the available biographical information or from the novels how Richardson resolved this cataclysmic event sufficiently to carry on a highly functional life. Possibly she did not resolve it at all.

The suicide is the last event described in *Honeycomb*, the third novel-chapter of *Pilgrimage*, but it is reported so subtly that it could be missed, or misconstrued. After Richardson worked as a teacher and governess in Germany, she returned to London and taught in a girls school. These experiences are captured in *Pointed Roofs* and *Backwater*, the first two novel-chapters. During the time in which Richardson was teaching in London, her mother had another in a series of severe nervous breakdowns. Richardson accompanied her to a seaside resort in order to escape from her detested job and to help her mother recuperate. As Mary was more attached to Dorothy than to anyone else in the world, the family pinned its last hope of Mary Richardson's recovery on Dorothy's being with her.

This same family hope and close relationship is repeated in *Pilgrimage*. In the book, the moment of the suicide is indicated by a blank space on the page the size of a narrow paragraph. In the passage following that space, Miriam returns from a short and desperately needed walk and finds her mother dead. The landlady of their hotel then enters and embraces Miriam, saying, "You must never, as long as you live, blame yourself, my gurl," but Miriam does blame herself (*Honeycomb*, 489). The fact that her mother slit her throat with a kitchen knife, as well as other details of the suicide, are omitted from *Pilgrimage*. After the landlady's embrace Miriam says, "Everything was dream; the world. I shall not have any life. I can never have any life; all my days" (*Honeycomb*, 489). It is then nearly impossible for Miriam to move her body which suddenly feels leaden, and she is unable to eat or imagine ever eating again. After this last paragraph of *Honeycomb*, *Pilgrimage* contains no further direct mention of, or direct reaction to, the suicide. Describing the event, Fromm provides some context:

> Lodgings were rented at 11 Devonshire Terrace in Hastings, and Dorothy and her mother arrived there late in November. The sea was rough, the air somewhat cool, but after a few days Dorothy thought her mother looked better. She did not leave her alone for a moment. There was always something her mother needed done for her or something she wanted to try to express. At night Mary Richardson found it hard to sleep. Dorothy heard her moans and tried to reassure her: she was not stupid, she was not sinful, she was not eternally damned. Dorothy wanted desperately [sic] to convince her mother of all this, but Mary Richardson had accumulated nearly thirty years of evidence to the contrary. And precisely because her husband would have found it incontrovertible proof of her stupidity that she believed in damnation, she was absolutely certain of both. Dorothy herself wanted to cry out in loathing and anguish. Instead, she went out one morning, to escape. It was Saturday, November 30. Hastings was quiet, the season long over. Dorothy wandered about for an hour or so, hoping to still the pounding in her head and erase from her mind's eye the image of self-loathing that was her mother's entire being, hoping she would not herself go mad. When she got back to Devonshire Terrace, her mother was dead. Somehow she had laid her hands upon a kitchen knife and cut her throat with it. She was fifty-two years old; Dorothy was twenty-two.[3]

Another significant event of Richardson's life that does not enter into *Pilgrimage* is her marriage. *Pilgrimage* ends before Miriam marries, although her marriage is imminent. As Richardson was married during the time in which she wrote part of *Pilgrimage*, and she wrote about almost all other events of her life, this omission stands out. It is in *March Moonlight*, the last novel-chapter, that Miriam meets her fiancé, Mr. Noble, the ironically named alias for Alan Odle, the man who became Richardson's husband. Dorothy and Odle married in 1917, when she was forty-four and he was twenty-nine. *Honeycomb* was published that year, and Richardson was in the midst of writing *The Tunnel*. Odle was quite ill when they married, and after he died she wrote to Henry Savage, "If at the time I had had the remotest inkling of the possibility of his surviving me, I would never have consented to marry him."[4] Perhaps the ambivalence about her marriage expressed in this statement contributed to her decision not to include Miriam's married life in *Pilgrimage*.

Dorothy Richardson and Alan Odle were so poor and Alan's health so bad that they lived in Cornwall in cheap rental cottages in the off season, winter, and in a few rented rooms in London in the summers. Alan was an artist and illustrator in the style of Aubrey Beardsley. His work was highly respected by those who knew it, but it was never widely known. When Richardson met him, he was in the habit of spending all night in the Cafe Royal talking, drinking, and smoking with other artists. The cafe was always filled with a varied collection of artists, sculptors, and poets such as Jacob Epstein, Augustus John, Henry Savage, and Wyndham Lewis. Savage was editor of a literary magazine called *The Gypsy*, of which Alan Odle was art director. Dorothy and Alan met at the rooming house in which they both lived. He was extremely eccentric looking with long fingernails, long hair and a long gaunt body dressed always shabbily but dramatically. He spent all his money at the cafe and had none for food. Although clearly tubercular, he didn't acknowledge or care for his condition.

After they were married Dorothy spent much of her time tending to him and to their economic and household affairs. He was frail and interested almost exclusively in drawing and talking. According to Fromm, only Dorothy's constant care enabled Odle to live as long as he did. She supported the two of them by doing translations and writing reviews and hack journalism. Their financial state was desperate, and Dorothy yearned for time away from the relentless work of providing for their survival.

Alan Odle died at sixty in Cornwall. Soon after, his sister-in-law Rose and other close friends persuaded Dorothy that it would be best to leave Cornwall rather than live alone. In the spring of 1954, after thirty-six winters spent there, Richardson reluctantly moved to a private nursing home in southeast London. She hated the first nursing home and was sent to another. Her visiting friends described her as

> aware and oblivious, vague and sharp, regal and pathetic. They were never sure whether she was paying attention to them, whether they were in touch with her or not, whether when she talked about the past she knew it was the past, or whether she had forgotten the present. Sometimes, after remarking (as she often did) that Wells was coming to see her, she would then announce, with some surprise but no sadness, that H.G. was dead. Most of the time she was impenetrable, but she was rarely obscure except at the very end.[5]

On June 17, 1957, she died. She donated her body to the Royal College of Physicians and Surgeons. Two years later her body was returned to her family and buried under a tombstone inscribed, "To the Memory of Dorothy Miriam Odle, Authoress D.M. Richardson." Dorothy's middle name was Miller, her mother's maiden name, but nobody noticed the mix-up in names until long after the tombstone was set.

NOTES: APPENDIX

1. Fromm, 8.
2. Fromm, 14.
3. Fromm, 22.
4. Letter from Dorothy Richardson to Henry Savage, May 3, 1947.
5. Fromm, 394.

SELECTED BIBLIOGRAPHY

Dorothy Richardson: Primary Sources*

The order of the *Pilgrimage* novel-chapters and the dates of publication are as follows:

Volume I: *Pointed Roofs*, London, Duckworth, 1915.
Backwater, London, Duckworth, 1916.
Honeycomb, London, Duckworth, 1917.
Volume II: *The Tunnel*, London, Duckworth, [Feb.] 1919.
Interim, London, Duckworth, [Dec.] 1919.
Volume III: *Deadlock*, London, Duckworth, 1921.
Revolving Lights, London, Duckworth, 1923.
The Trap, London, Duckworth, 1925.
Volume IV: *Oberland*, London, Duckworth, 1927.
Dawn's Left Hand, London, Duckworth, 1931.
Clear Horizon, London, J. M. Dent & Cresset Press, 1935.
Dimple Hill, vol. I-IV, London, J.M. Dent & Cresset Press; New York: Alfred A. Knopf, 1938. First collected edition of *Pilgrimage*.
March Moonlight, published in the 1967 edition that Dent reissued.
Pilgrimage has been reissued in four volumes (London: Virago, 1979).

Close Up articles appear in chronological order:

"Continuous Performance," *Close Up* 1 (July 1927): 34-37.

"Continuous Performance 2: Musical Accompaniment," ibid. (Aug. 1927): 58-62.

"Continuous Performance 3: Captions," ibid. (Sept. 1927): 52-56.

"Continuous Performance 4: A Thousand Pities," ibid. (Oct. 1927): 60-64.

"Continuous Performance 5: There's No Place Like Home," ibid. (Nov. 1927): 44-47.

"Continuous Performance 6: The Increasing Congregation," ibid. (Dec. 1927): 61-65.

"Continuous Performance 7: The Front Rows," ibid. 2 (Jan. 1928): 59-64.

"A Note on Household Economy," ibid. (Feb. 1928): 58-62.

"Continuous Performance 8," ibid. (Mar. 1928): 51-55.

"Continuous Performance 9: The Thoroughly Popular Film," ibid. (Apr.): 44-50.

"Continuous Performance 10: The Cinema in the Slums," ibid. (May): 58-62.

"Continuous Performance 11: Slow Motion," ibid. (June 1928): 54-58.

"Continuous Performance 12: The Cinema in Arcady," ibid. 3 (July 1928): 52-57.

"Films for Children," ibid. (Aug.) 21-27.

"Continuous Performance: Pictures and Films," ibid. 4 (Jan. 1929): 51-57.

"Continuous Performance: Almost Persuaded," ibid. (June 1929): 51-57.

"Continuous Performance: Dialogue in Dixie," ibid. 5 (Sept. 1929): 211-18.

"The Censorship Petition," ibid. 6 (Jan. 1930): 7-11.

"Continuous Performance: A Tear for Lycidas," ibid. 7 (Sept. 1930): 196-202.

"Continuous Performance: Narcissus," ibid. 8 (Sept.1931): 182-85.

"Continuous Performance: This Spoon-Fed Generation?" ibid. (Dec. 1931): 304-8.

"Continuous Performance: The Film Gone Male," ibid. 9 (Mar. 1932): 36-38.

"Continuous Performance," ibid. 10 (June 1933): 130-32.

---

*The books cited here in no way comprise a comprehensive bibliography of Dorothy Richardon's work. For such a bibliography please see Gloria Fromm's book, *Dorothy Richardson, A Biography*, Chicago, IL: University of Illinois Press, 1977. This is the most comprehensive Richardson bibliography, including both primary and secondary sources, of which I am aware.

"About Punctuation," *Adelphi* 1 (Apr. 1924): 990-96. "*De la ponctuation*," trans. Sylvia Beach and Adrienne Monnier, Mesures (Jan. 15, 1935): 155-56.

Gleanings from the works of George Fox, London: Headley, 1914.

John Austin and the Inseparables, London: William Jackson, 1930.

The Quakers Past and Present, London: Constable; New York, Dodge, 1914.

Review of *Psycho-Analysis: A Brief Account of the Freudian Theory*, by Barbara Low, Dental Record, 40 (Aug. 2, 1920): 522-23.

"Talkies, Plays and Books: Thoughts on the Approaching Battle Between the Spoken Pictures, Literature and the Stage," *Vanity Fair* 32 (Aug. 1929): 56.

"What's in a Name?" *Adelphi* 2 (Dec. 1924): 606-9.

"Women in the Arts: Some Notes on the Eternally Conflicting Demands of Humanity and Art," *Vanity Fair* 24 (May 1925): 47.

"Women and the Future: A Trembling of the Veil before the Eternal Mystery of 'La Giaconda' [sic]," *Vanity Fair* 22 (Apr. 1924): 39-40.

DOROTHY RICHARDSON: SECONDARY SOURCES*

Abel, Elizabeth, Hirsch & Langland, eds., *The Voyage In, Fictions of Female Development*, Hanover and London: Dartmouth College, University Press of New England, 1983.

Allen, Walter, Introduction to *Pilgrimage*, vol. I, by Dorothy M. Richardson, Knopf, 1967: 3-8.

Allentuck, Marcia, "Dorothy Richardson on William Blake and the Broadside: An Unrecorded Appraisal." Blake Studies, Spring 1971: 195-96.

Bangs, Carol Jane, "The Open Circle: A Critical Study of Dorothy Richardson's *Pilgrimage*," *Dissertation Abstracts International* 38, 1977: 1376A.

---

*As Fromm's bibliography is comprehensive, I only list here work that she does not cite, in order to avoid needless duplication. Duplication will only occur when I have also used a book that is cited in the Fromm bibliography.

Beach, Joseph Warren, "Imagism: Dorothy Richardson," in *The Twentieth Century Novel: Studies in Technique*, New York: Appleton-Century-Crofts, 1932, 385-400.

Bell, Millicent, "The Single Self," *New Republic*, October, 1973, 23-27.

Blake, Caesar R., *Dorothy M. Richardson*, Ann Arbor: University of Michigan Press, 1960.

Bryher, Winifred, *The Heart to Artemis, A Writer's Memoirs*, New York: Harcourt, Brace & World, 1962.

Bryher, Winifred, "Dawn's Left Hand," [review], *Close Up* 8, December 1931: 337-38.

Cooke, Judy, "Pleasing Mamma," *New Statesman*, April 11, 1980: 557-58.

Craig, Patricia, "Dorothy Richardson—'The Damned Egotistical Self,'" *Books and Bookmen* 18, September, 1973: 246-47.

DuPlessis, Rachel Blau, *Writing Beyond the Ending; Narrative Strategies of Twentieth-Century Women*, Bloomington: Indiana University Press, 1985.

Deutsch, Babette, "Adventure in Awareness," *Nation* 148, Feb. 18, 1939: 210. [Review of *Pilgrimage*]

Eagleson, Harvey, "Pedestal for Statue," *The Sewanee Review*, vol. XLII, no. 1, Winter, 1934 42-53.

Edel, Leon, "Notes and Discussion: Dorothy Richardson 1882-1957," *Modern Fiction Studies*, vol. IV, no. 2, Summer 1958: 165-68.

Edel, Leon, *The Modern Psychological Novel 1900-1950*, London: Rupert Hart-Davis, 1961.

Fleishman, Avrom, *Figures of Autobiography: the Language of Self-Writing in Victorian and Modern England*, Berkeley: University of California Press, 1983.

Ford, Ford Madox, *The March of Literature*, London: Allen & Unwin, 1939.

Fromm, Gloria, *Dorothy Richardson: A Biography*, Urbana, Chicago, London: University of Illinois Press, 1977.

Fromm, Gloria Glikin, "What Are Men to Dorothy Richardson?" Janet Todd, ed. *Men by Women*, New York and London: Holmes and Meier Publishers, 1981, 168-188.

Gilbert, Sandra M., "A Painful Case," *Nation*, Sept. 1975: 246-47.

Gillespie, Diane Filby, "Political Aesthetics: Virginia Woolf and Dorothy Richardson," *Virginia Woolf: A Feminist Slant*, Jane Marcus ed., Lincoln and London: University of Nebraska Press, 1983.

Greene, Graham, "The Saratoga Trunk," in his *Collected Essays*, 1951, reprinted, Viking Penguin, 1969: 149-52.

Gregory, Horace, *Dorothy Richardson: An Adventure in Self-Discovery*, New York: Holt, Rinehart and Winston, 1967.

Hanscombe, Gillian, *The Art of Life: Dorothy Richardson: And the Development of Feminist Consciousness*, London: Owen, 1982; Athens: Ohio University Press, 1983.

Haule, James Mark, "The Theme of Isolation in the Fiction of Dorothy M. Richardson, Virginia Woolf, and James Joyce." *Dissertation Abstracts International*, 35, 1975: 7905A-6A, Wayne State.

Heath, Stephen, "Writing for Silence: Dorothy Richardson and the Novel," *Teaching the Text*, eds., Kappler and Bryson, London: Routledge & Kegan Paul, 1983.

Henke, Suzette, "Male and Female Consciousness in Dorothy Richardson's Pilgrimage," *Journal of Women's Studies in Literature*, 1, 1979: 51-60.

Kaplan, Sydney Janet, "Featureless Freedom or Ironic Submission: Dorothy Richardson and May Sinclair," *College English*, 32, May 1971: 914-17.

Kaplan, Sydney Janet, *Feminine Consciousness in the Modern British Novel*, Urbana: University of Illinois Press, 1975.

Kelly, Robert Glynn, "The Strange Philosophy of Dorothy M. Richardson," *The Pacific Spectator*, vol. XIII, no. 1, Winter 1954: 76-82.

Kelly, Robert G., *The Premises of Disorganization: A Study of Literary Form in Pound, Eliot, Joyce and Dorothy Richardson*, Stanford, 1952.

Mansfield, Katherine, "Dragonflies," *Athenaeum*, Jan. 9, 1920: 48. Reprinted in *Novels and Novelists*, ed. J. Middleton Murry, London: Constable, 1930. [Review of *The Tunnel*]

Manning, Olivia, "The Future of the Novel," *John O'London's*, December, 1962 556-60.

Miller, Jane, "In the Element of Language," *Times Literary Supplement*, July 14, 1978: 788.

Miller, Jane, "'Feminine' Time in Dorothy Richardson's *Pilgrimage*," *IJWS*, 1 1978: 211-19.

Odle, R. I., "Dorothy Richardson," *New York Times Book Review*, October 22, 1967: 48.

Pritchett, V. S., "Moral Gymnasium," *New Statesman*, May 5, 1967: 619.

Radford, Jean, *Dorothy Richardson*, Bloomington and Indianapolis: Indiana University Press, 1991.

Richard, Janis Marie, "The Modern British Bildungsroman and the Woman Novelist: Dorothy Richardson, Rosamond Lehmann, Elizabeth Bowen, and Doris Lessing," *Dissertation Abstracts International*, vol. XLII, no. 8, February 1982: 3612A-13A.

Rose, Shirley, "Dorothy Richardson's Theory of Literature: The Writer as Pilgrim," *Criticism*, vol. XII, no. 1, Winter 1970.

Rose, Shirley, "Dorothy Richardson's Focus on Time," *English Literature in Transition* 17, 1974: 163-72.

Rose, Shirley, "Dorothy Richardson Recalls Yeats," *Ireland* 7, Spring, 1972: 96-102.

Rose, Shirley, "Dorothy Richardson: The First Hundred Years, A Retrospective View," *Dalhousie Review* 53, Spring, 1973: 92-96.

Rose, Shirley, "The Unmoving Center: Consciousness in Dorothy Richardson's *Pilgrimage*," *Contemporary Literature*, vol. X, no. 3, The University of Wisconsin Press, 1969, 366-382.

Rosenberg, John, *Dorothy Richardson: The Genius They Forgot*, London: Duckworth, 1973.

Showalter, Elaine, *A Literature of Their Own: British Women Novelists from Bronte to Lessing*, Princeton: Princeton University Press, 1977.

Showalter, Elaine, "New Woman as Artist," *New York Times Book Review*, December 11, 1977: 12 +.

Smyers, Virginia L., "Dorothy M. Richardson: Some Uncollected Authors," *Book Collector* 27, 1978: 60-70.

Staley, Thomas F., *Dorothy Richardson*, Boston: Twayne, 1976.

Swinnerton, Frank, "Post Freud: May Sinclair, Dorothy Richardson, Rebecca West, E. M. Forster, D. H. Lawrence, James Joyce," in *The Georgian Scene: A Literary Panorama*, Farrar and Rinehart, 1934: 379-420.

Taylor, Nancy McKeon, "Conscious Construction: The Concept of Plot in Five Novels by Women," *Dissertation Abstracts International* 38, 1977: 2115A.

Tiessen, Paul, "A Comparative Approach to the Form and Function of Novel and Film: Dorothy Richardson's Theory of Art," *Literature Film Quarterly*, vol. III, no. 1, Winter 1975, 83-90.

Thorn, Arline R., "'Feminine' Time in Dorothy Richardson's Pilgrimage," *International Journal of Women's Studies*, 1, 1978: 211-19.

Tudor, Kathleen R., "The Androgynous Mind in W. B. Yeats, D. H. Lawrence, Virginia Woolf and Dorothy Richardson," *Dissertation Abstracts International* 35, 1974: 1126A-27A (Toronto).

Wallace, Doris Blumenthal, "The Fabric of Experience: A Psychological Study of Dorothy M. Richardson's *Pilgrimage*," *Dissertation Abstracts International* vol. XLII, no. 11, May 1982: 4565B (Rutgers University).

West, Rebecca, "Dawn's Left Hand," *Daily Telegraph*, Dec. 4, 1931. [Review]

FEMINIST THEORY

Adams, Parveen, "A Note on the Distinction Between Sexual Division and Sexual Differences," m/f, no. 3, 1979.

Baron, Dennis, *Grammar and Gender*, New Haven and London: Yale University Press, 1986.

Berg, Elizabeth, "The Third Woman," *Diacritics*, Summer 1982.

Bernheimer and Kahane, eds., *In Dora's Case, Freud-Hysteria-Feminism*, New York: Columbia University Press, 1985.

Butturoff, Douglas and Epstein, Edmond L., eds., *Women's Language and Style*, Studies in Contemporary Language #1, Department of English, University of Akron, Ohio, 1978.

Carrruthers, Mary, "Imaging Women: Notes Towards a Feminist Poetic," *Massachusetts Review* vol. XX, no. 2, Summer 1979, 281-407.

Cixous, Helene and Clement, Catherine, *The Newly Born Woman*, trans. Betsy Wing, Minneapolis, MN: University of Minnesota Press, 1986.

DuPlessis, Rachel Blau and members of Workshop 9, "For the Etruscans: Sexual difference and Artistic Production—The Debate Over a Female Aesthetic," in *The Future of Difference*, Eisenstein and Jardine, eds., New Brunswick: Rutgers University Press, 1985.

Ecker, Gisela, ed., *Feminist Aesthetics*, Boston: Beacon Press, 1985.

Flax, Jane, *Thinking Fragments Psychoanalysis, Feminism and Post Modernism in the Contemporary West* Berkeley, Los Angeles, Oxford: University of California Press, 1990.

Friedman, Susan Stanford, "When a 'Long Poem' is a 'Big Poem': Self-Authorizing Strategies in the Twentieth-Century Women's 'Long Poem,'" paper delivered at MLA, 1986.

Gallop, Jane, *Thinking Through the Body*, New York & Oxford: Columbia University Press, 1988.

Greene and Kahn, eds., *Making a Difference, Feminist Literary Criticism*, London and New York: Methuen, 1985.

Heath, Stephen, "Difference," *Screen* vol XIX, no. 3, Autumn 1978.

Heilbrun, Carolyn G. and Higonnet, Margaret R., eds., *The Representation of Women in Fiction*, The John Hopkins University Press, 1983.

Hejinian, Lyn and Watten, Barrett, eds., Women and Language edition of *Poetics Journal* no. 4, Berkeley: Inland Book Co. and Small Press Distribution, Inc., May 1984.

Homans, Margaret, "'Her Very Own Howl': The Ambiguities of Representation in Recent Women's Fiction," *Signs* vol. IX, no. 2 Winter 1983.

Irigaray, Luce, *This Sex Which Is Not One*, trans. Catherine Porter, Ithaca: Cornell University Press, 1985.

Irigaray, Luce, *Speculum of the Other Woman*, trans. Gillian C. Gill, Ithaca: Cornell University Press, 1985.

Jacobus, Mary, ed., *Women Writing and Writing About Women*, including essay: "Towards A Feminist Poetics," New York: Barnes and Nobles Imports, 1979.

Lakoff, Robin, *Language and Women's Place*, New York: Harper and Row, 1975.

de Lauretis, Teresa, ed., *Feminist Studies, Critical Studies*, Bloomington: Indiana University Press, 1986.

McConnell-Ginet, Borker and Furman, *Woman and Language in Literature and Society*, New York: Praeger, 1980.

Miller, Nancy K., and Heilburn, Carolyn, eds., *The Poetics of Gender*, New York: Columbia University Press, 1986.

Parker, Rozsika and Pollock, G., *Old Mistresses: Women, Art and Ideology*, New York: Random House, 1981.

Russ, Joanna, *How to Suppress Women's Writing*, Austin: University of Texas Press, 1983.

Schenck, Celeste, "All of a Piece: Women's Poetry and Autobiography," in *Life/Lines, Theorizing Women's Autobiography*, eds., Brodzki & Schenck, Ithaca and London: Cornell University Press, 1992.

Stewart, Grace, A New Mythos, *The Novel of the Artist as Heroine 1877-1977*, Montreal: Eden Press, 1981.

FILMIC POETICS

Andrew, Dudley, *The Major Film Theories*, London, Oxford, New York: University of Iowa, Oxford University Press, 1975.

Arnheim, Rudolf, *Film As Art*, Berkeley: University of California Press, 1957.

Barthes, Roland, *Image—Music—Text*, trans. Stephen Heath, New York: Noonday Press, 1977.

Benjamin, Walter, "The Work of Art in the Age of Mechanical Reproduction," *Illuminations*, ed. Hannah Arendt, trans. Harry Zohn, New York: Schocken Books, 1969.

Bland, Lucy, "The Domain of the Sexual: A Response," *Screen Education*, no. 39, Summer 1981.

Burgin, Victor, et al. ed., *Formations of Fantasy*, London: Methuen, 1986.

Cohen, Keith, *Film and Fiction—The Dynamics of Exchange*, New Haven and London: Yale University Press, 1979.

de Lauretis, Teresa, *Alice Doesn't: Feminism, Semiotics, Cinema*, Bloomington: Indiana University Press, November, 1984.

de Lauretis, Teresa, and Heath, Stephen, eds., *The Cinematic Apparatus*, London: Macmillan, 1980.

Doane, Mary Ann, *The Desire to Desire—The Woman's Film of the 1940s*, Bloomington: Indiana University Press, 1987.

Doane, Mary Ann, "The Moving Image" *Wide Angle*, vol. VII, nos. 1 & 2, Athens Center for Film and Video.

Doane, Mary Ann, and Williams, Linda, eds., *Revision: Essays in Feminist Film Criticism*, University Publications of America and the American Film Institute, 1984.

Eisenstein, Sergei, *Film Form*, ed. trans. Jay Leyda, New York: Harcourt, Brace & Company, 1949.

Ellsworth, Elizabeth "Illicit Pleasures: Feminist Spectators and Personal Best," *Wide Angle*, vol. VIII, no. 2, 1986.

Freud, Sigmund, "A Note on the 'Mystic Writing Pad,'" XV, 1925, *Collected Papers, 1988-1938*, vol. V, ed. James Stratchey, New York: Hogarth Press, 1959.

Friedberg, Anne, "Because they speak separate languages: Dorothy Richardson and the Film Gone Male," *Framework*, no. 20.

Friedberg, Anne, *Window Shopping: Cinema and the Post Modern*, Berkeley: 1993.

Friedberg, Anne, *Writing About Cinema: Close Up 1927-1933* (cinema) (Ph.D. 1983, N.Y.U.) 372, 44/12A, 3522.

Heath, Stephen, *Questions of Cinema*, Bloomington: Indiana University Press, 1980.

Herring, Robert, "A New Cinéma, Magic and the Avant Garde," *Close Up*, vol. IV, no. 4, April 1929.

Kern, Stephen, *The Culture of Time and Space, 1880-1918*, Cambridge: Harvard University Press, 1983.

Kuhn, Annette, *Women's Pictures Feminism and Cinema*, London: Routledge and Kegan Paul; Boston: Melbourne and Henley, 1982.

Low, Rachel, *History of the British Film, 1918-1929*, London: Allen & Unwin, 1971.

Lowe, Donald, *The History of Bourgeeois Perception*, Chicago: University of Chicago Press, 1982.

Metz, Christian, *The Imaginary Signifier, Psychoanalysis and the Cinema*, trans. Britton, Williams, Brewster, Gouzzetti, Bloomington: Indiana University Press, 1977.

Rose, Jacqueline, *Sexuality in the Field of Vision*, London: Verso, 1986.

Tyler, Stephen, "The Vision Quest in the West, or What the Mind's Eye Sees," *Journal of Anthropological Research*, vol. XL, no. 1, Spring 1973: 29.

LITERARY AND CULTURAL THEORY

Abrams, M.H., *The Mirror and the Lamp: Romantic Theory and the Critical Tradition*, New York: Oxford University Press, 1953.

Aries, Philippe, *The Hour of Our Death*, New York: Vintage Books, 1982.

Barthes, Roland, *Mythologies*, London: Cape, 1972.

Barthes, Roland, *S/Z*, trans. Richard Miller, New York: Hill and Wang, 1974.

Barthes, Roland, *A Lover's Discourse*, trans. Richard Howard, New York: Hill and Wang, 1978.

Benjamin, Walter, "The Storyteller" in *Illuminations*, ed. Hannah Arendt, trans. Harry Zohn, New York: Shocken Books, 1969.

Beebe, Maurice, *Ivory Towers and Sacred Founts, The Artist as Hero in Fiction from Goethe to Joyce*, New York: New York University Press, 1964.

Bruss, Elizabeth, W., *Autobiographical Acts, The Changing Situation of a Literary Genre*, Baltimore and London: Johns Hopkins University Press, 1976.

Clifford, J. and Marcus, G., eds., *Writing Culture, The Poetics and Politics of Ethnography*, Berkeley, Los Angeles, London: University of California Press, 1986.

Culler, Jonathan, *Structuralist Poetics*, Ithaca: Cornell University Press, 1975.

Curtius, Ernst Robert, *European Literature and the Latin Middle Ages*, Harper Torch Books, 1963.

Derrida, J., "The Law of Genre," *Critical Inquiry* 7, Autumn 1980: 57.

de Saussure, Ferdinand, *Course in General Linguistics*, Bally, Sechehaye and Riedlinger, Wade Baskin, trans., New York, Toronto, London: McGraw-Hill Books, 1959.

Fabian, Johannes, *Time and the Other: How Anthropology Makes its Object*, New York: Columbia University Press, 1983.

Felman, Shoshana, *Writing and Madness, Literature/Philosophy/ Psychoanalysis*, trans., Evans and Masssumi, Ithaca: Cornell University Press, 1985.

Felman, Shoshana, ed., *Literature and Psychoanalysis: The Question of Reading—Otherwise*, Baltimore: Johns Hopkins University Press, 1982.

Fletcher, Angus, *Allegory: The Theory of A Symbolic Mode*, Ithaca: Cornell University Press, 1965.

Greenblatt, Stephen, ed., *Allegory and Representation*, Baltimore: Johns Hopkins University Press, 1981.

Heath, Stephen, *The Nouveau Roman: A Study in the Practice of Writing*, London: Elek, 1972.

Henriques, Julian; Hollway, Wendy; Urwin, Cathy; and Walkerdine, Valerie, *Changing the Subject: Psychology, Social Regulation and Subjectivity*, London: Methuen, 1984.

Macherey, Pierre, *A Theory of Literary Production* London: Routledge & Kegan Paul, 1978.

Said, Edward, *Beginnings: Intention and Method*, Baltimore: Johns Hopkins University Press, 1975.

Turner, Victor, *Drama, Fields and Metaphors: Symbolic Action in Human Society*, Ithaca: Cornell University Press, 1974.

Van Ghent, Dorothy, *The English Novel: Form and Function*, New York: Holt, Rhinehard and Winston, 1953.

White, Hayden, *Tropics of Discourse*, Baltimore, London: Johns Hopkins University Press, 1978.

White, Hayden, *The Content of the Form*, Baltimore, London: Johns Hopkins University Press, 1987.

MODERNIST CONTEXT

Allot, M., *Novelists on the Novel*, London: Routledge & Kegan Paul, 1965.

Altick, Richard D., *The English Common Reader: A Social History of the Mass Reading Public, 1800-1900*, Chicago: The University of Chicago Press, 1957.

Barrett, Michele, "Ideology and the Cultural Production of Gender," in *Feminist Criticism and Social Change*, ed., Judith Newton and Deborah Rosenfelt, New York: Methuen, 1985.

Beauman, Nicola, *A Very Great Profession: The Woman's Novel 1914-1939*, London: Virago, 1983.

Beresford, J. D., "Experiment in the Novel," in *Tradition and Experiment in Present Day Literature*, London: Oxford University Press, 1929: 23-25.

Blau Du Plessis, Rachel, "Romantic Thralldom in H.D.," *Contemporary Literature* vol. XX, no. 2, the Board of Regents of the University of Wisconsin System, 1979.

Bryher, Winifred, *The Heart to Artemis: A Writer's Memoirs*, New York: Harcourt Brace & World, 1962.

Burke, Carolyn, "Supposed Persons: Modernist Poetry and the Female Subject," *Feminist Studies*, vol. XI, no. 1 (Summer 1985).

Cavaliero, Glen, *The Rural Tradition in the English Novel 1900-1939*, London: Macmillan & Co., 1977.

Cobbe, Frances Power, "The Final Cause of Woman," in *Women & Women's Culture*, ed. Josephine E. Butler, London: Macmillan & Co., 1869.

Derrida, J., "The Theory of the Proper," *Margins of Philosophy*, Chicago: University of Chicago Press, 1982.

Edel, Leon, *Writing Lives, Principia Biographica*, New York and London: Norton, 1984.

Gilman, Charlotte Perkins, *Women & Economics: A Study of the Economic Relation Between Men & Women as a Factor in Social Evolution* (1898), New York: Harper & Row Publishers, 1966.

Green, Martin, *Dreams of Adventure, Deeds of Empire*, London: Routledge, 1980.

Helsinger, Sheets and Veeder, *The Woman Question: Society and Literature in Britain and America 1837-1883*, New York: Garland, 1983.

Hinz, Evelyn, "Hierogamy Versus Wedlock: Types of Marriage Plots & Their Relationships to Genres of Prose Fiction," *PMLA*, vol. XCI, no. 5, October, 1976.

Krauss, Rosalind. *The Originality of the Avant-Garde and Other Modernist Myths*, Cambridge and London: Massachusetts Institute of Technology Press, 1986.

Kristeva, Julia, *The Novel as Polylogue*, Paris: Seuil, 1977.

Mansfield, Katherine, *Novels and Novelists*, ed. J. Middleton Murry, New York: Alfred Knopf, 1930.

Marcus, Jane, "Middle Brow Marxism," *Virginia Woolf Miscellany*, Spring-Summer 1976.

Marcus, Jane, "No More Horses, Virginia Woolf and Propaganda," *Women's Studies* vol. IV, nos. 2-3, 1977.

Marcus, Jane, ed., *Virginia Woolf: A Feminist Slant*, Lincoln and London: University of Nebraska Press, 1983. Including essay: "Political aesthetics: Virginia Woolf and Dorothy Richardson," by Diane Filby Gillespie.

Mayhew, *London Labour and the London Poor*, London: 1861; reprinted Cass, 1967.

Meyers, Jeffrey, *Fiction and the Colonial Experience*, Ipswich: Boydell Press, 1973.

Mill, John Stuart & Taylor, Harriet *Essays on Sex Equality*, ed. Alice S. Rossi, Chicago: University of Chicago Press, 1970.

Mitchell, J., "Femininity, Narrative and Psychoanalysis," in *Women: the Longest Revolution*, London: Virago, 1984.

Poggioli, Renato, *The Theory of the Avant-Garde*, translated from Italian by Gerald Fitzgerald, Cambridge: Belknap Press of Harvard University Press, 1981.

Poovey, Mary, *The Proper Lady and the Woman Writer, Ideology as Style, in the Works of Mary Wollstonecraft, Mary Shelly, and Jane Austen*, Chicago and London: University of Chicago Press, 1984.

Scott, Bonnie Kime, ed., *The Gender of Modernism, A Critical Anthology*, Bloomington and Indianapolis: Indiana University Press, 1990.

Showalter, Elaine, ed., *These Modern Women: Autobiographical Essays from the Twenties*, Old Wesbury: Feminist Press, 1978.

Showalter, Elaine, *The Female Malady: Women, Madness and Culture in England 1930-1980*, New York: Pantheon, 1985.

Trevelyan, George Macauley, *English Social History: A Survey of Six Centuries, Chaucer to Queen Victoria*, third ed., London: Longmans, 1961.

Woolf, Virginia, *The Death of the Moth and Other Essays*, New York and London: Harcourt, Brace, Jovanovich, 1942.

Woolf, Virginia, "Manifesto for the New Novelist," "Women & Fiction," and other essays, *Granite & Rainbow*, New York: Harcourt, Brace & Jovanovich, 1958.

Woolf, Virginia, *Women and Writing*, ed., with an introduction by Michelle Barrett, New York and London: Harcourt, Brace & Jovanovich, 1979.

Woolf, Virginia, "Women Novelists" in *Contemporary Writers*, New York and London: Harcourt, Brace & Jovanovich, 1965 (Review dates from 1918).

Woolf, Virginia, *Three Guineas*, New York: Harcourt, Brace & Company, 1938.

PILGRIMAGE AND RELATED

Amelincx, Frans C., and Megay, Joyce N., eds., *Travel, Quest and Pilgrimage As A Literary Theme*, the Imprint Series, Ann Arbor: University Microfilms International, 1978.

Atkinson, Clarissa W., *Mystic and Pilgrim: The Book and World of Margery Kempe*, Ithaca: Cornell University Press, 1983.

Bunyan, John Paul, *The Pilgrim's Progress*, London: Cresset Press, 1928.

Dowse, Ivor, *The Pilgrim Shrines of England*, London: Faith Press, 1963.

Finucane, Ronald C., *Miracles and Pilgrims, Popular Beliefs in Medieval England*, Totowa: Rowman and Littlefield, 1977.

Fox, George, *A Journal or Historical Account of the Life, Travels, Sufferings, Christian Experiences and Labour of Love, in the Work of the Ministry of George Fox*; in two volumes, Leeds: printed by Anthony Pickard, 1988.

Fox, George, *The Book of Miracles*, Cambridge: Cambridge University Press, 1948.

Gardiner, F. C., *The Pilgrimage of Desire: A Study of Theme and Genre in Medieval Literature*, Leiden: G. G. Brill, 1971.

Gingras, George E., ed., trans. & annot., *Egeria: Diary of a Pilgrimage*, Ancient Christian Writers, The Works of the Fathers in Translation, no. 38, New York: Newman Press.

Greene, Graham, "Journey Without Maps," from *The Collected Graham Greene*, William Heinemann and the Bodley Head, 1978.

Hunter, J. Paul, *The Reluctant Pilgrim: Defoe's Emblematic Method and Quest for Form in Robinson Crusoe*, Baltimore: Johns Hopkins Press, 1966.

Howard, Donald R., *Writers and Pilgrims: Medieval Pilgrimage Narratives and Their Posterity*, Berkeley: University of California Press, 1980.

Mathews, W. H., *Mazes and Labyrinths: Their History and Development*, first edition 1922; reprinted, New York: Dover, 1970.

Paulson, Ronald, "The Pilgrimage and the Family: Structures in the Novels of Fielding and Smollett," in G. S. Rousseau and P. G. Bouce, eds., *Tobias Smollett: Bicentennial Essays Presented to Lewis M. Knapp*, Oxford: Oxford University Press, 1971. (essays on travel)

Paulson, Ronald, "Life as Journey and as Theater: Two Eighteenth-Century Narrative Structures," *New Literary History* 7, 1976: 43-58.

Reiss, Edmond, "The Pilgrimage Narrative and the Canterbury Tales," *Studies in Philogy* 67, 1970: 295-305.

Ropen, Georg and Sommer, Richard, "Strangers and Pilgrims: An Essay on the Metaphor of Journey," *Norwegian Studies in English*, no. 11, Oslo: Akademisk Forlag, 1964.

Travel, Quest and Pilgrimage as a Literary Theme, Society of Spanish and Spanish-American Studies; Ann Arbor: University Microfilms Intl., 1978.

Turner, Victor, *Image and Pilgrimage in Christian Culture: Anthropological Perspectives*, New York: Columbia University Press, 1978

Turner, Victor, *Process, Performance and Pilgrimage: A Study in Comparative Symbology*, New Delhi: Concept, 1979; Ranchi anthropologies series; 1.

Valenze, Deborah, *Prophetic Sons and Daughters: Female Preaching and Popular Religion in Industrial England*, Princeton: Princeton University Press, 1985.

POETICS AND PHENOMENOLOGY

Bachelard, Gaston, *Poetics of Reverie, Childhood, Language and the Cosmos*, Boston: Beacon Press, 1960.

Bachelard, Gaston, *The Poetics of Space*, trans. Maria Jolas, New York: The Orion Press, 1964.

Barthes, Roland, "Literature & Discontinuity," *Salmagundi*, no. 18, Winter, 1972.

Barthes, Roland, "Proust and Names," in *New Critical Essays*, trans. Richard Howard, New York: Hill and Wang, 1980.

Beaujour, Michel, *Miroirs d'encre: rhetorique de l'autoportrait*, Paris: Seuil, 1980.

Beaujour, Michel, "Some Paradoxes of Description," New Haven: Yale French Studies, 1981.

Beja, Morris, *Epiphany in the Modern Novel*, Seattle: University of Washington Press, 1971.

Bergson, Henri, *The Creative Mind*, trans. Mabelle L. Andison, New York: Greenwood Press, 1968.

Bergson, Henri, *Matter and Memory*, trans. Nancy Margaret Paul & W. Scott Palmer, New York: Zone Books, 1988.

Bergson, Henri, *Time and Free Will; an essay on immediate data of consciousness*, trans. Pogson, London: Allen & Co., 1950.

Black, Max, *Models and Metaphors, Studies in Language and Philosophy*, Ithaca: Cornell University Press, 1962.

Cohen, Murray. *Sensible Words: Linguistic Practice in England 1640-1785*, Baltimore: Johns Hopkins University Press, 1977.

de Certeau, Michel, *Heterologies, Discourse on the Other*, trans. Brian Massumi, Minneapolis: University of Minnesota Press, 1986.

de Certeau, Michel, *The Practice of Everyday Life*, trans. Steven Kendall, Berkeley, Los Angeles and London: University of California Press, 1984.

Freud, Sigmund, "Creative Writers and Day-Dreaming" (1908), *The Standard Edition of the Complete Psychological Works of Sigmund Freud*, vol. IX, London: Hogarth Press, 1959.

Freud, Sigmund, *The Psychopathology of Everyday Life*, New York and London: Norton, 1965

Kermode, Frank, *The Sense of an Ending*, New York: Oxford University Press, 1967.

Kirkegard, *Either/Or*, translated by Swenson and Swenson, Princeton: Princeton University Press, 1959.

Kripke, Saul, *Naming and Necessity*, Cambridge: Harvard University Press, 1980.

Lockhart, Russell A., *Words as Eggs Psyche in Language and Clinic*, Dallas: Spring Publications, 1983.

Poulet, Georges, *The Metamorphosis of the Circle*, Baltimore: Johns Hopkins Press, 1967.

Poulet, Georges, *Proustian Space, The Phenomenology of Reading*, trans. Elliott Coleman, Baltimore: Johns Hopkins University Press, 1977.

Quinn, Arthur, *Figures of Speech: 60 Ways to Turn a Phrase*, Salt Lake City: G. M. Smith, 1982.

Sacks, Sheldon, *Fiction and the Shape of Belief: A Study of Henry Fielding, with Glances at Swift, Johnson and Richardson* [not DR], Berkeley: University of California Press, 1964.

Smith, Barbara Hernstein, *Poetic Closure, On the Margins of Discourse: The Relation of Literature to Language*, Chicago: University of Chicago Press, 1978.

Tomkins, Jane, *Reader-Response Criticism: From Formalism to Post-structuralism*, Baltimore: Johns Hopkins University Press, 1980.

Walden, Anthony, *The Language of the Self: The Function of Language in Psychoanalysis*, Baltimore: Johns Hopkins University Press, 1968.

Yates, Frances Amelia, *The Art of Memory*, Chicago: Chicago University Press, 1966.

THEOLOGY AND SPIRITUALITY

Arnold, J. H., ed. *Anglican Liturgies*, London: Oxford University Press, 1939.

Armistead, Wilson, *Journal of George Fox: Being an historical account of 7th edition with notes, biographical and historical background*, London: W. & F. G. Cash (late Gilpin), 1852.

Biggs, Reverend Louis Couciar, ed., *Hymns Ancient and Modern For Use in the Services of the Church, with Annotations, Originals and References*, London: Novello & Co., 1867.

Bradshaw, Paul F., *The Anglican Ordinal, Its History and Development From the Reformation to the Present Day*, London: William, Clowes & Sons, 1971.

Brown, R.E. et al., eds., *Mary in the New Testament*, Philadelphia: Fortress, 1978.

Cockshut, A.O.J., *Anglican Attitudes, A Study of Victorian Religious Controversies*, London: Collins, 1959.

de Mendieta, Emmanuel Amand, *Anglican Vision*, London: Talbot Press, 1971.

The Dialogue on Miracles, trans. Scott and Bland, 2 vols., London, 1929.

Durkheim, Emile, *The Elementary Forms of the Religious Life*, trans. J. S. Swain, New York: Collier. [first published 1912]

Fiorenza, Elisabeth Schussler, *In Memory of Her, A Feminist Theological Reconstruction of Christian Origins*, New York: Crossroad, 1983.

Funk, R., *Language, Hermeneutic and the Word of God*, New York: Harper & Row, 1966.

Gauld, Alan, *The Founders of Psychical Research*, New York: Schocken Books, 1968.

Hampson, Daphne, *Theology and Feminism, Signposts in Theology*, Oxford and Cambridge: Blackwell, 1990.

Handelman, Susan, *The Slayers of Moses, The Emergence of Rabbinic Interpretation in Modern Literary Theory*, Albany: State University of New York Press, 1982.

McTaggart, John, *The Nature of Existence*, Cambridge: Cambridge University Press, 1921. Grosse Point Michigan Scholarly Press, 1968.

Pagels, Elaine, *Adam, Eve, and the Serpent*, New York: Vintage Books, Random House, 1988.

Rose, Gillian, *Judaism and Modernity: Philosophical Essays*, Oxford and Cambridge: Blackwell, 1993.

Ruether, R. R., ed., *Religion and Sexism: Images of Women in the Jewish and Christian Tradition*, New York: Simon and Schuster, 1974.

Ryan, Frank Jamieson, *Protestant Miracles, High Orthodox and Evangelical Authority for the Belief in Divine Interposition in Human Affairs*, Stockton: Record Publishing Company, 1899.

Starr, George, *Defoe and Spiritual Autobiography*, Princeton: Princeton University Press, 1965.

Steere, Douglas V., ed., *Quaker Spirituality*, Selected Writings, New York: Paulist Press, 1984.

Thorndike, Lynn, *A History of Magic and Experimental Science*, New York: Columbia University Press, vol. 1, 1923.

Turner, Edith and Victor, *Image and Pilgrimage in Christian Culture: Anthropological Perspectives*, New York: Columbia University Press, 1978.

Turpin, Joanne, *Women in Church History*, Cincinnati: St. Anthony Messenger Press, 1990.

Twelve Churchmen, *Anglican Liberalism*, London: Williams & Norgate, 1908.

Underhill, Evelyn, *Modern Guide to the Ancient Quest for the Holy*, ed. Dana Greene, Albany: State University Press of New York, 1988.

Von Franz, Marie-Louise, *The Passion of Perpetua*, Spring Publications, Inc., Irving: University of Dallas, 1980.

TRAVEL AND TRAVEL THEORIES

Adams, Percy G., *Travelers and Travel Liars, 1660-1800*, Berkeley: University of California Press, 1962.

Adams, William Henry Davenport, *Celebrated Women Travellers of the 19th Century*, New York: E. P. Dutton, 1903.

Baedeker, K., *Baedeker Guide to Great Britain, Handbook for Travellers*, Leipsic, 1897.

Baedeker, K., *Baedeker Guide to London and Its Environs*, 1911.

Butor, Michel, "Travel and Writing," *Mosaic*, vol. VIII, no. 1, 1974.

Chambers, Ross, *Nerval et la poetique du voyage*, Paris: Corti, 1969.

Cox, Edward G., *A Reference Guide to the Literature of Travel*, 3 vols., Seattle: University of Washington, 1935-49.

Dumont, Jean Paul, "A Matter of Touristic Indifference," *American Ethnologist*, vol. II, no. 1, 1984.

Fussell, Paul, *Abroad: British Literary Traveling Between the Wars*, New York: Oxford University Press, 1980.

Gladwin, Thomas, *East Is A Big Bird; Navigation and Logic on Puluwat Atoll*, Cambridge: Harvard University Press, 1970.

Keith, W. J., *The Rural Tradition*, Hassocks: Harvester, 1975.

Khazanov, A. M., *Nomads and the Outside World*, trans. Julia Crookenden, Cambridge: Cambridge University Press, 1984.

McCannell, *The Tourist—A New Theory of the Leisure Class*, New York: Schocken Books, 1976.

Michael, M. A., *Traveller's Quest, Original Contributions Toward A Philosophy of Travel*, essays by Henri Bordeaux, Peter Freuchen, and others, London: W. Hodge, 1950.

Middleton, Dorothy, *Victorian Lady Travellers*, London: Routledge & Kegan Paul, 1965.

Rice, Warner, G., ed. & intro., *Literature as a Mode of Travel: Five Essays and a Postscript*, New York: New York Public Library, 1963.

"Traveling Theories: Traveling Theorists" issue of *Inscriptions*, James Clifford and Vivek Dhareshwar, eds., Group for the Critical Study of Colonial Discourse and The Center for Cultural Studies, U.C. Santa Cruz, 5:1989.

Tinling, Marion, *Women Into the Unknown: A Sourcebook on Women Explorers and Travelers*, New York: Greenwood Press.

Turner, Louis, *The Golden Hordes: International Tourism and the Pleasure Periphery*, London: Constable, 1975.

Travels of Lady Hester Stanhope, 3 vols., Salzburg Studies, Dover, NH: Longwood Publishing, 1983.

Van Den Abbeele, Georges, "Sightseers: The Tourist As Theorist," *Diacritics*, vol. X, December 1980.

Van Gennep, *The Rites of Passage*, London: Routledge & Kegan Paul. First published 1908.

Yale French Studies, special issue on travel, including "Writing vs. Time: History and Anthropology in the Works of Lafitau," by Michel de Certeau, 59, 1980.

TRAVEL, SPACE/PLACE, AND NARRATIVE

Alcorn, John, *The Nature Novel from Hardy to Lawrence*, London: Macmillan, 1977. (With a chapter on "The Spirit of Place in the Travel Book.")

Bernstein, Carol, "Nineteenth-Century Urban Sketches: Thresholds of Fiction," *Prose Studies*, 1980.

Bradbury and McFarlane, eds., *Modernism*, England and New York: Penguin Books, 1976. "A Geography of Modernism: London 1880-1920."

de Man, Paul, *Critical Writings 1953-78*, Lindsay Waters, ed., Minneapolis: University of Minnesota Press, 1989.

Greimas, A. J., *Semiotique et Sciences Sociales*, aux Editions du Seuil, Paris: Semantique Structurale, Larouse, 1966.

Hoskins, *The Making of the English Landscape*, London: Hodder & Stoughton, 1955; reprinted Pelican, 1970.

Jakobson, Roman, *Verbal Art*, *Verbal Sign*, *Verbal Time*, Krystyna Pomorska & Stephen Rudy, eds., Minneapolis: University of Minnesota Press, 1985.

Keating, Peter, ed., *Into Unknown England 1866-1913; Selections from the Social Explorers*, London: Fontana, 1976.

Kirchoff, "City as Self: Henry James's Travel Sketches of Venice," *Prose Studies*, 1979.

Lyons, John, "Locative Subjects" and "Spatial Expressions" in *Semantics*, New York: Columbia University Press, 1977.

Peacock, James L., "Society as Narrative" in *Forms of Symbolic Action*. ed. Robert F. Spencer, Seattle: University of Washington Press, 1969.

Ricoeur, Paul, *Time and Narrative*, vol. II, trans. Mclaughlin and Pellauer, Chicago: University of Chicago Press, 1986.

Schwarzbach, F. S., "Terra Incognita"—An Image of the City in English Literature, 1820-1855," *Prose Studies*, vol. 5, no. 1, May 1982, Special Issue on Travel Writing, London: Frank Cass Publishing. Also includes: "The Spectacle of Reality in Sea and Sardinia, Sabin, Margery; "Debunking the Jungle: The Context of Evelyn Waugh's Travel Books 1930-19399," Stannard, Martin; "The Views of Travellers: Travel Writing in the 1930's," Dodd, Philip; "Travel Writing Victorian and Modern: A Review of Recent Research," Shattock, Joanne.

Seidel, Michael, *Exile and The Narrative Imagination*, New Haven and London: Yale University Press, 1986.

Smith, Carl S., "James's Travels, Travel Writings and the Development of his Art," *Modern Language Quarterly*, 1977.

Sopher, "The Landscape of Home, Myth, Experience, Social Meaning," in *The Interpretation of Ordinary Landscapes, Geographical Essays*, ed., Meinig, D. W., New York and Oxford: Oxford University Press, 1979.

Squiers, Susan Merrill, *Virginia Woolf and London: The Sexual Politics of the City*, Chapel Hill: North Carolina Press, 1985.

Squiers, Susan Merrill, *Women Writers and the City: Essays in Feminist Literary Criticism*, Knoxville: University of Texas Press, 1984.

Tuan, Yi-Fu, ed., *Topophilia: A Study of Environmental Perception, Attitudes and Values*, Englewood Cliffs: Prentice Hall, Inc., 1974.

Williams, Raymond, *The Country and the City*, London: Chatto and Windus, 1973.

Errata

for Narrative's Journey
by Susan Gevirtz

One page 167, the date of Barbara Guest's visit to Byher was 1978, not 1948.